SHIFTING IDENTITIES
SHIFTING RACISMS

A Feminism & Psychology Reader

edited by

KUM-KUM BHAVNANI and ANN PHOENIX

SAGE Publications
London • Thousand Oaks • New Delhi

This Collection first published 1994

All items appeared first in *Feminism & Psychology* 4(1) 1994, the Special Issue on Shifting Identities Shifting Racisms. The Introduction and the contribution by Kum-Kum Bhavnani and Donna Haraway have been slightly revised for this Collection.

SAGE Publications Ltd
6 Bonhill Street
London EC2A 4PU

SAGE Publications Inc
2455 Teller Road
Thousand Oaks, California 91320

SAGE Publications Pvt Ltd
32, M-Block Market
Greater Kailash — I
New Delhi 110 048

British Library Cataloguing in Publication data

Shifting Identities Shifting Racisms:
Feminism and Psychology Reader
I. Bhavnani, Kum-Kum II. Phoenix, Ann
305.8
ISBN 0–8039–7786–7
ISBN 0–8039–7787–5 (pbk)

Library of Congress catalog card number 93–087792

Typeset by Editorial Enterprises, Torquay, Devon
Printed by Cromwell Press, Melksham, Wiltshire

SHIFTING IDENTITIES
SHIFTING RACISMS

A Feminism & Psychology Reader

Edited by Kum-Kum BHAVNANI and Ann PHOENIX

CONTENTS

_____ OBSERVATIONS & COMMENTARIES

INTRODUCTION

Kum-Kum BHAVNANI and Ann PHOENIX

Shifting Identities Shifting Racisms[1]

The title of this volume, *Shifting Identities Shifting Racisms: Issues for Feminist Psychology*, is an attempt to signal the questions which we consider to be important for feminist approaches to psychology at the present time, and in the near future. The four word phrase of the title is without punctuation in order that we may point to a relationship between multiple identities and multiple racisms — a relationship which travels in both directions, however apparently tenuous at times. The word 'shifting' is used deliberately also with two meanings. Firstly, we wanted to indicate that identities are constantly variable and renegotiable, as are racisms. The second sense we wished to convey through this phrase is that the shifting of identities, whether intentional or not, may also shift the boundaries of racisms, and vice versa. For example, as people of South Asian and African-Caribbean origin in Britain together embraced the word 'black', racist definitions of black, aimed at dividing these populations, were weakened. Similarly, as racisms have come to connote ideas associated with nationhood and belonging, the strength of sympathy and identification with black diasporic identities has increased from the 'first' world, to the 'second' and 'third' worlds, which means a development of obstacles or resistances to the apparently smooth processes of reproduction of racisms.

The forms of racism are varied and, indeed, racism itself is a set of processes whose parameters are shifting away from mainly biologistic considerations to include cultural and national ones (see e.g. Wetherell and Potter (1993) for a recent study on the content of this, arguably more recent, type of racism). To suggest and show that the forms of racism are varied and shifting is not to deny that racism as practice also provides points of stasis and moments of ignition when thinking about, and acting against the inequalities which racism legitimates. However, we wanted this book to embrace both aspects of racism — the

Feminism & Psychology © 1994 SAGE (London, Thousand Oaks and New Delhi), Vol. 4(1): 5–18.

seemingly enduring and fixed ones as well as its apparently newer and more fluid forms.

Similar processes, with rather different histories and content, may be apparent as gendered identities shift. The influence of the second wave women's movements in Europe and the United States has been considerable. In this period of negotiation and change, the consequent shift in identities — a refusal of the category 'lady' as a means of dividing women or a determination to insist that we are black (i.e. not white) women — may also be pointed to as examples of the two way relationship between identities and structured inequalities. In other words, we want to suggest, through the title of this volume, that the shifting of identities may contribute to a shifting of racisms, and vice versa, and thus provide a challenge to racisms, as well as an important set of issues for feminist psychology.

'Identity' is a word which is much used in both academic and political contexts. Its strength is that it captures succinctly the possibilities of unravelling the complexities of the relationship between 'structure' and 'agency'; perhaps, one could say it is the site where structure and agency collide. From the late 1970s, identity has become a term which is meaningful across disciplinary boundaries, and forms the site of many discussions, for example, within feminism (see e.g. Asian Women United of California, 1989), psychology (see e.g. Hogg and Abrams, 1988), sociology (see e.g. Giddens, 1991), literature (see e.g. Spillers, 1991), and contemporary cultural studies (see e.g. Chow, 1993; the Special Issue of *October* Number 61, 1992). It is now clear that to imagine the notion of identity as static, and therefore, unchanging, is one which is not fruitful in discussing the construction of, the reproduction through, and the challenge to unequal social relationships. Racism or, more accurately, racisms, is one means through which unequal social relationships are constructed and reproduced. It is for these reasons that we wanted the title to indicate that this collection was conceived as being one which contained articles that discussed the implications of racism for the development of feminist psychologies.

'Feminism' as a body of ideas, and as a set of political practices implies more than simply 'adding women in' to the subject matter of the human and material sciences (see Wood Sherif (1979) for an early exposition of this type of argument). Thus, when feminism is added on to psychology, so that they become one phrase, the phrase comes to imply not only an academic rethinking of that universe of discourse which is known as psychology but, also, a political project which may provide elements for this rethinking, as well as being itself rethought. It is for these reasons, the academic and the political, that we use *Shifting Identities Shifting Racisms* as the title.

The articles in this book were originally sought for a Special Issue of the journal *Feminism & Psychology*, a journal which first appeared in February 1991. A brief history of the journal is therefore important in the contextualization of this volume. The earlier publication in 1984 of *Changing the Subject* and, in 1986, of *Feminist Social Psychology*, helped to create an atmosphere which would make the project of producing *Feminism & Psychology* more feasible. The possibilities of setting up the journal were initiated by Sue Wilkinson and discussed with other feminist social psychologists between 1987 and 1990, a period when *Significant Differences* (1989) and *Feminists and Psychological Practice* (1990) were also produced. In the first issue of the journal, Sue Wilkinson, along with the rest of the Editorial Group, argued that the aim of the journal was to move away from being only a critique of psychology to a reconstruction of the subject/discipline. She also indicated that the journal would want to pay particular attention to forms of inequality other than gender, such as sexuality, 'race' and class (Editorial, *Feminism & Psychology*, 1991). For example, the journal adopted the policy of not having South African links while universal suffrage was absent in that country. This judgement, based on the African National Congress' call for an academic boycott between South Africa and other nation states also followed in the wake of heated and furious debates within the British Psychological Society about this academic boycott (Henwood, 1989). In the second issue of the journal it was announced that, in addition to keeping constantly at the forefront, issues of 'race' and sexuality as particular forms of inequality, the journal would also be producing Special Issues on these topics. It was soon after that decision that we decided to accept the invitation to be Guest Editors for a special edition of the journal and a book on the same issue. We signal these points in the journal's history to indicate that to discuss racism was always one element of the journal's aim.[2]

Within many feminist discourses such a sympathetic awareness of some of the problems of racism has not always been present. The arguments and debates, in the United States between women of colour and white women, and in Britain between black women and white women have often been sharp and, at times, bitter (see Anzaldua and Moraga (1981) for an example from the USA, and, in Britain, *Many Voices One Chant* (1984), a Special Issue of *Feminist Review*). These arguments often included aspects of class as well as racialization, and issues of sexuality were never far removed from any of these discussions (see e.g. Carmen et al., 1984). Many black women and black feminists in Britain felt unhappy both with white socialist feminists, and with radical feminists, for both of these seemed determined to ignore 'race' as one key organizing principle of inequalities amongst women (see e.g. Carby, 1982; Bhavnani and Coulson, 1986; Bryan et al., 1985, for further discussion of this point). It was argued, often, that white feminists refused to see that theories produced within feminisms were specific to, for example, white women, or white women who were middle class, or heterosexual women, or able-bodied women, or a combination of all of these (see e.g. Lorde, 1984; Parmar, 1982; Phoenix, 1988). Such arguments and the insistence of many black feminists that we were making these points from within the feminist movements, rather than from outside, gave rise to a productive rethinking of what is meant by the category 'woman'. The tensions generated by these debates served to move feminist theorizing away from its implicit assumption of a universal woman towards a recognition of differences amongst women, with the consequent complexities and contradictions that such rethinking implies (see e.g. Bhavnani, 1993; Essed, 1990; Hill Collins, 1990; Phoenix, 1991). Thus the idea that feminist work should begin not only from identity but also from difference, not only from agreement but also from conflict began to take hold, and forms the basis of some recent invigorating writing (e.g. Frankenberg, 1993; Grewal et al., 1988; Haraway, 1989; Sharpe, 1993; Ware, 1992).

In the period discussed above, the crisis of knowledge, which is part of the heritage of current poststructuralist theorizing, was also gaining ground. In the social sciences, the critiques of positivism were intensifying (see e.g. Parker (1989) for an outline of this crisis of knowledge, and its implications for psychology). In the humanities, the work of Derrida (1978, for example), and others, forced a reflection on the nature of a text, its authority and the way in which its meaning is constructed. The claim that a particular text is objective — either as a scientific or as a literary work — lost much of its power, and the argument that standpoint is a necessary ingredient in the development of insights into human relationships has become almost commonplace in feminist work. Nancy Hartsock (1983), in one of the first discussions of feminist standpoints, demonstrated that a key effect of feminist standpoint work is that it provides a means of grounding our insights into social relationships by locating those insights themselves within structures of power inequalities (of gender, 'race', class, for example) and inequalities of resource distribution (see Haraway, 1988; Hill Collins, 1990; Harding 1987, 1991; Lather, 1991 for further development of these ideas).

The development of the idea of feminist standpoints urged further movement on points of identity, ideology and cultural practice. As a result, difference emerged as an important matter and, thus, came into the foreground of feminist theory and politics. If objectivity, in the sense of being a taken-for-granted essential aspect of analysis, as it was within positivism, could no longer be accepted as a viable concept in feminist and poststructuralist accounts of the world (but see Harding (1993) for a recent argument about 'strong objectivity'), it meant that discussions had to occur on how to understand the standpoints of writers and of analysts. Identity — the concept and the process — appeared to provide one site, a crucial one, from which to discuss these issues (see e.g. Ferguson et al., 1990).

The current interest in identity also follows social psychological concerns with social identity, which developed from earlier discussions of identity within psychology. These earlier discussions located identity in the apparently broader area of 'personality', and viewed identity as 'a person's essential, continuous self, the internal, subjective concept of oneself as an individual' (Reber, 1985: 341). It was this notion of a continuous and essential personality trait, limited to subjective definitions of its content that the social identity researchers were trying to challenge when developing their theories and studies about identity and social relationships. For example, Tajfel's pioneering work (1978), developed by Brown (1984), Reicher (1984), Turner (1982) and Williams (1984) became one area within psychology which attracted many who were interested in shifting psychology away from its individualist frames to ones which made up structural axes of inequality. It was only in this way that it was thought that it would become possible to discuss psychic processes (see e.g. Armistead (1974) for an early collection of writings which implied the need for this movement in social psychology). Feminist interest in issues of identity have been rekindled both through discussions of identity politics (Bourne, 1987; Adams, 1989) and the re-examination of psychoanalytic approaches to issues of subjectivity (see e.g. Brennan, 1989; Mitchell and Rose, 1982). While the languages used in these different areas of academic specialism vary considerably, for example the empirical (and often empiricist) approaches within social psychology, as well as the sometimes abstract and obscure terminology used in analysing identity, along with the experiences that identities seem to engender, the point is that it is this issue, identity, which has captured the political imagination of the present time.

One consequence of these discussions is that the notion of identity as a static and unitary trait which lies within human beings, rather than as an interactional and contextual feature of all social relationships, has been laid to rest. Identity as a dynamic aspect of social relationships, is forged and reproduced through the agency/structure dyad, and is inscribed within unequal power relationships. In other words, identity is not one thing for any individual; rather, each individual is both located in, and opts for a number of differing, and at times, conflictual, identities, depending on the social, political, economic and ideological aspects of their situation — 'identity emerges as a kind of unsettled space ... between a number of intersecting discourses' (Hall, 1991: 10). This conception of identity thus precludes the notion of an authentic, a true or a 'real self'. Rather, it may be a place from which an individual can express multiple and often contradictory aspects of ourselves (see e.g. Griffin, 1989, 1991; Condor, 1988, 1989 for examples of how two feminist psychologists have discussed this point).

Feminist work on deconstructing the category of 'woman' — necessitated by the charges of racism levelled at much feminist writing often by black feminists (but see e.g. Spelman (1988) for an exception) — combined with the development of ideas on standpoint, and on identity largely discredited essentialist explanations for human behaviour within the academy. The reliance on social constructionism as a total, and therefore adequate explanation is also not considered satisfactory however (e.g. Brah, 1992; Burman, 1989; de Lauretis, 1987; Fuss 1989, 1991). The reasons provided by writers for their reservations about social constructionism and deconstruction as totalizing narratives are varied, and include issues of politics and subjectivities. These arguments, about not viewing social constructionism or essentialism as opposite ends of a spectrum but rather as a couplet each of whose parts contains the seeds of the other, also echo a debate which occurred in the late 1960s, and in the early 1970s. At that time, 'heredity and environment' or 'nature and nurture' were discussed in this way — namely, there was some agreement that a totally environmental approach to human development (as in B.F. Skinner's work) was not an adequate means for understanding individual differences amongst human beings. Rather, it was shown that the two processes of 'heredity' and 'environment' were related dialectically to each other. This attempt at describing the interactional aspects of 'nature' and 'culture' was much discussed by anti-racist psychologists, biologists and some feminists who were trying to challenge the writings of Jensen (1969), of Eysenck (1971), as well as of writers like Buffery and Gray (1972) and Corinne Hutt (1972) (see e.g. Griffiths and Saraga, 1979; Richardson et al., 1972). In addition, some women anthropologists were also discussing similar issues, most frequently as 'nature' and 'culture': this can be seen in the highly influential collection of chapters edited by Rosaldo and Lamphère (1974).

Thus, the debate which began by using 'environment/nurture' (that is, social constructionist) arguments to challenge the 'heredity/nature' (that is, essentialist) thesis moved on to question the very basis of the distinction between 'environment' and 'heredity' in the first place, that is it entailed what can be referred to as a double move between studying both modes of construction and already constructed categories. In short, these debates created possibilities for both deconstruction and reconstruction simultaneously.[3] A concern to examine 'heredity and environment', or essentialism and social constructionism within this double move, and, therefore, as *processes* of human development and interaction is often expressed in discussions of identity — influenced as these are by postcolonial and feminist writings and politics. In other words, feminist writings on standpoint, on identity and difference, and on racisms seem to us to be worthwhile points from which we can discuss human behaviours. It is those key axes which this collection seeks to address.

While the articles in this issue are written mainly by feminist psychologists, we did not intend to ignore the point that inter-disciplinary approaches have contributed significantly to developing thinking about these issues. Therefore, the articles include writers who rely not only on psychological perspectives alone but also on sociological perspectives (Yuval-Davis) and on the intersection of critical psychology and cultural studies (e.g. Räthzel and Squire). It is thus, from a variety of different perspectives, as well as two continents, that the articles in this volume address a range of themes pertinent to issues to be considered by, and engaged with, in feminist psychology. The fact that a number of themes recur across articles reflects the current theorizing in the area, and the concerns of feminist psychologists. We would like to highlight five of these cross-cutting themes.

PSYCHOLOGY AS REPRODUCER AND AMPLIFIER OF RACISM AND SEXISM

A recurrent focus is on the discipline of psychology, itself. It is no longer novel for feminist authors to produce analyses of psychology which demonstrate its shortcomings or the crises in which it finds itself at the end of the 20th century.

However, several articles in this book are innovative in demonstrating the implicit ways in which psychology has served to reproduce societal power relationships in which racist and sexist inequalities are maintained, even in explicit attempts to change the subject.

Kum-Kum Bhavnani and Donna Haraway depict ways in which the clear-cut focus on black people's intelligence in the 'race' and IQ debate has constituted a key form of racism which has been influential beyond the bounds of psychology. Two other authors illustrate the more indirect racist impact of psychology. Karen Henwood documents the ways in which the British Psychological Society's responses to calls for an academic boycott of South Africa served, in the name of neutrality and professionalism, to undermine resistances to racism within psychology. L. Mun Wong analyses journal articles to illustrate how apparently innocuous investigations of the impact of 'race' on cognition themselves operate to perpetuate stereotypical constructions of black people, and the domination of white people.

Even perspectives which developed within a spirit of critique, and which attempted to address racial prejudice and discrimination, such as Social Identity Theory, have not proved progressive since they have, for example, omitted black people's experiences of racism — see Karen Henwood's article. In a similar way, Erica Burman cautions feminist psychologists against a too easy acceptance of the 'Psychology of Women' as an additional area of psychology. She demonstrates that such an acceptance results in an essentializing of women as a fixed, unitary category, that is likely to reproduce the structures which feminists seek to change. In addition, an uncritical reception of a 'Psychology of Women' will reproduce the absence of a focus on racism which is characteristic of the psychological agenda. Both these authors demonstrate ways in which racisms within psychology shift over time, and how new theoretical perspectives shift the identities of the discipline.

MULTIPLE SHIFTING IDENTITIES

In their examination of the shifting nature of identities, and in keeping with the point that identities are both structural and agentic, many contributions demonstrate the intersection of individual histories and political imperatives in producing identities. Bhavnani and Haraway, and Henwood use autobiographical narratives to trace routes to, and reasons for, resisting the traditional tenets of psychology with regard to anti-racism and feminism. Henwood shows how the structures of the British Psychological Society have served to promulgate ways of thinking about 'race' and racism as well as feminism, which have acted to silence white women psychologists like herself who, only through struggle, can declare their allegiances and stand against racism. Bhavnani and Haraway relate their histories to their current intellectual identities exploring the commonalities and differences that have led each to be feminists within the US academy. They discuss how identities shift, and, therefore, how the constituents of racist discourses do so. In this way, new ways of thinking and social changes emerge, so that there can no longer be one static form of racism but a multiplicity of racisms which are in a constant process of formation.

Burman and Essed also use personal biographies to situate the ways in which identities are multiple, relational, historically located and potentially contradictory. Essed uses a case study approach to show that the category of 'black woman' is not a monolithic one; that black women's life experiences are the result of the interweaving of gender and 'race' and that it is simultaneously possible to consider oneself as very different from other people who are deemed to constitute part of the same group, in this case black people, while still experiencing a sense of group responsibility. The article by Woollett, Marshall, Nicolson and Dosanjh provides an empirical exploration of the varied strategies of bringing up children employed by women living in London, who, in the British context, are constituted as 'Asian'. Woollett and her colleagues argue that the plurality of identities of the women they studied show how the ascription 'Asian woman' is not a singular nor a homogeneous category.

Corinne Squire's piece engages with a topic that touches the lives and interests of millions of people who view it in Britain and in the USA — the *Oprah Winfrey Show*. The huge popularity of this chat show, hosted by a black woman who regularly confronts her audience with intimate details of issues popularized from psychology, demonstrates a tension also touched on in Burman's article. How do the actions of particular members of minority groups — either through assimilation (Burman) or through respect and adulation (Squire) — lead to a shift in majority constructions and identities? Squire engages with the question of whether the *Oprah Winfrey Show*, with its carefully formulated psychological appeal, can be said to be feminist or anti-racist. Her argument is consistent with that of many articles in this issue in showing the complexities and contradictions the above question raises.

AGENCY AND COLLECTIVE ACTION AS FEMINIST PSYCHOLOGISTS

Questions of identity and difference, along with how these can be harnessed for positive political change, continue to exercise feminist psychologists. How can non-exploitative alliances between different groups of women be fostered? In the articles in this issue, the identity politics of the last two decades are examined and found wanting in terms of both explanatory power and of political action. Postmodernist notions of fragmented identities are also partially criticized in this context for their encouragement of a solipsistic focus on difference, rather than on political alliances and action (see e.g. the pieces by Burman and by Yuval-Davis). Although recognizing the importance of the concept of identity, Burman expresses a preference for the idea of 'positionality' — the process of constructing identifications which treat identities as produced rather than as fixed, personal attributes. This concept can potentially allow alliances between, for example, black women and white Jewish women. From a sociological perspective, Nira Yuval-Davis highlights the shortcomings of academic and grass-roots notions of empowerment. Her argument points to the usefulness of the term 'transversalism', as espoused by the group 'Women in Black'. The process is one which creates room both for individual 'rootedness' in identity, while permitting empathy with identifications different to one's own. Her piece uses the concept of feminist standpoint, as do Henwood, and Bhavnani and Haraway as a means of theorizing collective identities and as an impetus for political action.

THE INTERROGATION OF WHITENESS

Until very recently, work on racisms and on identities did not examine 'whiteness' as a problematic.[4] Rather, 'whiteness' and white identities were used as tacit backdrops to highlight the difficult and pathological nature of 'blackness' and black identities. One of the advances in such work, inspired largely by black feminist writing, has been the recognition that the absence of focus on whiteness is not only unsatisfactory in an academic sense, but also serves to perpetuate racisms. In this book, Mun Wong demonstrates ways in which the silent signifier, whiteness, serves to maintain, and obfuscate its privileged position within psychological texts. As a result, it is whiteness and white identities which continue to define the direction of psychology and the treatment of black and other minority peoples. Burman's article is centrally concerned with disaggregating whiteness as a global category. She argues that Jewish identities are themselves diverse, multiple and contradictory and that although Jewish people in the West[5] are frequently white, their identities and the ways in which they are positioned differ from those of non-Jewish white people. She develops the phrase 'different degrees of otherness' to signal this point. The two pieces in the Observations and Commentary section also discuss whiteness; Shari Tarver-Behring and Barbara Trepagnier each suggest and speculate upon ways in which whiteness can be unpacked and analysed in order to initiate change with regard to racisms.

POLITICAL IMPLICATIONS OF IDENTITIES

We mentioned, earlier in this introduction, that psychological interest in identity has tended to treat it as a personality trait, at the expense of ignoring its structural features. Many of the articles in this volume, however, have addressed the political implications of the ways in which identities are theorized and experienced, specifically with regard to the production and reproduction of racisms. Nora Räthzel grapples with these political implications in her article by focusing on the treatment of people who are seen as foreigners/outsiders ('Ausländer') in Germany — an issue which has generated some media coverage particularly in

Europe. Räthzel examines constructions of 'Heimat' (approximating to the notion of 'home' in English) and of 'Ausländer' in the conceptions of groups of Swiss and German people, many of whom have some commitment to anti-racism. She demonstrates the necessity of dealing politically with contradictory identifications in order to shift racisms. Her article makes some suggestions about the political interventions that would be necessary to reduce the distance between 'Heimat' and 'Ausländer' felt by many Swiss and German people.

CONCLUDING THOUGHTS

We began this piece by discussing the commitment of the journal *Feminism & Psychology* to exploring anti-racism, and to the desire to see more feminist discourses which genuinely incorporate these issues. The aim of this volume is to make a contribution to the present stages of this on-going project — a project which, given the variety of arguments developed in our introduction is not simply of academic but also of political significance. We trust that it will make a contribution to thinking about how to understand identities and racisms by exploring the shifting nature of these two concepts, and interrogating them in a constructive way. The articles do not set out to present clear-cut solutions to the questions raised above, and, indeed, the questions themselves are not so clear-cut. Multiple and often contradictory constructions of the political and academic strategies are required to shift currently powerful relationships articulated around and against racisms. We hope, however, that whatever their intellectual and political sympathies, readers will reflect on the varied nature of the articles in this collection, and use them to develop discussion/debate within and outside of psychology.

NOTES

1. We would like to thank the Editor and the Associate Editors of *Feminism & Psychology* for their interest and enthusiastic encouragement during the production of this Introduction, for their prompt reviewing of articles, and their commitment to this book. We are also grateful to the other 50 women who acted as reviewers, as well as to the authors who frequently revised their pieces within a very short space of time, and without whom, this volume would not have been possible.
2. We are aware that running a special issue of any journal with 'racisms' in the title risks marginalizing the constellation of questions about power inequalities, agency and structure which the word connotes. For all too often, focusing on these areas in one edition can seem to be a token gesture rather than a sincere recognition of the importance of highlighting them throughout academic discourses. Yet the sustained interrogation of a topic such as racism can also serve to highlight its importance and signal to readers and potential contributors the weight a journal gives to this area. We would suggest that this is the case for *Feminism & Psychology*.

3. We are grateful to Christine Griffin and Margaret Wetherell for helping to clarify this point.
4. We will use the term 'whiteness' here, but always with the proviso that, just as 'blackness' is not a homogeneous category, nor is 'whiteness'. Indeed the unsatisfactory character of these two terms requires considerable interrogation, along with the issues they connote. However, this section will focus mainly on the issues, rather than the unspecified quality of each term.
5. While we are not happy with the use of this term to refer to an imagined entity (Said, 1978), we use it here in order to keep the argument succinct.

REFERENCES

Adams, Mary Louise (1989) 'There's No Place Like Home: On the Place of Identity in Feminist Politics', in *The Past Before Us. Twenty Years of Feminism* Special Issue of *Feminist Review* No. 31 (Spring): 22–3.

Anzaldua, Gloria and Moraga, Cherríe Moraga eds (1981) *This Bridge Called My Back. Writings by Radical Women of Colour.* Watertown, MA: Persephone Press.

Armistead, Nigel ed. (1974) *Reconstructing Social Psychology.* Harmondsworth: Penguin.

Asian Women United of California eds (1989) *Making Waves. An Anthology of Writings By And About Asian American Women.* Boston: Beacon Press.

Bhavnani, Kum-Kum (1993) 'Talking Racism and the Editing of Women's Studies', in Diane Richardson and Victoria Robinson (eds) *Introducing Women's Studies. Feminist Theory and Practice*, pp. 27–48. London: Macmillan.

Bhavnani, Kum-Kum and Coulson, Margaret (1986) 'Transforming Socialist Feminism: The Challenge of Racism', in *Socialist Feminism — Out of the Blue* Special Issue of *Feminist Review* No. 23: 81–92.

Bourne, Jenny (1987) 'Homelands of the Mind: Jewish Feminism and Identity Politics', *Race and Class* XXIX (1, Summer): 1–24.

Brah, Avtar (1992) 'Difference, Diversity and Differentiation', in James Donald and Ali Rattansi (eds) *Race, Culture and Difference*, pp. 126–45. London and Milton Keynes: Sage and Open University Press.

Brennan, Teresa ed. (1989) *Between Feminism and Psychoanalysis.* London: Routledge.

Brown, Rupert (1984) 'The Effects of Intergroup Similarity and Co-operative vs. Competitive Orientation on Intergroup Discrimination', *British Journal of Social Psychology* 23: 21–33.

Bryan, Beverley, Dadzie, Stella and Scafe, Suzanne (1985) *The Heart of the Race. Black Women's Lives in Britain.* London: Virgao.

Buffery, A. W. H. and Gray, J. A. (1972) 'Sex Differences in the Development of Spatial and Linguistic Skills', in C. Ounstead and D.C. Taylor (eds) *Gender Differences: Their Ontogeny and Significance.* Edinburgh: Churchill Livingstone.

Burman, Erica (1989) 'Differing With Deconstruction: A Feminist Critique', in Ian Parker and John Shotter (eds) *Deconstructing Social Psychology,* pp. 208–20. London: Routledge.

Burman, Erica ed. (1990) *Feminists and Psychological Practice.* London: Sage.

Carby, Hazel (1982) 'White Women Listen! Black Feminism and the Boundaries of Sisterhood', in Centre for Contemporary Cultural Studies (eds) *The Empire Strikes Back. Race and Racism in 70s Britain*, pp. 212–35. London: Hutchinson.

Carmen, Gail, Shaila and Pratibha (1984) 'Becomining Visible: Black Lesbian Discussions', in *Many Voices, One Chant*: Special Issue of *Feminist Review* No. 17 (Autumn): 53–74.

Chow, Ray (1993) *Writing Diaspora. Tactics of Intervention in Contemporary Cultural Studies*. Bloomington, IN: Indiana University Press.

Condor, Susan (1988) 'Race Stereotypes and Racist Discourse', *Text* 8 (1–2): 68–89.

Condor, Susan (1989) '"Biting Into the Future": Social Change and the Social Identity of Women', in Suzanne Skevington and Deborah Baker (eds) *The Social Identity of Women*. London: Sage.

Derrida, Jacques (1978) *Writing and Difference*. London: Routledge and Kegan Paul.

Essed, Philomena (1990) *Everyday Racism. Reports from Women of Two Cultures*. Claremont, CA: Hunter House.

Eysenck, Hans (1971) *Race, Intelligence and Education*. London: Temple Smith.

Ferguson, Russell, Gever, Martha, Trinh, T. Minh-ha and West, Cornel eds (1990) *Out There: Marginalization and Contemporary Cultures*. New York and Cambridge, MA: The New Museum of Contemporary Art and MIT Press.

Frankenberg, Ruth (1993) *White Women Race Matters*. London: Routledge.

Fuss, Diana (1989) *Essentially Speaking: Feminism, Nature and Difference*. New York and London: Routledge.

Fuss, Diana ed. (1991) *Inside/Out. Lesbian Theories, Gay Theories*. New York and London: Routledge.

Giddens, Anthony (1991) *Modernity and Self-Identity. Self and Society in the Late Modern Age*. Stanford: Standford University Press.

Grewal, Sahbnum, Kay, Jackie, Landor, Liliane, Lewis, Gail and Parmar, Pratibha eds (1988) *Charting the Journey. Writings by Black and Third World Women*. London: Sheba Feminist Press.

Griffin, Christine (1989) '"I'm Not a Women's Libber But ...".. Feminism, Consciousness and Identity', in Suzanne Skevington and Deborah Baker (eds) *The Social Identity of Women*. London: Sage.

Griffin, Christine (1991) 'Experiencing Power: Dimensions of Gender, Race and Class', Unpublished Paper presented at the Women and Psychology Conference University of Edinburgh, Scotland.

Griffiths, Dorothy and Saraga, Esther (1979) 'Sex Differences in Cognitive Abilities: A Sterile Field of Enquiry?', in Oonagh Hartnett, Gill Boden and Mary Fuller (eds) *Sex Role Stereotyping*, pp. 17–45. London: Tavistock.

Hall, Stuart (1991) 'Ethnicity: Identity and Difference', *Radical America* 23 (4): 9–20.

Haraway, Donna (1988) 'Situated Knowledges: The Science Question in Feminism and the Privilege of Partial Perspective', *Feminist Studies* 14 (3): 575–99.

Haraway, Donna (1989) *Primate Visions*. New York and London: Routledge.

Harding, Sandra ed. (1987) *Feminism and Methodology*. Milton Keynes: Open University Press.

Harding, Sandra (1991) *Whose Science? Whose Knowledge? Thinking From Women's Lives*. Ithaca, NY: Cornell University Press.

Harding, Sandra (1993) 'Rethinking Standpoint Epistemology: "What is Strong Objectivity?" ', in Linda Alcoff and Elizabeth Potter (eds) *Feminist Epistemologies*. New York and London: Routledge.

Hartsock, Nancy (1983) 'The Feminist Standpoint: Developing the Ground for a Specifically Feminist Historical Materialism', in Sandra Harding and Merrill Hintikka (eds) *Discovering Reality*. Dordrecht: Reidel.

Henriques, Julian, Hollway, Wendy, Urwin, Cathy, Venn, Couze and Walkerdine, Valerie (1984) *Changing the Subject*. London: Methuen.

Henwood, Karen (1989) 'Moral and Legal Issues in the South African Boycott', Letter in *Psychologist* 2 (8): 329.

Hill Collins, Patricia (1990) *Black Feminist Thought. Knowledge, Consciousness and the Politics of Empowerment*. London: Harper Collins.

Hogg, Michael and Abrams, Dominic (1988) *Social Identifications. A Social Psychology of Intergroup Relations and Group Processes*. London: Routledge.

Hutt, Corinne (1972) *Males and Females*. Harmondsworth: Penguin.

Jensen, Arthur R. (1969) 'Environment, Heredity and Intelligence', *Harvard Educational Review* 39 (1): 1–123.

Lather, Patti (1991) *Getting Smart. Feminist Research and Pedagogy With/In the Postmodern*. New York: Routledge.

de Lauretis, Theresa (1987) *Feminist Studies, Critical Studies*. Bloomington, IN: Indiana University Press.

Lorde, Audre (1984) *Sister Outsider. Essays and Speeches*. Trumansburg, NY: The Crossing Press.

Many Voices, One Chant. Black Feminist Perspectives (1984) Special Issue of *Feminist Review* No. 17 (Autumn).

Mitchell, Juliet and Rose, Jacqueline eds (1982) *Feminine Sexuality — Jacques Lacan and the Ecole Freudienne*. New York: Pantheon.

October (1992) Special Issue on Identity No. 61.

Parker, Ian (1989) *The Crisis in Modern Social Psychology — And How to End It*. London: Routledge.

Parmar, Pratibha (1982) 'Gender, Race and Class: Asian Women in Resistance', in Centre for Contemporary Cultural Studies (eds) *The Empire Strikes Back*, pp. 236–75. London: Hutchinson.

Phoenix, Ann (1988) 'Narrow Definitions of Culture: The Case of Early Motherhood', in Sallie Westwood and Parminder Bhachu (eds) *Enterprising Women*. London: Routledge.

Phoenix, Ann (1991) *Young Mothers?* Cambridge: Polity Press.

Reber, Arthur (1985) *The Penguin Dictionary of Psychology*. Harmondsworth: Penguin.

Reicher, Steven (1984) 'The St Paul's Riot: An Explanation of the Limits of Crowd Action in Terms of a Social Identity Model', *European Journal of Social Psychology* 14: 1–21.

Richardson, Ken, Spears, David and Richards, Martin eds (1972) *Race, Culture and Intelligence*. Harmondsworth: Penguin.

Rosaldo, Michelle Zimbalist and Lamphère, Louise eds (1974) *Women, Culture and Society*. Stanford: Stanford University Press.

Said, Edward (1978) *Orientalism*. New York: Pantheon.

Sharpe, Jenny (1993) *Allegories of Empire. The Figure of Woman in the Colonial Text*. Minneapolis and London: University of Minnesota Press.

Spelman, E. (1988) *Inessential Woman: Problems of Exclusion in Feminist Thought.* Boston: Beacon Press.

Spillers, Hortense ed. (1991) *Comparative American Identities. Race, Sex and Nationality in the Modern Text.* New York: Routledge.

Squire, Corinne (1989) *Significant Differences — Feminism in Psychology.* London: Routledge.

Tajfel, Henri ed. (1978) *Differentiation Between Social Groups.* London: Academic.

Turner, John (1982) 'Towards a Cognitive Redefinition of the Social Group', in Henri Tajfel (ed.) *Social Identity and Intergroup Relations.* Cambridge: Cambridge University Press.

Ware, Vron (1992) *Beyond the Pale. White Women, Racism and History.* London: Verso.

Wetherell, Margaret and Potter, Jonathan (1993) *Mapping the Language of Racism. Discourse and the Legitimation of Exploitation.* New York: Columbia University Press.

Wilkinson, Sue ed. (1986) *Feminist Social Psychology. Developing Theory and Practice.* Milton Keynes: Open University Press.

Williams, Jennie (1984) 'Gender and Intergroup Behaviour: Towards An Integration', *British Journal of Social Psychology* 23: 311–16.

Wood Sherif, Carolyn (1979) 'Bias in Psychology', in Julia A. Sherman and Evelyn Torton Beck (eds) *The Prism of Sex: Essays in the Sociology of Knowledge.* Madison: University of Wisconsin Press.

Kum-Kum BHAVNANI is Associate Professor in the Department of Sociology at the University of California, Santa Barbara, CA 93106, USA. She teaches cultural studies, feminist theory and epistemology and social psychology and has published articles in all of these areas. Her book, *Talking Politics*, was published by Cambridge University Press in 1991.

Ann PHOENIX is a black feminist whose political activity has been mainly in black and feminist campaigns. She spent ten years engaged in policy relevant research at the Thomas Coram Research Unit, in London, and now teaches psychology in the Human Sciences Department at Brunel University, Uxbridge, Middlesex UB8 3PH, Britain.

Kum-Kum BHAVNANI and Donna HARAWAY

Shifting the Subject :[1] A Conversation between Kum-Kum Bhavnani and Donna Haraway on 12 April, 1993, Santa Cruz, California
Transcribed by Justine MEYERS

FOREWORD

Donna HARAWAY has worked extensively on the relationships between the history and practices of science, their relationship to feminist theorizing, and their place in the construction of future cultures. She often uses metaphors based in science fiction in order to express her conviction that to conduct critical work on the present and the past requires that such work also be inscribed within the future.

Kum-Kum BHAVNANI has written on racism, gender and class inequalities within methodologies, on the processes of racialization in feminist theorizing, and used cultural studies frameworks to interrogate the views of politics expressed by working class youth. She was active in community and political issues from 1970 to 1990 in Britain.

REHISTORICIZING OURSELVES

KK: Donna, you and I are talking together because you were invited to contribute to this volume. You suggested a conversation between us. We've known of each other's work for some time, although we met for the first time only last month. In some ways, we could say our identities are very different. You are a white woman, born in the United States, and living in the United States, while I am a woman of colour, born in India, migrated to Britain, and now a migrant in

Feminism & Psychology © 1994 SAGE (London, Thousand Oaks and New Delhi), Vol. 4(1): 19–39.

California since 1991. Despite this apparent gulf in our experiences, we share an interest, if not a passion, in reflecting on identities and the ways in which they shift. So, why don't we begin this conversation on shifting identities for this collection by telling a narrative story about ourselves. Why don't you tell ...

DH: The story of the kind of work we've done, the kinds of places we've come from and the kind of imaginative and material world within each of us, in which we see ourselves living among shifting identities. As I approach this question, I think of the moment when I began my full-time teaching career, in 1970, at the end of graduate school, in Honolulu at the University of Hawaii in the General Science Department. I think teaching 'general science' in Honolulu is a bit like the folks in Britain who have come out of adult education as opposed to maybe more explicitly elite pathways into university life. Also, I am an Irish Catholic, Euro-American, middle-class woman with a PhD in Biology. Because of the cold war and Sputnik and the tremendous American economic hegemony after the war, people like me became national resources in the national science efforts. So, there was money available for educating even Irish Catholic girls' brains. [Laughter from both.]

After graduate school I found myself in Honolulu. I think Hawaii, unlike many of the other states of the United States, has a particular kind of relationship to imperialism and colonialization, that for me foregrounded questions of racial, colonial and postcolonial positioning in a way that my growing up in Colorado didn't: not that it shouldn't have, but that it *didn't*. Denver was composed from Mexicano, Chicano, worlds; African-American worlds. Irish, Italian, Mexicano and Chicano Catholics populated the parochial elementary and high schools. Now I grew up in that world, but I had the skewed awareness of an unmarked white girl, and I didn't have a very conscious racial identity. They weren't part of what I was turning into, a way of thinking consciously, a way of interrogating, until much later. Hawaii, in the early 1970s, was the center of the Pacific Strategic Command at the end of the Vietnam war, and I was on that island where the population was minority Anglo, minority European ancestry. Hawaii is a very polyethnic world, one which is intimately tied to indigenous land and cultural struggles, to waves of labor history through the Pacific, and the history of the military in the Pacific. It was a whole different world compared to that which I had known until then. I was teaching general science to non-science majors. So Japanese American kids, Hawaiian kids, Chinese American kids, some Samoans, some Euro-Americans were taking general science from a person like me. It was a bizarre introduction to the historical positioning of endeavors like biology, and brought out clearly the racial, geographic, historical positioning that is inscribed in these endeavors. I was also developing professionally as a historian of biology, working with a colleague who now lives in London named Dorothy Stein. She was a very smart, savvy, complex person. In June 1971 we taught a course together called the Biology and the Psychology of Sex Differences. We taught it for a couple of years although neither of us was theorizing racial formations in our work at that time. We were doing what most white women were doing in that period, which was thinking of sex differences in an unmarked fashion. But it was a very important moment for putting together the politics, the theories and the experiences of identity in our teaching as Women's Studies people in a colonial university.

We taught this course to fill a science requirement for non-science majors, so we had a very general population who weren't all Women's Studies students by any means. And we taught it as a Women's Studies course in Biology and Psychology. Out of that experience, and using that as a core story to rethink what I'm about as a worker in those areas, I find myself compelled by the way we repeatedly rehistoricize ourselves by telling a story; we relocate ourselves in the present historical moment by reconfiguring our identities relationally, under-standing that identity is always a relational category and that there is no such thing as a subject who pre-exists the encounters that construct that subject. Identity is an effect of those encounters — identity is that set of effects which develop from the collision of histories. It is not an abstraction. It's an extraordi-narily complex kind of sedimentation, and we rehistoricize our identities all the time through elaborate story-telling practices, in my view. And those story telling practices themselves are ways of trying to interrogate, get at, the kinds of encounters, historical moments, the kinds of key moments of transition for us — both individually and collectively.

KK: How does the history that you've been telling and your rehistoricizing your-self, how does that relate to your work now, 20 years later?

DH: Well, let me tell it by a series of professional moves. The job in Hawaii was a time in which I was married to a man who was actively gay. During that period we decided that marriage was not a good form for the intense complex friendship and sexual relationship we had with each other. In 1974, he lost a tenure case in Honolulu, and that was deeply involved with homophobia — very painful stuff. We both left Honolulu traumatized, and got jobs in different places.

I got a job at the History of Science Department at Johns Hopkins University in the city of Baltimore, a very elite institution, quite a contrast to the job in Honolulu. Johns Hopkins has a well known powerful medical school, a powerful applied physics laboratory that has been very important in the history of defense and nuclear research, and a policy school that has played a significant role in the development of American foreign policy. So, it's a place deep in the history of the reform and modernization of American medicine, and public health policy — in other words a place of power and money. And that's where I became a historian of science. I had not previously really studied the subject. I had taught it in this other context in Hawaii, and I had done some history of science in my dissertation, which was in the Biology Department at Yale University, on scholarship. Again the kind of money that was available in the United States, through the 1960s and 1970s just can't be underestimated in making people like me into intellectuals.

At Johns Hopkins I was also part of the Women's Union — a socialist feminist organization — in a neighborhood that was bi-racial, African-American and Euro-White. Not especially multi-racial, but Black and White. Baltimore was very much a scene where the category White and the category Black dominated other categories of possible racial complexity. The university did not have a strong feminist core and, also, had so few women working as academics, that we were very much, and quite rightly, thrown into the community for our feminist politics. [Laughter from both.] This was a good thing. [More laughter.]

There are many places in the United States where partly because of the size of this society and the size and wealth of its universities, many feminists in the United States were able to form a good enough community inside the university. I think it's one of the aspects of the history of American feminism that's been a problem. I think it's one of the reasons that we lost some of the organic connections between community organizing, social movements and intellectual and theoretical development that we did. So many, many, many of us became well enough supported in the universities that we really didn't need the kind of everyday psychological, physical connection with the larger communities.

But that wasn't really true in Baltimore, not in the late 1970s anyway: I'm talking mid-1974 to 1980. And it was a period when, as a historian of biology, a historian of science, I became much more aware of the history of Marxist discourse in the history of science, the development of feminism in science-related issues, the importance of the struggle against racism embedded in the history of science, the *very* important radical science history against the electronic battlefield, chemical and biological warfare, biological racism and sexism — those kinds of issues became the core of my intellectual work, my writing.

And at the same time, I was part of a socialist feminist city organization that was more attuned to some of the racial dynamics than was true in some other places in the United States in that period. The neighborhood I was in was more racially mixed than most other neighborhoods. This was partial, but it was important. It was in that period that I started working on *Primate Visions* (Haraway, 1989).[2] I began to think of primates as 'figures', as these germinal entities into which many people's imaginations are condensed. I saw primates as these creatures on the boundary between what counted as nature and culture, onto which a great deal of racial discourse was projected in the United States in the 1960s and after. I began to see how primates were part of popular cultures, movies, technical field studies, part of social psychology, part of evolutionary biology, and part of zoo management. These creatures existed at the boundaries of many constituencies that figured and carried the meanings of many kinds of stories in their bodies.

The western animal/human boundary story was, from the start, a heavily racialized story. Think of the entry of the white woman to Africa, women such as Jane Goodall or Dian Fossey, who became the surrogate for man, and who went to make contact with the animals, across the chasm between nature and culture. They were figured as *alone* in nature. And this was happening in the early 1960s, when the very areas of the world in which these animals lived were gaining national independence as the culmination of decolonizing struggles. So fifteen African nations achieved national independence and UN membership the year Jane Goodall goes to nature to be alone with the chimpanzee? [Both laugh.] She goes at just the moment of repossession of territory on the part of African nationalists, who, of course, developed very different stories about the plants and animals inside their own national boundaries and very different stories about the peoples and about ethnicities.

Well, anyway, I saw the monkeys and the apes as extremely interesting figures to carry a lot of these discussions, so I could write about them in a way that would hopefully compel a lot of audiences to want to read it.

I moved from Johns Hopkins to the History of Consciousness Board at the University of California at Santa Cruz in 1980 and took up a position in feminist theory; I think it was the first position in the US called that. History of Consciousness was an interdisciplinary, or even anti-disciplinary, department. By this I mean that it was deeply committed not to naturalizing its own objects of discourse. It was here that I started doing the cyborg work (Haraway, 1985), the work on hybridizations and fusions among the organic, human and technical, and the way the material, the literal and the tropic implode into each other. I started to see how the metaphoric and material are not opposites but really collide into each other and can create potent historical transformations. I began to understand how machines and bodies are historically specific tools and metaphors, without for a second losing their fierce materiality. Popular culture, like science fiction films, plays off of this consciousness, but so do science-based industry, biotechnology especially, and medicine. I became committed in the regions of technosciences to the project of contesting for anti-racist feminist meanings and bodies.

I also learnt from my feminist theory classes; for example Gloria Watkins, who writes as bell hooks, as a graduate student made very effective and courageous interventions in these classes that made me pay much more attention to the questions of racism in my own discourse and the discourse of people like me. Also, wonderful graduate students like Ruth Frankenberg (1993), Chela Sandoval (1991), Katie King (1986), Caren Kaplan (1987), Lata Mani (1987), and many others made quite an impact on me and my work. They were people who had a deep political, emotional and intellectual impact on each other, and who provoked each other to rethinking and redoing our theoretical work as feminists in response to these issues of shifting identities. We all engaged with issues such as the point that not all identities shift. What does it cost to stabilize which identities? Questions like that. Not all things are shifting at the same rate and the specificities of who shifts and at what costs really matter.

KK: Knowing a little bit of your biography has made your work come alive, and has made it have a depth which …

DH: … doesn't necessarily show up in the surface of the text.

KK: When we talk about identity we are also able to talk about ourselves — the person who is producing the ideas. We do this as we define our identities, although, obviously, not at the expense of talking about the social contexts.

DH: We're narrating. These are instances of rehistoricizing ourselves in order to come to some kind of changed consciousness as well as to interrogate the kind of consciousness that we have had. It's in these constant passages of stories that I think we produce the effects called identities. I think of these story-telling processes, and these passings back and forth, and rehistoricizing as very fundamental operations both for critical and intellectual work, but also just for daily life. I've been playing around with the image of cat's cradle. The making of string figures? I think of cat's cradle as a very interesting image for passing back and forth the patterns. You can build some of them yourself, but on the whole you can't, because you need more than two hands.

KK: You can't change these patterns?

DH: You can only to some degree change them. And you can, in a sense, interrupt or add to each other's patterns, you can take or accept the string pattern and do something else with it. I think of that as a powerful metaphor for conversation among us. And the knots in the string figures I think of as metaphors for identities. The knots that are formed out of these pattern makings. You can focus on those knots. You can be caught in them too. [Laughter.] You may not know how to undo them. If these become metaphors for developing our protocols in social psychology, our ways of configuring our empirical work, or our theoretical work, then what kind of trope, what kind of figural language do we use to try to describe what we're getting at? I think of a lot of my work as an attempt to imagine relationality differently. And I think the language we use to figure what we mean by 'relationality' really matters.

So let me turn the tables and ask you to tell me the stories of how in this context you narrate your own stories.

KK: I always insist that I am a migrant to Britain while claiming Britain as my home. We moved to Britain when I was seven, in 1958. I actually remember very little of my life in India apart from occasional flashes of an event. My mother and father and two older sisters and myself came to London, where I attended a local school. At the age of eleven I got a scholarship to a girls' school in north-west London, in Hampstead. I was one of only three or four black women in the school, black young girls.

So here we're talking from about 1962 to 1968. In 1968 I came to the United States — to Buffalo, New York — for a year on an American Field Service (AFS) Scholarship; this was another international move for me — which was not a migration. In the AFS programme, 16 year olds came to the United States from all over the world, lived with a family and attended high school. In

England, I had gone to a girls' school which, although a third of the girls were on scholarships, was semi-private; I had wanted to come to the United States so that I could attend a regular comprehensive school. Both my sisters, for example, went to the local grammar school, and I'd always been quite envious of them going to a regular school, a state school. Well, the American Field Service programme placed me in a private girls' school!

Yet, despite and perhaps because of that, Buffalo in the late 1960s was where I learnt a lot about politics. It was 1968, so Miami and the siege of Chicago had happened by the time I had arrived in the US. Nixon got elected in November, 1968. At the same time there were two other (I say 'other', because I didn't really count), there were two other women of colour in the class of 40 seniors — both of whom were on scholarships, both of whom were African-American and both of whom I became close friends with. The thing that I remember strikingly was that at that stage in 1968, in Buffalo, people were genuinely intrigued by the fact that I was Indian. Nowadays I would talk about the ways of expressing that interest as being derived from the processes of exoticization of India, of eroticization of the East, and of the engendering of Asia. At that time, those vocabularies and perhaps those categories as well were not available to me. All I remember is that I was related to as a young woman from India — The Orient — who had an English accent. All perfectly accurate, of course!

So, I was not racialized in the way I was racialized in England. I wasn't Black in the United States, not in the way in which that word is used in Britain. Yet, I thought I knew what the two young Black women in my class were going through because I thought I could identify racism even though those things were not happening to me in the same way.

Migrating to Britain at the age of seven, and being in the US at the age of sixteen are two key biographical markers for me. After I did my 'A' Levels I went to Bristol University, and became politically involved very quickly. This was because a strike of refuse collectors, dustbin workers, began during my first three months at Bristol. It seemed so self-evident to me, that, here were people who were doing jobs which many of us would not choose to do, were not being paid enough to have a decent standard of living and were merely asking for that. I became involved because the refuse collectors were members of the same union as the porters at the University, who were supporting the refuse collectors. This support was expressed by the porters refusing to do their own jobs, such as opening up buildings at the University. The student union was divided on whether to support the porters — some argued the strike was nothing to do with university students, while others of us spoke at lengthy meetings arguing that the University was part of the town of Bristol, one section of whose population was on strike and, therefore, was something to do with us, university students. It was at Bristol in 1970 that I was introduced to second-wave British feminism, almost at its inception. My active involvement in feminist groups began, however, when I was doing my MA at Nottingham University, in 1973.

At Bristol I pursued a three-year honours degree course in psychology, and studied philosophy, politics and sociology as my subsidiary subjects. In my second year I came across Jensen's (1969) *Harvard Education Review* article, and didn't understand a word! I did know, however, that Jensen had provided an academic way of legitimizing the racist idea that black people were genetically inferior to white people in terms of intelligence. I had done enough biology at 'A' Level to know that such an argument was flawed, to put it mildly. But I didn't know much more than that. And it seemed important to undermine that argument. I asked our lecturer if he would go through the Jensen article for the whole class. Now, this is a 200-page article, full of equations — basically rather turgid reading — and he said, 'You want me to prepare for this?' And I said yes please. I think that the lecturer couldn't believe my request because I was known as being on the left, and here I was wanting to know what it was that Jensen, a racist psychologist, had said. I am really very grateful to him that he agreed to do so — I think it was Peter Powesland — for I then understood what Jensen was saying and was able to argue against his ideas, both from within and outside of psychology.

It was from that lecture, and later discussions that I saw that intelligence is too frequently equated with IQ, despite the caveats some psychologists wrote into their work. One of the assumptions about IQ is that it is distributed amongst populations according to a Gaussian (what used to be called a 'normal' — and there's a story to be written on that sometime!) distribution; that is, that some people have a lot of this characteristic, some have very little and most have a middling amount. But this assumption — also very powerful in everyday understandings of intelligence, not just of IQ — is just that — an assumption. The reason most often provided for this assumption is that IQ/intelligence is considered to be genetically controlled. So the process, as far as I can still see, is that IQ/intelligence is assumed to be genetically controlled; the tools to measure IQ reflect that assumption, and when the IQ scores of populations are plotted, one gets a Gaussian distribution. This distribution is then used to *demonstrate* that IQ/intelligence is genetically controlled, losing sight of the history, namely that the means devised to measure this concept based themselves on an assumption of genetic control. So, an assumption about IQ/intelligence came to be translated as a truth about intelligence. It all seemed like a sleight-of-hand to me. I also have never, to this day, understood why intelligence has to be measured. The familiar question of whose interests does such measurement serve seems to be manifestly avoided in most discussions of intelligence within psychology.

The other major insight I developed at that time was that 'heredity and environment' or 'nature and nurture' — these were the terms in use at that time — were not oppositions. It was through looking at intelligence that I saw how the meanings of each term are inscribed within the other — it was probably my first insight into the processes of deconstruction, although I certainly did not have such language available to me then.

As you can see, conquering the Jensen article was a significant intellectual development for me. I learnt the necessity of struggling to understand arguments with which I didn't agree, as well as how to discuss those with which I did agree. So, migration, living in the US and a determination to undermine the ideas in the Jensen article were central for me in the early 1970s.

After my BSc in Psychology, I did an MA in Child and Educational Psychology at Nottingham University. It was at that time (1973–74) that I became very involved with feminist groups — particularly in terms of talking about women's relationships to the means of production, and what that meant about domestic labour and women. There was some writing which emerged around that time which I read avidly, for example, on the domestic labour debates (Coulson et al., 1975) which happened at roughly the same time. I then got a job at Leeds Polytechnic, in Britain. So, from the age of 23 I was a lecturer and began to teach and research within Higher Education. Between then and now I've done a number of jobs. I went from Leeds Polytechnic to working as an Educational Psychologist in Sheffield, and from there, I went to the Open University for twelve months as a Project Officer in Race Relations Education. This was in September 1979. I had the exciting task of setting up a project which would produce anti-racist materials for use by trades union and community groups, or so I thought. It became much harder to implement the project than I had thought six months earlier, for, by now, Margaret Thatcher had been elected in May and the Conservatives began to run down publicly funded education early on in their tenure. There were also petty tensions around the project — for example, bitter discussions as to whether I would have academic terms and conditions of employment or not — an issue which bedevils the employment conditions of all contract researchers in universities. Exactly twelve months later, at the age of 29, I was appointed as a Senior Lecturer in Developmental Psychology at Preston Polytechnic; I decided I wanted that job. I had set the Race Relations Education project in place, raised funds for it and was now ready to move on.

Preston Polytechnic was a place where I also learnt a lot! I became very close friends with Meg Coulson there; for most of my time there, I was the only woman lecturer in a department of 12 lecturers, and also the only person of colour employed in the department. All the support staff, including the technicians, were white women, with one exception. At least half the students were women, and most of the students were white. My work load was very high, as you can imagine. At one point, 1982, I think, I developed a syllabus in Life Span Developmental Psychology. I was told by some of the other lecturers who had looked at that syllabus that if I wanted to introduce ideas about 'race', gender and class into the curriculum, a psychology department was not the place to do so. I was horrified — I couldn't see how anyone could make sense of human psychological development without understanding the economic, social and political inequalities into which all people were born. In 1983 I taught one class which had a student who was a card-carrying member of a fascist organization.

The complicated power relationships which developed — a black woman lecturer, whose authority defined the academic interactions, and yet whose authority could potentially be undermined by a student bringing in fascist literature
into the classroom — all this provided a demanding set of challenges for me. He
accused me of stifling his freedom of speech when I challenged his racism.
Woman–man, black–white, teacher–student — these were some of the relationships of inequality which could not be read off easily from each other. In those
days, strategies for dealing with these situations had not been discussed very
widely — perhaps because there were even fewer black women teaching in
British Higher Education at that time than there are now.

It was from Preston that I went to Cambridge to do my PhD in 1983; I was a
student at Cambridge University — a very elite institution. I was there despite
being black and a woman. My time at Cambridge, while almost unbearable at
times, provided me with a large number of intellectual challenges, such as being
forced to explain myself, being pushed to argue for my intellectual positions in a
way that might *just* convince someone. So, I went from a permanent Senior
Lectureship to becoming a student. After Cambridge, I taught at Bradford
University for a number of years, spent a year (1989–90) at Oberlin College and
came to Santa Barbara in 1991.

I was politically active from 1970 onwards — in trades unions, anti-racist and
black groups, as well as women's groups. The groups rarely worked on issues
together, although some of us tried to make that happen, and we were beginning
to do this *as* black women. For example, it was in 1978, I think, that I wrote an
early piece with Pratibha Parmar on racism in the women's movement, which
we presented to a Socialist Feminist conference that year.

Overall, being an immigrant to Britain at the age of seven, going to the US in
1968, the strike at Bristol, contesting the Jensenite arguments, doing a PhD at
Cambridge in my mid-thirties, all while struggling with the intersections of race,
gender and class in my academic, personal and political concerns have been significant markers in shaping my intellectual concerns and hopes of today.

INTELLIGENCE

KK: There have been many shifts within psychology, some of which we will
discuss later in our conversation, but one area where I feel that there has been
virtually no shift is on the topic of intelligence. The campaigns against the racist
conclusions of Jensen and Eysenck (1971) were successful two decades ago; but
it feels to me as if a social amnesia has developed, including amongst progressive individuals, over the need to undermine the ways in which intelligence is
used to justify social inequalities. This justification takes place when the concept
of intelligence — a highly valued characteristic which is supposed to reside
within people — is used to explain the creation and/or the perpetuation of material and political inequalities, through denying rationality and competence to

people when they are positioned as subordinate. What I mean is that many arguments use discourses of intelligence, uncritically, to describe people — as being either 'bright' or not, 'smart' or not and, of course, 'intelligent' or not. The use of intelligence as an apparent explanation for inequality can then permit a side-stepping of discussions of racialized inequalities. What I mean by this is that intelligence is inscribed within the stereotypical definitions of some ethnicized and racialized groups — groups are defined as possessing or as not possessing it. For example, if you can argue that someone is not 'clever enough' to become a graduate student or not give a job to someone in a university for the same reason, these descriptions ensure that there is then no demand to *explain* why that individual is not being allowed to enter the institution. I realize these are very shorthand arguments I am putting together here, but it seems to me that intelligence is an idea which provides a place of condensation for racialized, gendered and class-based inequalities by using discourses associated with rationality and abilities. This is important because the concept of intelligence is a powerful example of how a discursive construction can be viewed as natural, as essential; such a presentation can then undermine projects which strive for greater democracy and equality.

DH: You can't avoid that discursive object — intelligence.

KK: I certainly can't!

DH: Is it true that African-Caribbean in the English/British context have that same kind of race and IQ edge that was true for African-Americans, and unlike, I would assume, what South Asian kids experienced in that regard?

KK: Yes, yes. It was similar to the North American experience. Bernard Coard (1971) wrote a book — *How the West Indian Child is Made Educationally Subnormal in the British School System* — which became a very significant book in challenging the racism of intelligence and its inscription in British educational policy. The issues of education and intelligence were presented differently for children of South Asian origin — it was assumed they/we had no language if we weren't fluent in English.

DH: Language and culture as opposed to the kind of literal animalization of people of African descent. I think of the IQ stuff as part of the animalization in a pretty blunt way.

KK: And yet they are both forms of racism — that is, there are racisms, plural — as Stuart Hall pointed out some time ago (Hall, 1976).

DH: Yes. Absolutely. They are the two key forms of racism, if you think of the history of colonialism from the point of view of the West. There is, on the one hand, the moves of orientalism and, on the other hand, the moves of naturalization or primitivization. On the one hand, the anxieties of the West as this fictional, powerful place — that kind of fiction which is real? I'm thinking of Edward Said's argument about the anxiety of the West with the East as its own birthplace (Said, 1978), the place of superior civilization, and the particular kind of anxiety around language and culture where the derivative culture is the West, vis-a-vis the East, and the forms of intellectual colonialism which, of course, are very different. Whereas vis-a-vis Africa, the form of intellectual colonialism and the form of anxiety are all in terms of the discourse of the primitive. These two issues of primitivity and orientalism converged as the key racializing discourses, with both being deeply involved with colonial practices; they seem to have converged in England in a way that they did not in the United States then. They both have histories; they're not one thing that marches through time. But it's useful to distinguish those kinds of colonizing discourses that work by primitivisation and those that work by culturalization, if you will; it's orientalizing versus naturalizing.

They're both modes of racialization. And in the United States, the complex kinds of racial formations in play in Californian politics now produce a different map from Britain in the 1970s. It is a map in which you can't do the Black/White dichotomy, in the American sense of Black/White.

This also gives me a way of reading your book *Talking Politics* (Bhavnani, 1991). Your passion about intelligence as a construct to be done away with helps me make more sense of some of the things in your book. I can now see the way you related to the young people, and the way you wrote about them, and the way you *engaged* their discourse as an engagement with them as *producers* of political discourse, as rational thinkers, as political theorists. You weren't giving them voice in some condescending way. You weren't studying them developmentally in some scientific way. You weren't essentializing them by giving them voice. You weren't scientizing them by studying their development of political reasoning, so that you were 'stage theorizing' them. You were, it seems to me, trying to develop a mode of relationship as a research worker and a descriptive language as a writer, that produces their discourse as *political* discourse. You didn't agree with them necessarily all the time. You're not romanticizing them. You were talking politics as they are talking politics. Now, in this sense, this is a book about political theory. Every bit as much as a book about social psychology or a book *of* social psychology. It is a book *of* political theory. Now, I think of that as one bit of the work that undoes the concepts of intelligence and redoes the concepts of rational discourse.

It's very interesting that for both of us, the Jensen paper was a kind of turning point and the race and IQ debates really have mattered to each of us as professionals in Biology and Psychology ...

KK: Why don't you expand on that a little?

DH: OK. The Jensen paper and the question of the race and IQ debates occurred as a kind of turning point in our own coming to maturity as critical intellectuals, to use bell hooks's phrase. I think for me, IQ in particular, but also the Moynihan Report on the African-Americans' supposedly pathological, matriarchal family (Moynihan, 1965) were two key events. It was the political struggles that surrounded them that taught me the meaning of the word discourse. Although I didn't have this language at the time, I saw IQ as a materialized fiction. It is an example of an apparatus for materializing the world, and these forms are themselves modes of domination. These apparatuses produce subjects with various adjectives attached to them who can then be measured, for example a student with particular scores or a pregnant teenager with a specific profile that puts her at risk for further surveillance. These sets of rules materialize the world within unlivable narratives, and it is these narratives *that are our object of struggle.*

'Intelligence' is incredibly important, which I think is the sense we both share here. As teachers, we're continually working with students who, in contextually specific ways, learn to produce themselves as 'dumb'. In contextually specific ways, folks learn to produce themselves as 'not entitled', 'not rational', 'not smart', 'dumb'. What happens next is that the contextual specificity of that production drops away and a person is left with a residual self-image of 'not entitled', 'not smart', 'not intelligent'. What we lose track of, institutionally, is that there is an *apparatus* for the producing and sorting of people, as distinct from a natural object which can be measured. That's the move that I think radical science movements made analytically. They forced an understanding of the difference between the natural object and the discursively produced real object. So that there's no opposition here between fact and fiction, between discursive and material. This is an example of the implosion of the material, tropic and literal I was talking about a few minutes ago.

KK: I agree that intelligence is a material fiction, and is part of those broad fictions that are established as racialized discourses, as sexualized discourses and so on.

DH: That's right. The world is *literally* naturalized as sexualized, as racialized. Bodies come that way. It is the word made flesh! [Laughter.]

IDENTITIES

KK: Let's turn to identity and subjectivity.

DH: I don't tend to engage psychoanalytic discourse as my own, very much, and I think of that as the major body of writing that has theorized subjectivity. I think of Theresa de Lauretis, who is my colleague, as a really strong, positive example here. These are not my languages though I read them, I engage them.

But, that caveat aside, I am more than a little interested in, and have been attempting to create a little trouble around, notions of identity and subjectivity or subject formation. I take seriously the notion of identity as an *effect*. I take seriously Judith Butler's (1992) notion of contingent foundations and the modes of production of subjects and subject positions in discourse.

KK: Could you explain that a little more?

DH: Well, a couple of things. One is a kind of catechism, a set of principles that I feel myself working with, working hypotheses, a tool kit. Namely, nothing, no sets of actors in the world are preconstituted with their skin boundaries already clearly pre-established. There are no pre-established actors in the world. Be those actors human, machine, other organisms, various kinds of machines, various kinds of humans. There are no pre-constituted entities. All the actors in the world aren't 'us', whoever you think of as like yourself. It is in relational encounters that worlds emerge, they emerge in plots of materialized stories. And the actors are the *result* of encounter, of engagement. So there is no pre-discursive identity for anyone, including machines, including the non-human. Our boundaries form *in* encounter, in relation, in discourse. Hold us still — outside social discourse — and try to measure us, and you get a mirage, a ghost or a projection of those doing the measuring. There is no pre-discursive or pre-relational, using discursive as a kind of synonym for relational. One of the problems with using the word discourse is that the metaphor of language can end up carrying too much weight. I'm willing to let it carry a lot of weight, but I'm not willing to let it then finally really *be* everything. There are non-language-like processes of encounter. But there's nothing pre-relational, pre-encounter. So it is only in engagement that we, and everybody else, get our boundaries and our skins drawn. That's what I mean by saying everything is relational.

KK: You had said that there are questions to be raised about the nature of shifting identities. You posed questions in our conversation earlier such as what is the rate of change for identities? For whom do identities change?

DH: The stabilization of identity is a world industry. [Laughter.] You can think of the history of capitalism as the stabilization of some identities and not others. Who gets to have a stable identity? Is it a good stable identity or a rather costly one? Seriously. How many identities does who get to have? Are you forced into your multiplicities or are you invited? Which ones, at which times of life? Which mobilities at what? For whom? What kinds of effects come readily? What kinds are subsidized? What kind of identity effects are practically impossible to avoid? Which ones are really hard to achieve? These are the questions that come to my mind in this context.

For example, Aihwa Ong, a few years ago, wrote extensively about young women of Malay ethnicity and Malaysian citizenship, in Malaysia, working in

Japanese and United States multinational electronics firms, in the export processing zones in Malaysia (Ong, 1987). These were young women whose Malay ethnicity was itself the result of British imperialism, as transplanted Javanese people earlier were brought as peasants into a British-plantation colonial system that also imported South Asian labor in another set of relationships, Chinese in yet another set of relationships. In other words, the traditional Malay identity was already historicized in this way. There is never an already existing racial, ethnic identity which is the tradition against which everything else happens. Ong subverts that kind of essentialism from the start.

The young women, they are Muslim. They are within Islam, but Islam is not homogeneous. The Islam of many of these young women produces an identity of a Muslim young person, who is also a wage-earning young woman, perhaps the only source of money income in the family, whose brothers might be unemployed or forced to migrate. They are young unmarried women, who are at a moment of their lives where lots of folks have an interest in them. Family lineages are being negotiated, and questions of honor are at stake. The women's self-identities are often reconfigured in the factory through beauty pageants, or cosmetic sales, or vacations to the city, or as young girls by the factory managers who consider themselves to be in loco parentis. All these things and more are going on; that's the point. These young women, in their embodiment, are the points of collision of all these powerful forces, including forces of their own. They're certainly not passive here. And I think of these young girls as not unlike the young people you wrote about. People at an age, and in an institutional setting, at a historical moment where all of the really interesting things implode, crash in. And I think these are stories about shifting identities. These are ways of asking: 'How might connections be formed in all these different worlds?' What are the possible feminist alliances between women in our locations and the young women Aihwa Ong is writing about? How can such alliances come about? What could that possibly mean? Marxists would have said that there surely was a position around questions of class solidarity in terms of the labor relationship and transnational capitalism, but we can see from her work that such arguments could only be one set of starting points.

KK: A question which I have is why is work like Aihwa Ong's not classified as psychology; it may be classified as feminist and as anthropology but not psychology. Why? If the subject matter of psychology is identity, then why does psychology refuse to deal with questions of identity in the way Aihwa Ong does?.

Let me say a little more. Social psychology has attempted to deal with identity as a place where variables [sic] such as class, gender, race, age, employment, status and many other elements come together. But, the problem is that because psychology demands clean and uncontaminated variables (here I'm using the language of psychology), the discipline is not able to cope with the idea that these issues, while named as variables, are not clear-cut or static; rather they are constantly shifting and changing, even as they are being assessed. Perhaps, because they are being assessed. Psychological approaches which rely on experimentation are therefore unable to assess or analyse identity in the ways in which someone like Aihwa Ong does. So, the subject, psychology, has to be shifted, as do many of the subjects who constitute psychology. The need for this to happen can be seen most clearly, I think, when identity is considered. Intuitively, psychology is the academic site where identity could be discussed and yet, when we turn to psychology, it becomes almost impossible to tackle, or even engage with, the complexities of the experience or the concept. Psychology stabilizes identity and so impairs those characteristics which are important in experiencing and analysing identity — its fluidity, for example. This is not to say that such engagement and shifting can't be achieved within psychology. The current generation of students whom I meet and who work in psychology seem determined to shift the subject, in all senses of the phrase. For example Barbara Trepagnier is focusing her doctoral dissertation to examine the identities of white feminists through their discussions of racism. It builds on Ruth Frankenberg's work, but also departs from it, in that Barbara is determined to harness social psychology in developing her empirical work as well as her theoretical insights. What I see, therefore, is a determination to shift psychology, through working on questions of identity — precisely because identity is the site where the material and the tropic implode. The implosion of the material and the tropic within psychology is merely an extension of your argument about the material, the tropic and identities — isn't that right, Donna?

DH: Yes. Let me approach this question from the point of view of a historian of the life sciences, one of which is psychology. Let me crudely schematize the history of 19th and 20th century psychology. The discourse is dominated by evolutionary frameworks, biologizing frameworks, the discursive production of the psychological subject as the measurable subject and by the construction of an individual subject. The history of psychology is replete with functionalism — namely the adding together of separate subjects, and claiming this reconstitutes the social. Well, contemporary postcolonial, anti-racist, feminist and neo-Marxist theory undermines all of that. *All of it.* The whole question of what counts as the unit of analysis is in play in those oppositional theoretical models. So the subject of psychology, the object produced by the discourse, which is the subject of psychology, has to be an object (or subject — an entity) whose boundaries are configured in the kinds of relationships being examined. And now we can see that what counts as an individual is far from self evident.

SOCIAL REPRESENTATIONS

KK: It is this conundrum, 'what can count as an individual?', which keeps me within psychology, while being critical of that universe of discourse known as psychology. It is challenging to have to deal with that question — not just in my own work but when I teach a course which has to act as an introduction to social psychology to 500 undergraduates.

My way of dealing with these puzzles is to view psychology as being located at the intersection of all the human sciences, just as each area of enquiry, for example, sociology, history, philosophy, is also located at just such an intersection for its own universe of discourse.

Perhaps the best way to explain this is to provide an example. As you know, my book is about the ways in which young working-class people discuss issues in the domain of the political. I used a social psychological theory, social representations theory, to unravel some of the ideas which developed. Basically, I suggest that the project of social representations is to cast light on the social, from the standpoint of the subject. But I don't see 'social' as a synonym for shared, consensual beliefs. Social, for me, refers to the conflictual economic, political and ideological systems, expressed through discourses, which constitute a society: the 'social' has embedded within it relations of subordination and domination.

My argument is that social representations are contradictory ideological elements which make up 'the common senses' of particular social groups. In order to understand these common senses, it is helpful to examine the contradictions in both their content and form. I argue, therefore, that social representations be recast as discursive configurations. In using 'discursive', it is clear I am influenced by Foucault. I suggest 'configurations' in order to retain the dynamic and shifting nature of those representations or elements. Discursive configurations provide a way to examine the manner in which power inequalities, shifting meanings and common sense frames are condensed in social issues. That is, discursive configurations are the elements which together make up discursive formations. And discursive formations are what I see as being appropriately analysed by social psychology.

It is social representations theory that has allowed me to claim the identity of psychologist and go to certain psychology conferences, even though I talk about configurations — even though I use the language that is more often associated with critical theory. It can be very hard to claim that identity — of a psychologist — when using the language and the arguments I do.

DH: I think that is very true. In the United States, the constant pull of psychology to be a science, like the natural sciences, is a big issue. It pulls psychology away from the critical discourses of social inquiry, on the one hand, and the hermeneutic interpretive discourse of the human sciences on the other. The drive for psychology to be a natural science, the institutional pressures, the many enticements and coercions for psychologists to be in the model of the so-called hard sciences, pushes psychology away from the kind of critical role that I think it could institutionally play in the American university. Now, this is a very crude generalization, because immediately I can think of a zillion exceptions. There are the traditions of humanistic psychology, for example. But anthropology, unlike psychology as an institutional formation in the United States, has much more easily been an active place for the making of alliances with the critical theoretical discourses, like the oppositional consciousness that Chela Sandoval (1991) theorizes. Anthropology has become a key site for the practices of cultural and social interrogation of cultural theory and cultural studies.

KK: Why?

DH: I do think it has a lot to do with the question of the hegemony of a model of knowledge-production processes in the natural sciences. Anthropology with its historical commitment to field work, its commitment to risking identity as part of doing research, is able to shift as a result of the critiques. You are at risk in your identity, as a knowing subject, as an anthropologist, in a way I don't think psychologists have been forced to be institutionally. Some of course have, and there's a long history of reflective participant observation in psychology. I want to say these things very carefully. There are deep literatures in psychology inquiring into the question of relationships in research. But, that said, I think psychology has undergone different kinds of pressures that push the discipline as a whole away from positions which are more common in anthropology and anti-racist cultural studies.

It seems as if psychology is inoculated against a certain kind of critical theory, or hermeneutics. I've been very interested in Sandra Harding's work, who is a philosopher of science, a feminist. She has a new book coming out called *The 'Racial' Economy of Science* (Harding, 1993). She has written extensively on both race and gender in scientific models. Her concept of 'strong objectivity' is what interests me. She's pushing natural scientists to take on board a concept of objectivity that I think is actually very similar to the notions that I tried to work out in 'situated knowledges' (Haraway, 1988), that you tried to work out with 'Tracing the Contours' (Bhavnani, 1993), that Chela works out with oppositional consciousness (Sandoval, 1991), in all these various languages circulating among us. I see Sandra Harding's argument about strong objectivity in all scientific pursuit as a taking on board the kind of critical inquiry into positioning, into relationality, into history, into the stakes. What kind of partiality, what kind of commitment, engagement, what way of life are you *for*, in your knowledge-production factors? This question insists on accountability. A kind of relentless situating as part of objectivity, so that objectivity is not maintaining the boundaries of the knower intact vis-a-vis what is studied, but is the opposite — is opening up the boundaries of the knower to a kind of accountability for positioning in all knowledge production. Call that 'strong objectivity'. It's an attempt to intervene in what's going to count as science. And I think psychology is in those struggles, ought to be in those struggles more explicitly, very strongly.

KK: Reading your 'situated knowledges' work, Donna, in which you look at notions of accountability, positioning and partiality in relation to standpoint, it became very clear that the concept of standpoint (which is a concept that is discussed in feminist writing) is not a given, and is certainly not the same as providing a list of social categories which describe oneself — age, sex, 'race', status and so on, and is not merely about an individual. Is that right?

DH: Right. Absolutely and I learned this from Nancy Hartsock, mainly (Hartsock, 1983). And the other folks who did this work, but for me personally I learned it from Nancy, and she wrote it very clearly in her feminist standpoint paper. She, out of Marxist materials really, and out of her engagement with both Lukács and Gramsci, in different ways, argues that standpoint is an achievement. That it is what is struggled *for*. Perhaps, being born into, or finding yourself in, certain situations produces a *potential* for standpoint, but the achievement of standpoint is the achievement of a critical take, and a *collective* critical take. Standpoint is crafted out of struggle, out of engagement, and then becomes a powerful possibility for fueling a different kind of knowledge in the world. And to go back to our discussion about IQ, standpoint theory becomes a way of producing — of materializing — the world differently. So in that sense, I think of standpoint theory as like the 'situated knowledges', 'tracing the contours' or 'oppositional consciousness' arguments. These are not all the same thing; and their fantasies and languages are different, their immediate audiences and stakes are different, but I think there's real cross-talk going on among all these different ways of thinking that have everything to do with seeing the possibility for learning how to craft with each other a critical social intelligence. For me, this is cat's cradle in practice! You know, a kind of critical practice that's accountable for our resistance, tries to remember our resistances, what we've inherited as well as what we've done, that isn't just premised on notions of deliberateness and choice, instrumentality and will, and understands the kind of deep structure of how we're positioned. Which understands that not everything is equally mobile, but none-the-less is a critical engagement that opens up possibilities. I appeal to a kind of science fictional quality of 'worlding', of making another world imaginable, and maybe just barely possible.

KK: Unexpected openings perhaps? …

DH: … Some kind of surprise. Production of surprises is, I think, critical political work.

KK: Yes. I usually call what you've been describing as counter-intuitive work. [Laughter from both.]

DH: Something we didn't know was possible. Maybe that's the hope for liberation. Maybe that's what liberation talk is about. That the established disorder is *not necessary*. It's that kind of conviction that I think we're about as critical intellectuals — it doesn't *have* to be this way.

NOTES

1. We would like to thank all those who provided comments on this piece.
2. This is a retrospective statement. I can see the germs were developing then, though I didn't formulate it this way till considerably later.

REFERENCES

Bhavnani, Kum-Kum (1991) *Talking Politics*. Cambridge: Cambridge University Press.
Bhavnani, Kum-Kum (1993) 'Tracing the Contours: Feminist Research and Feminist Objectivity', *Women's Studies International Forum* 16 (2): 95–104.
Butler, Judith (1992) 'Contingent Foundations: Feminism and the Question of "Postmodernism" ', in Judith Butler and Joan W. Scott (eds) *Feminists Theorize the Political*. New York: Routledge.
Coard, Bernard (1971) *How the West Indian Child is Made Educationally Sub-Normal in the British School System*. London: New Beacon Books.
Coulson, Margaret, Magas, Branca and Wainwright, Hilary (1975) 'The Housewife and Her Labour Under Capitalism — A Critique', *New Left Review* No. 89: 59–71.
Eysenck, Hans (1971) *Race, Intelligence and Education*. London: Temple Smith.
Frankenberg, Ruth (1988) 'The Social Construction of Whiteness', PhD dissertation, University of California at Santa Cruz.
Hall, Stuart (1976) 'Racism and Reaction', in *Five Views of Multi-Racial Britain*. London: Commission for Racial Equality.
Haraway, Donna (1985) 'Manifesto for Cyborgs: Science, Technology and Socialist Feminism in the 1980s', *Socialist Review* No. 80: 65–104.
Haraway, Donna (1988) 'Situated Knowledges: The Science Question in Feminism as a Site of Discourse on the Privilege of Partial Perspective', *Feminist Studies* 14 (3): 575–99.
Haraway, Donna (1989) *Primate Visions*. New York: Routledge.
Harding, Sandra (1993) *The Racial Economy of Science*. Bloomington, IN: Indiana University Press.
Hartsock, Nancy (1983) 'The Feminist Standpoint: Developing the Ground for a Specifically Feminist Historical Materialism', in Sandra Harding and Merrill Hintikka (eds) *Discovering Reality*. Dordrecht: Reidel.
Jensen, Arthur R. (1969) 'How Much Can We Boost IQ in Scholastic Achievement?', *Harvard Educational Review* Vol. 39 No. 1 pp 1–123.
Kaplan, Caren (1987) 'Deterritorializations: The Rewriting of Home and Exile in Western Feminist Discourse', *Cultural Critique* No. 6: 187–98.
King, Katie (1986) 'The Situation of Lesbianism as Feminism's Magical Sign: Contests for Meaning and the US Women's Movement', *Communication* 9 (1): 65–92.
Mani, Lata (1987) 'The Construction of Woman as Tradition in Early Nineteenth Century Bengal', *Cultural Critique* No. 7: 119–56.
Moynihan, Daniel (1965) *The Negro Family: The Case for National Action*. Washington, DC: US Department of Labor.
Ong, Aihwa (1987) *Spirits of Resistance and Capitalist Discipline: Factory Workers in Malaysia*. Albany, NY: State University of New York Press.
Said, Edward (1978) *Orientalism*. New York: Pantheon.

Sandoval, Chela (1991) 'US Third World Feminism: The Theory and Method of Oppositional Consciousness in the Postmodern World', *Genders* No. 10: 1–24.

Stein, Dorothy (1985) *Ada, A Life and a Legacy.* Cambridge, MA: MIT Press.

Kum-Kum BHAVNANI is Associate Professor in the Department of Sociology at the University of California, Santa Barbara, CA 93106, USA. She teaches cultural studies, feminist theory and epistemology and social psychology and has published articles in all of these areas. Her book, *Talking Politics*, was published by Cambridge University Press in 1991.

Donna HARAWAY is at the University of California at Santa Cruz, where she teaches feminist theory, cultural and historical studies of technoscience, and women's studies. She is the author of *Crystals, Fabrics and Fields: Metaphors of Organicism in Twentieth Century Developmental Biology* (Yale University Press, 1976), *Primate Visions: Gender, Race, and Nature in the World of Modern Science* (New York and London: Routledge, 1989; London: Verso, 1992), and *Simians, Cyborgs, and Women: The Reinvention of Nature* (New York: Routledge and London: Free Association Books, 1991). She is currently working on a book called *Worldly Diffractions: Feminism and Technoscience*. She can be contacted at the Board of History of Consciousness, Oakes College, University of California at Santa Cruz, Santa Cruz, CA 95064, USA.

Karen L. HENWOOD

Resisting Racism and Sexism in Academic Psychology: A Personal/Political View

The article discusses resistance to racism and sexism within academic psychology. Its contents are linked together by the chronology of my own experiences, presenting a personal/political view. Focusing upon Social Identity Theory in particular, I point out that even critical perspectives in the social psychology of prejudice and discrimination tend to neglect black people's experiences of racism and represent an impoverished approach to the social construction of 'race'. I pay special attention to the culturally pervasive problem of new racism, and to psychology's commitment to a purportedly apolitical professional identity and value-free science. Both are implicated in academic psychology's lack of a clear commitment to anti-racism, as illustrated in my account of the British Psychological Society's handling of the call for an academic boycott of apartheid South Africa. I touch on various ways of moving forward to an anti-racist psychology in respect of theory, research and the institution of psychology. One possibility is to work within a version of feminist standpoint epistemology which seeks to re-vision knowledge by starting from the multiplicity and diversity of women's experiences and conditions of our lives.

INTRODUCTION

Conjoining the notions of shifting identities and shifting racisms provides a fruitful starting point for a consideration of the relationship between feminism and psychology. The tension in this relationship has been widely discussed within feminist scholarship, given that severe difficulties exist in maintaining a personal/political commitment within the confines of the academy (see e.g. Unger, 1982; Kitzinger, 1990). As part of this debate, the issue has been raised of whether feminist research can remain as a perspective within psychology or whether it must necessarily transform psychology in some quite radical ways.

Feminism & Psychology © 1994 SAGE (London, Thousand Oaks and New Delhi), Vol. 4(1): 41–62.

However, increasingly, it has become clear that the reasons for this tension also include the construction which is to be put on the notion of feminist identity/political commitment itself. Feminist research is conducted *for* (rather than on) women, thereby empowering (see e.g. Bhavnani, 1988, 1990) us in our everyday lives. But the category 'women' includes within it a variety of other social positions including black/white, lesbian/heterosexual and disabled/able-bodied. Therefore feminist research must involve challenging racism(s), hetero-sexism(s) and the bias toward women who are able-bodied and so on, as well as sexism(s). Any individual woman may be the subject of multiple, perhaps contradictory, positions in wider society. Consequently, identity — including feminist identity — is probably best described as plural, fragmented and with a propensity to shift contextually and over time.

The foregoing remarks outline some of the general theoretical considerations which form the background to this article, the major purpose of which is to present a personal/political view of my own commitment to anti-racism and subsequently to feminism in academic research and within the institution of academic psychology. Like Burman (1990), I believe that it is important to make public our private stories to provide a commentary on the operation of psychology, in order to make available to others those ideas and strategies which enable us to do the research that we want to do, and to illuminate the ways in which we can resist — and yet may be periodically rendered powerless by — the wider institution of psychology. The article is comprised of three sections, the contents of which are linked together by the chronology of my own experiences. The first section is a critical commentary on social psychological research on prejudice, discrimination and latterly racism, focusing in particular on the 'social identity theory' of relationships between social groups and the problem of new racism. In the second I consider the events that took place during the campaign for the academic boycott of apartheid South Africa, pointing out how the British Psychological Society's handling of and position on this issue is inconsistent with a commitment to anti-racism. In the third section I provide a more detailed account of how the need to include the perspectives and voices of black women is beginning to alter the complexion of feminist scholarship, and how this change has confirmed my belief in the need for a specifically feminist form of social research.

THE SOCIAL PSYCHOLOGY OF PREJUDICE, DISCRIMINATION AND RACISM

Starting Out in Psychology: Social Identity Theory

In recalling her early experiences as a female undergraduate, Jane Ussher (1990) describes her feelings of 'disillusionment' with psychology. I was similarly perplexed by many areas of psychological investigation; however, one area convinced me of psychology's human and social relevance — social psychological studies of prejudice and discrimination. Some researchers were clear in their view that social psychological research should be evaluated for its ability to provide strategies for challenging racism and for promoting social change (called 'action research') (see e.g. Billig, 1978). Consequently, I was enthusiastic about specializing, both in my final year of undergraduate studies and postgraduate work, in the social psychology of prejudice and discrimination.

Of course, the broad base of social psychological research on prejudice and discrimination is not without its limitations. Focusing upon prejudice and discrimination as the object of study implicitly conceptualizes a problem which has a widespread and inherently social dimension, in terms of individual attitudes and behaviours (Henriques 1984). Therefore, as Husband (1986) has argued, the problem for social psychology is best considered as one of 'racism' in both its institutional/structural (Howitt, 1991) and symbolic/everyday aspects (Essed, 1988, 1991). The value of Social Identity Theory — the framework within which I began to conduct my early research — was that it sought to open up a space for a genuinely *social* social psychology, by focusing upon relationships between persons not as individuals but as members of groups within a stratified society (Tajfel, 1978a, 1978b, 1981; Tajfel and Turner, 1979).[1] The theory states that by categorizing persons socially and locating oneself within this pattern of wider social relationships, a sense of social identity or selfhood — and hence a basis for social action — can be achieved. Within this approach, primacy is afforded to the principles of social categorization and identification in order to undermine the view that prejudice is due to the unconscious psychological dynamics involved in the character formation of bigoted authoritarian individuals (see e.g. Adorno et al., 1950) or to a human instinct for aggression in response to frustration (see e.g. Berkowitz, 1962). However, the strategy of simply excluding unconscious psychological processes from consideration would not be judged a satisfactory solution to the problem of reductionism by many anti-racist researchers today (see e.g. Donald and Rattansi, 1992; cf. Widdicombe, 1992).

Cognitive Social Psychology and the Problem of 'New Racism'

Despite the fact that advocates of Social Identity Theory (SIT) continue to distinguish it from other more individualistic and reductionist approaches in social psychology, there are some significant points of concordance with other contemporary cognitive social psychological accounts of prejudice and discrimination. First, while glossed as research on a social problem which therefore requires some analysis of social context, prejudice and discrimination are nevertheless perceived to have a psychological origin which can be traced back to the fundamental cognitive process of categorization (see references to SIT and texts on social cognition, e.g. Fiske and Taylor, 1984; Hamilton, 1981; Miller, 1982).[2] Prejudice, in this sense, is a form of prejudgement — a cognitive filing system (Billig, 1985) which is necessary if human beings are to be able to comprehend, act and survive (Allport, 1954; Tajfel, 1969). Second, in time honoured fashion for psychology and in common with other social categories, 'race' is treated practically as an operationalizable, measurable and contrastive experimental variable.[3]

Social psychology is a constitutive and productive social activity which occupies the same plane as everyday thought and understanding: accordingly it can be 'deconstructed' to establish what is taken for granted within it (Parker, 1989; Parker and Shotter, 1990). This has begun to occur in social psychological research on prejudice and discrimination, with the result that hidden racist and sexist practices and assumptions are being revealed. The problem is not one of overt hostility and disparagement, nor in most cases of malicious intent, but of the 'new racism' (see e.g. Barker, 1981). Unlike old style racism, which tends to posit crude notions of 'racial' and cultural inferiority, the new racism asserts that differences between groups are simply natural, intractable and non-negotiable, and that for this reason groups are best kept apart. It is proving itself to be a potent means by which dominant groups can discriminate, and yet apparently save face by denying racism (van Dijk, 1984, 1992), within a liberal democratic society or culture (see e.g. Billig, 1988). Therefore, instances of new racism in contemporary social psychology have to be documented and 'faced up to' (Howitt, 1991: 119) if racism is to continue to be challenged and, hopefully, undermined.

In the case of using 'race' as an experimental variable, Steven Reicher (1986) has considered the practice in research on intergroup contact, and pointed out that it may, unintentionally, represent an example of new racism since it takes the category of 'race' for granted. Susan Condor (1988) has also found some striking and alarming parallels between new racism and social cognitive research on social stereotypes. One example — of the practice that she calls 'metalevel racism' — is the quite fundamental argument in social cognitive research that categories of people (e.g. 'race' and sex), like categories of objects, are more or less useful to the extent that they allow for the accurate, empirical prediction of behaviour. The argument is problematic because, in the manner of new racism, the racist insults which can accompany the deployment of such categories are effectively naturalized, obscured or denied. Condor's second form of new racism, called 'reification of "race" categories' again involves a treatment of 'race' not as a social construct but as a highly 'visible' or 'distinctive' physical characteristic (see e.g. Taylor, 1981; McArthur, 1982). Undesirable stereotypical attributes are explained as resulting from associations (including temporal and metaphorical connections) between salient physical (e.g. black/white faces, thick/thin lips) and corresponding psychological/social characteristics (laziness/endeavour) (McArthur, 1982). A flawed and rigid commitment to naïve empiricism in this case reinforces a highly racialized view of external reality, together with the racist view that the attribution of undesirable characteristics to certain groups merely reflects certain objective facts about them. From other traditions of social psychological investigation this would be called 'blaming the victim'.

The assumption that the use of categories and categorization is some neutral act of biological significance also has the unfortunate effect of implying the inevitability of prejudice (Billig, 1985). Just as this assumption can be shown to function as a rhetorical strategy in the promulgation of new racism, however, so can it be undermined at the level of social psychological theory. As Billig explains, any concept such as categorization can be seen to imply its opposite — in this case particularization; instances can be filed into boxes only if the boxes and the instances are particularized or distinguished along some dimension from others of an otherwise similar kind. On grounds of argument, therefore, categorization can have no greater biological priority than particularization. The fortunate consequence of this being the case is that prejudice can appear as neither natural nor inevitable. As part of the deconstruction of the link between categorization and prejudice, Billig also points to the lack of universally held prejudice within society, given the existence of what he calls 'tolerance'. The problem with this notion of tolerance is that it implicitly assumes that there is, indeed, something about minority groups which is to be tolerated — that majority groups have genuine fears. This is an instance, therefore, where even an explicitly anti-racist social psychological analysis is incomplete as a challenge to the liberal discourse of new racism (Husband, 1986).

Reappraising Social Identity Theory

In seeking to avoid the pitfalls of assuming the natural, objective facticity of 'race', SIT can return to its theoretical conception of race as a social position or category within a stratified society. Attempts have also been made to theorize the relationship between the psychological and the social in dialectical terms (Turner and Oakes, 1986), which is required in order to overcome the assumption of the psychological origins to, and hence inevitability in the determination of, intergroup conflict. Over the years I have become increasingly despairing, however, of the idea that such problems could be solved by means of high level theoretical recapitulation and revision alone.

As early as 1974 Godfrey Harrison had pointed to a bias in social psychological accounts of prejudice, for neglecting the experiences of the targets of prejudice in their own terms. Given the power asymmetries involved, where the majority of researchers are white, male and middle class, there are of course some good reasons for researchers 'studying up' the hierarchy (Gorelick, 1991) — not least of which is to avoid an excessive problematizing of minority groups. However, by neglecting the experiences and views of those who suffer most, one risks generating a partial and quite possibly distorted account (e.g. Harding, 1986, 1991). Thus, for example, as far as I am aware, SIT has thrown little light on the issue of what it means for black people to live under threat of racist abuse and attack, prompting comments on its emptiness in this respect (Husband, 1984). SIT has also been deconstructed to reveal an implicit masculinist bias in privileging competition and differentiation (agency) over cooperation and similarity (communion) in relationships between groups (Williams, 1984). While I would not concur with the view that communion and agency reflect essential differences between women and men, as cultural codes they do function to fix and differentiate feminine and masculine values and modes of being (Wetherell, 1986). From the perspective of cultural constructionism, therefore, SIT would seem to approach intergroup relationships from a specifically masculinist point of view (Michael, 1991).

Historically, SIT has been proposed as a theory of inter- (and intra-) group relationships which takes social and historical relationships, power and ideology fully into account. Its overwhelming predilection for experimental control, universal psychological processes and highly predictive/generalizable theory[4] has, however, posed a barrier to research which can illuminate the more contextually grounded, culturally constructed and therefore socially meaningful aspects of human functioning and social life (Henwood and Pidgeon, 1992a). Yet, presumably, this is vital if social psychology is to contribute to understanding how social identities and/or psychological subjectivities become formed within, and fashion resistance to, broader social structures, construed as complexes of relationships of ideology and power. In order to overcome past barriers, a new paradigm for research has emerged at the critical margins of social psychology, focused upon the concept of discourse, together with its potentialities for doing research differently (Potter and Wetherell, 1987; Parker, 1991). This approach problematizes the concepts/theories and methods deemed acceptable within a positivist–empiricist framework of science and makes alternative proposals in their wake. It has generated a new perspective in the study of racism, breaking with the prejudice problematic of the past (Wetherell and Potter, 1992). Instead, this research seeks to map out the contours and shape of the language of racism, teasing out the discursive practices that operate to 'legitimize' the exploitation of minorities.

THE LIMITS OF A 'PSYCHOLOGICAL IDENTITY': LESSONS FROM THE CAMPAIGN FOR THE ACADEMIC BOYCOTT OF SOUTH AFRICA

During the mid to late 1980s I completed my PhD and stayed on to work as a research associate at the University of Bristol. My PhD had argued for a reconceptualization of social stereotypes as signifying practices, and I was finding it increasingly difficult to work effectively within the social identity paradigm. However, the most significant and formative event for me at this time was the campaign for the academic boycott of apartheid South Africa.

Many sections of the international community world-wide were supporting the call by the African National Congress (ANC) and the mass democratic movement (MDM) for a comprehensive boycott of diplomatic, economic, sporting and other cultural (including academic) links with the apartheid state, as part of a strategy to undermine the illegitimate regime and replace it with a government representative of the majority of people. This general strategy was supported by the United Nations General Assembly, by the Commonwealth and by the EEC. Therefore, one might have thought that the issue for psychologists in Britain would be quite simple — how to enforce the academic boycott most effectively and appropriately. Unfortunately, this did not turn out to be the case, and the campaign itself became a focus of a struggle against racism within the discipline of psychology.

A brief account of some of the events which occurred as part of the campaign at this time is as follows. The question of what to do about the extensive contacts which existed between the British Psychological Society (BPS), individual university departments in Britain and their equivalents in South Africa was first raised formally at the Annual Conference of the Social Psychology Section in 1986. At this meeting it was decided to promote an open, public debate on the issue of the need to break institutional links with apartheid, and how this could be achieved. To this end a letter was sent to the house journal of the BPS (the then *Bulletin of the British Psychological Society*, now the *Psychologist*, publication date January 1987) supporting the call by the MDM for a boycott of institutional links with apartheid South Africa, and signed by 96 psychologists. It was followed by a prolonged series of exchanges between supporters of the academic boycott and those who opposed it.[5]

During 1988, discussion of the problem of maintaining links with apartheid was superseded by concerted demands for action from sections of the membership. The Social Psychology Section, for example, made the decision at its AGM to ballot its membership on a resolution to implement the academic boycott. A group of (then trainee) clinical psychologists based at the Institute of Psychiatry proposed a 'compromise' proposal of a 'selective' boycott of those academics in South Africa who did not object to the apartheid regime (Baron-Cohen et al., 1988). Subsequently, these two groups (plus other individuals totalling over 100 UK psychologists) joined together to form a pressure group called Psychologists Against Apartheid (PAA), which was affiliated to the Anti-Apartheid Movement (AAM). (For details of the current status of AAM solidarity work and PAA see note 12.)

The position of the BPS at this time was that no resolution could be voted upon which is inconsistent with the 'key object' of the Royal Charter of the Society (that is Clause 3 (ii) — to promote 'the advancement and diffusion of a knowledge of psychology pure and applied'), since it would be rendered vulnerable to proceedings in the courts restricting it from acting ultra vires (see e.g. Newman, 1989). Agreement *was* reached with advocates of the boycott, however, on the point that it would not be ultra vires to vote on a resolution to break links on the grounds that the racism of apartheid is inconsistent with the Code of Conduct of the Society. Accordingly, the Social Psychology Section agreed to abandon its plans for a ballot in favour of a postal ballot of the entire membership organized by the BPS. Shortly thereafter the following resolution was voted upon, passed and confirmed at the AGM of the BPS on 1 April 1989:

> The Code of Conduct of the British Psychological Society requires psychologists 'Not to allow their standards of professional responsibilities or standards of practice to be diminished by considerations of religion, sex, race, age, nationality, party politics, social standing, class or other extraneous factors'. The racism of apartheid is incompatible with the Society's Code and the Society therefore condemns apartheid and resolves to avoid all links with psychologists and psychological organisations and their formal representatives that do not affirm and adhere to the principles in this clause of its Code of Conduct.

At least two features of these events are of concern to anti-racist psychology: the nature of the arguments levelled against the imposition of sanctions and the position finally adopted by the BPS on the issue. They lead me to conclude that arguments for the impartiality and neutrality [sic] of scientific and professional psychology can be used rhetorically to undermine resistance to racism within the discipline.

Arguments Used Against the Imposition of Sanctions

One argument frequently levelled against the call for the imposition of the academic boycott was that it posed a direct threat to academic freedom. Clearly, academic freedom is a cherished value for all psychologists, as teachers, researchers and clinicians, since its purpose is to defend us from unjustified interference from external agencies whose activities are structured by different and often incompatible goals. For this reason it must be protected vigorously. However, the case of apartheid South Africa shows that it must be protected not as an abstract slogan but at the practical level at which it is intended to operate in people's everyday lives. Academic freedom, in this respect, did not exist at all in apartheid South Africa, where the majority of people were excluded from receiving even the most basic education if they were classified racially as 'non-white'.[6] Those academics who had opposed the apartheid regime had been victimized, subjected to harassment and torture; some were even murdered. And they and their writings had been banned, thus limiting academic freedom even in the most limited sense in which it is understood in western democratic countries. Conversely, the continuance of academic relationships as usual with external institutions had allowed the apartheid regime to conclude that no fundamental threat to academic values was perceived by the academic community beyond South Africa. Hence, objections to the call for the boycott could not be sustained on the grounds of some (false) ideal of protecting academic freedom alone (Reicher, 1988a).

In order to explain the vociferous opposition of certain psychologists to the imposition of sanctions, one must consider the closely related argument that sanctions unfairly punish/discriminate against/mistreat some of those individuals who would be affected. Expressed as the view that individuals should not be blamed for the racism of the society in which they live, it also at times included the accusation that advocates of the academic boycott were making an arrogant, ostentatious, callous and inhuman judgement to subject people to isolation if they suggested otherwise. The nature and strength of feeling associated with such a view is well illustrated in the following quotation:

> How can we, with relatively secure jobs at British Universities, who have free-dom of speech and expression, make judgements as to what is best for people such as these? What do we know about them as persons living under constant pressure and fear, and about their fights with the regime? We usually hear about people who are members of anti-apartheid organisations and about those who are actively involved. However, we must be aware that there are different ways of being involved, that people are suited to different kinds of activity, and that some contribute in one way in producing change while others contribute in other ways. Some ways, of course, are more ostentatious than others. Some people remain uninvolved, but that is true in any walk of life. I do not believe that individuals whose 'crime' is that they live in a country with a racist gov-ernment should be punished with isolation by those who have the privilege, without any effort of their own, of living in a country where such inhuman practices do not exist (Markova, 1988a: 3–4).[7]

The latter argument is based on the logical contradiction of arguing against the arrogance of making a judgement on this issue, but then proceeding to make the opposite judgement of supporting those people in South Africa who opposed the boycott. It also amounts, of course, to choosing in favour of the minority of mainly white, relatively privileged professionals and against the majority of mainly black, underprivileged people — whose suffering by any reasonable standard of comparison is no less extreme (Reicher, 1988b).

This is not to deny that those who opposed the campaign for the boycott con-fronted a painful and difficult moral dilemma. It was not an easy or pleasant task to contemplate the possibility of breaking contacts with people abroad that one possibly knew, with whom one had possibly developed friendships and with whom one was likely to share some interests and values in common. However, their dilemma took a specific form which devalued acts of solidarity with the people who had been targeted by the racism of apartheid, because it rested on a narrow academic/professional definition of psychological relationships and identity (Reicher, 1988b). Ivana Markova (1988b) focuses upon the issue of how messages about her actions would reach her colleagues (p.21), and how the actions of social psychologists should be guided by the need for 'our credibility as social scientists (is) to be upheld and increased by scientists and professionals in other fields' (p.22). But in so doing the wider moral dilemma posed by the need to show solidarity with those people in South Africa who were struggling against the racism of apartheid is effectively set aside. The question of who is deserving of psychology's support and who, when choices have to be made, will be subject to relative isolation is one that should be at the heart of discussions of our 'professional' psychological identity. Ignorance or wilful neglect of this issue can only make psychology a very one-sided political concern.

The Position of the BPS

An analysis of the response of the professional body representing psychologists in the UK — the British Psychological Society — is also instructive in respect of psychology's ability to resist racism. The resolution against apartheid was welcome as a long overdue statement of the Society's position in relation to the apartheid regime (Henwood et al., 1989). Unfortunately, at a practical level it was undermined, however, by a lengthy explanation of how the policy would be interpreted (for details of the explanation see Newman, 1989). Contact was, in effect, *permitted* with all but the government of the Republic of South Africa and its various agencies (e.g. civil service, police force), individuals serving as official representatives of those agencies, and individuals who were not prepared to affirm the Society's Code of Conduct. Hence the BPS's chosen strategy amounted to the least wide-ranging of the options adopted by other institutions and outlined in Aitkenhead (1988).[8]

In justification of its choice of strategy, the BPS's argument was that breaking links with any other South African citizens would represent an act of discrimination against them as individuals 'simply because they were employed by a government agency or were members of a particular racial group' (p.328), and hence would be against the Code of Conduct. However, the adoption of such an undifferentiated and relativistic approach to the character of human rights violations simply serves to trivialize and minimize the specificity of crimes against humanity, such as apartheid, by equating them with other sorts of crimes, committed by 'others' and 'elsewhere' (Seidel, 1988). Drawing upon Aitkenhead's (1988) observations of modes of institutional regulation, it is quite possible that this argument could have been devised, at least in part, as a public version of morality, the purpose of which was to quell dissent within the ranks of the discipline.[9] If this was the case, it was a very ill chosen and disturbing strategy, however, since it parallels some of the claims made by the New Right in co-opting the notion of human rights for its own ends — which include undermining the anti-fascist consensus that has existed since the Second World War (Seidel, 1988). To repeat what should be unrepeatable, here the argument is that since all parties commit crimes in war, all are victims, and hence no person or group can be considered more culpable than any other during the period of Nazi rule. The ideology of human rights is in this case, as in the case of the argument against breaking links with individual beneficiaries of apartheid, reduced to the idea that all suffering is equal, thereby 'serving to exculpate what it sets out to incriminate' (Levy, 1987; quoted in Seidel, 1988: 118).

The boycott of academic links was lifted by the ANC at their National Executive Committee meeting in October 1991, except against organizations and institutions that continued to practise apartheid and exchanges that involved military and security technology transfers.[10] At the time of writing the expectation was also widespread that the date of 27 April 1994 would soon be set for democratic and non-racial[11] elections. However, many compromises have had to be made by the MDM in protracted negotiations to achieve this end. Therefore, the cautious optimism that followed the release of Nelson Mandela has been replaced by the sober realization that even an election victory for the majority of black people as represented by the ANC will result in a government with many unwelcome legacies. Accordingly it is likely that requests for help and acts of solidarity will continue to be made to the international community, particularly by those non-governmental agencies for reconstruction and development whose roots lie in the structures of resistance to apartheid.[12]

Should this be the case, the BPS will not be in a strong position to respond. Having adopted a 'technicist fix' (Husband, 1992) to the pressure from its membership to implement the academic boycott, and fallen into a relativist and reductionist line of reasoning on the character of human rights violations, the actions of the BPS will have to be monitored on matters of 'race' and racism to ensure that it does not retrench further into the ideology of the New Right. One pro-active step might be to campaign to include within the Royal Charter a clause — equal in status to Clause 3 (ii) quoted above — stating that the discipline of psychology is actively concerned with the protection and promotion of human rights.[13] The problem of how such a commitment would be interpreted would also have to be addressed.[14] The achievement of a genuinely anti-racist psychology will ultimately require that psychology has a starting point in interpretations of the world as seen from the perspectives of black people, together with those of other marginalized groups. This will necessitate a break with the narrow view and identity of psychology as a wholly neutral, objective and value-free science, and as an entirely apolitical professional concern. The groundwork for such a radical epistemological change is already in place within feminist social science, including feminist psychology.

ANTI-RACISM AND CHOOSING TO DO RESEARCH FROM A FEMINIST STANDPOINT

A further course of action for psychologists with a commitment to anti-racism is to explore the various ways in which we necessarily become caught up in the institutional practices of the discipline — if not within wider structures such as the BPS then at least in terms of the micro-politics of the departments in which we work. Personally speaking, I developed a strong feeling of alienation from the discipline of psychology over the reaction of many psychologists and the BPS to the issue of imposing sanctions, and felt that finding a way of doing what I wanted to do would be difficult. If anything, my misgivings have increased still further in subsequent years, particularly in view of the publication of an article in the *Psychologist* espousing a crude form of biological racism (Rushton, 1990). The editors subsequently agreed with letters pointing out that the article should not have been published (e.g. Antaki et al., 1990; Lea et al., 1990; Fatkmilehin et al., 1990), but only on the grounds that 'the scientific content was below the standard required' (Breakwell and Davey, July, 1990: 318). Moreover, an agenda was set for a follow-up debate, between Rushton and his original critic Flynn, which centred upon the threat to academic freedom and the evil of censorship versus the desire to bring politics and values into research. In this way, the evil of giving succour to racism was relegated to a peripheral and lesser concern (McCullough, 1991).[15]

Since starting my lecturing post at Brunel University, I have been aware of 'playing safe', and channelling the most obvious manifestations of my commitment to anti-racist practice through activities outside my academic work (see note 12). I was persuaded to take on the administrative task of undergraduate admissions for psychology, and hence have been able to strive to implement a policy of equal opportunities in our admissions procedures. However, given that an ever increasing amount of my time, and indeed so much of myself, is necessarily taken up with being an academic psychologist, I have become all too aware of the creeping effects of 'institutional cognitive bondage' (Aitkenhead, 1988: 44).

Against this background, I 'discovered' feminist scholarship, and particularly the concept of doing research from the 'standpoint' of women's experiences and lives (Hartsock, 1983; Smith, 1974; Harding, 1986, 1991), with a marked sense of relief. Whereas psychologists in Britain who have a commitment to anti-racism still tend in my experience to conduct their research in relative isolation, formal structures for feminist psychologists (e.g. the Psychology of Women Section of the BPS) and the publication of *Feminism & Psychology* (together with many other feminist psychology publications, mainly in the USA) provide a strong sense of support for research that refuses to accept a false and naïve dichotomy between science/professionalism and political practice. Within this framework it should, therefore, be possible to do research that is *for* rather than on women and other socially disadvantaged or marginalized communities.

There is no need to rehearse in any detail the arguments for adopting a feminist perspective in research here. Briefly, however, the strength of the feminist position derives from many rigorous and scholarly analyses of androcentrism in scientific practice, which have pointed to the partiality and distortion of knowledge that is generated solely from the perspective of men's lives (for a brief account of some of these analyses see Nielsen, 1990). This argument shares some important similarities with social studies of science which also point to the origins of knowledge in social activity, including wider social, historical and cultural relations (see e.g. Knorr-Cetina, 1981). Within feminist scholarship, however, attention is drawn specifically to the gendered nature of this activity, together with the inextricable link between its personal/experiential and political aspects (for a review of the distinctive features of the feminist epistemological critique see Cook and Fonow, 1986). Feminist social science takes particularly strong objection to the tendency for the meaning of women's experiences to be appropriated by so-called objective (but in fact male-biased and hence highly political) systems of meaning (see e.g. Stanley and Wise, 1983). This fuels the conviction within feminist research that women's experiences are valid in our own terms (see e.g. Duelli-Klein, 1983).

These insights have enabled me to continue my research with a renewed sense of confidence and vigour, since I was able to justify conducting social psychological investigations into adult mother–daughter relationships by starting from the perspective of women's lives (Henwood and Coughlan, 1993; Henwood, 1993). I have been stimulated to think critically about research practice, developing an approach called 'grounded analysis', one aim of which is to generate accounts from the standpoint of women (Henwood and Pidgeon, 1992b, 1993c). Feminist critiques of the idea that absolute foundations to knowledge can be found in women's experience (see e.g. Griffin, 1986; Hollway, 1989), together with other perspectives that alert us to the dangers of naïve realism (e.g. discourse analysis in social psychology; Potter and Wetherell, 1987), make it clear that a 'constructivist' version of the principle of grounding must be used (Henwood and Pidgeon, 1992b, 1993a). Hence, two of the analytic strategies used in my research on mothers and daughters are to focus upon contradictions within and between women's experiences and accounts (see e.g. Currie, 1988) and to draw upon feminist analyses (so far in my research mainly of representations of motherhood), in order to deconstruct the taken for granted in women's lives (Henwood and Pidgeon, 1993b).

The irony (and sadness) of such research developments is that they give no consideration to the way that women's experiences of disadvantage and oppression are gendered in highly racialized ways. The issue of shifting identities highlighted in the title of this special issue is therefore particularly revealing for me, since a developing commitment to feminist standpoint analysis in my case did not translate automatically into a concern for anti-racism in my ensuing research. In one sense this is not surprising; black women have for many years pointed to feminism's neglect of the diversity of women's experiences, grounded in the very different social conditions of their lives (see e.g. hooks, 1981; Lorde, 1984). A similar point has been made by lesbian feminists, concerned with the bias towards heterosexuality in research (see e.g. Kitzinger et al., 1992). In this respect, black and lesbian women are closely aligned with advocates of feminist poststructuralism (e.g. Flax, 1987) who argue strongly that the category 'woman' must itself be deconstructed.

Ultimately, however, the tendency toward relativism within feminist poststructuralism would be resisted by many black feminists, whose concern would therefore be for multiple standpoints. Whereas poststructuralist thought is distinctive in its view of the partiality of all knowledge, black feminists are often committed to the notion that special insights can be gained by oppressed peoples when they occupy the position of 'outsiders within' who can therefore see what is ordinarily invisible within the dominant order (see e.g. Collins, 1986). In addition, the view has been expressed that on occasion there may be a need for strategic essentialism (Brah, 1992). A strong case can be made, therefore, that one of the most urgent tasks for feminist social scientists is to be able to theorize the plurality and diversity of women's standpoints, but within a framework of alliances that can mobilize political action on behalf of all women (Stanley and Wise, 1990; Phoenix, 1990). One appealing suggestion in this regard is that knowledge generated from the perspective of black women must be used to re-vision that of women as a whole (Gorelick, 1991). I can see considerable scope for this in my own research on adult mothers and daughters. Feminist standpoint theory in this guise can provide a wide open space within which it is possible to combine a concern for feminist *and* anti-racist research.

CONCLUSION

This article presents a view of the difficulties and necessity of maintaining an anti-racist and feminist commitment within academic psychological research. Its contents are linked together by my own struggles to cope with, resist or change the theoretical perspectives and institutional practices of psychology, so that the aims and principles of anti-racist and feminist scholarship seem less alien to the settings in which I work. Hence it includes critical discussions of (i) social psychological research on prejudice, discrimination and latterly racism; (ii) the problem of new racism in both social psychological theory and professional practice (the example of the BPS's handling of the campaign to implement sanctions against apartheid South Africa features strongly here); and (iii) the question of how feminist standpoint research can be responsive to — and indeed how it must be revisioned by — the different experiences and lives of black women and members of other marginalized groups.

One of my main arguments is that psychological research is both an academic function and a political practice. It is therefore appropriate to end with a comment upon the position of women in the national liberation struggle of the people of South Africa, since in my view this contains a message which is relevant to western psychologists seeking to do anti-racist and feminist research. In making these comments I draw extensively upon the analysis in Kimble and Unterhalter's (1983) article on ANC women's struggles.

For many white, western feminists the struggle of black women in South Africa is not one to be envied nor is their example one to be followed, since it is just one part of a global struggle for national liberation for the whole people. Only as women have become politically mobilized has the arena of struggle broadened to include sexual politics, and women have tended to assume that through the main struggle they will gain their rightful place.

In order to understand the position of South African women we must look, however, at the actual conditions within which it has been necessary to organize, and which necessarily link women's interests with the struggle for all black people. The guiding principle has to be one of unity in action, for without it the racist regime would be better able to continue to divide and rule.

Kimble and Unterhalter cite the following poem by Dora Tamane, then an 80-

year-old member of the Federation of South African Women and still campaigning in South Africa:

> Let us share our problems so that we can solve them together.
> We must free ourselves.
> Men and women must share housework.
> Men and women must work together in the home and out in the world.
> There are no creches and nursery schools for our children.
> There are no homes for the aged.
> There is no one to care for the sick.
> Women must unite for these rights.
> I opened the road for you.
> You must go forward.

White, western women have opened the road to feminist scholarship on many topics. Black women have opened it further by initiating feminist scholarship on previously neglected issues and by promoting the realization that most existing knowledge must be reappraised in the light of their experiences. Each has opened the road for the other. We must go forward together.

NOTES

My thanks to Ann Phoenix, Chris Griffin and Eva Lloyd for their helpful comments on an earlier draft of this paper, and to Ann Phoenix, in particular, for the idea of putting pen to paper for this special issue.

1. For a more up to date review of criticisms of individualistic theories from the social identity perspective see Hogg and Abrams (1988).
2. Within the social identity framework, reference is made to a parallel psychological motive — that of seeking to maintain and enhance self-esteem through differentiation between groups. The version of social cognition research which has its origins in information processing theory has also recognized the limitations of an overly cognitive approach, and has begun to investigate the relationship between cognition and affect in prejudice and stereotyping (see e.g. Mackie and Hamilton, 1993).
3. Hence, a prototypical social psychological study would involve presenting a sample of white, and perhaps black, 'subjects' (either individually or in groups, and under one or more experimental treatments) with stimuli (e.g. persons, activities or traits), which are also classified by researchers and/or participants in terms of 'race'. Questions investigated in this way include: 'What is the effect of social categorization on perception, judgement and behaviour?', 'Is there a tendency towards bias in favour of one's own group?' and 'What makes particular social categories salient?'
4. For a significant exception see the fieldwork study of the St Paul's riot (Reicher, 1984).
5. The various points made against implementing the boycott were that 'it is not the place of a scientific society to get involved in politics (Deregowski, *BPS Bulletin*, April 1987), that a boycott would itself be a form of discrimination (Callias, *BPS Bulletin*, May 1987), that a boycott would deprive South African psychologists of

their right to "academic freedom" (Michael, *BPS Bulletin*, March 1987; Lowenstein, *Psychologist*, January 1988), that a boycott would abandon and isolate psychologists in South Africa who need our support (Bloom, *BPS Bulletin*, March 1987) and that it would be ultra-vires the Royal Charter of the BPS (Hayes, *Psychologist*, February 1988)' (for the review see Baron-Cohen et al., 1988).

6. Repeal of the laws of 'petty apartheid' in recent years has removed some impediments to children's learning, for example the disruption of classroom activity in order to check for possession of 'passes'. However, the gross inequalities in resources for education, and the social conditions which detract from children's physical and psychological health, still remain unchanged.

7. In addition to the argument in the text, there are at least two more minor points of inaccuracy in this statement. First, not all of those who supported the proposal for an academic boycott had secure academic jobs: some were on temporary contracts and certainly did not help their chances of securing a more long term appointment by their actions! Second, as I argue in this article, British institutions, including the teaching and professional practice of psychology, are not free from racism. Therefore, it does require some 'effort of our own' to counteract it.

8. The BPS's course of action was in large part to permit contact whilst using the resolution to draw attention to the issue of apartheid. Aitkenhead's two other possible tactics were (i) to issue statements to individuals condemning apartheid, and simultaneously asking them to think seriously about the implications of breaking the boycott requested by the MDM; and (ii) withdrawing recognition from the equivalent professional body in South Africa (namely the Psychology Association of South Africa, PASA); this latter tactic was adopted by the Royal Institute of British Architects (RIBA).

9. It may also simply have been useful in apparently strengthening a position that required the BPS to take no more action than arranging for the Code of Practice to be sent out routinely with conference information, etc. Consequently, it enabled the Society to experience very little disruption to its normal institutional functioning.

10. The lifting of sanctions was conceptualized as a phased process; with sanctions on trade linked to the installation of an interim government and diplomatic sanctions to free and fair elections for a non-racial parliament and representative government.

11. Throughout this article I have used the term *anti*-racist in preference to the alternative *non*-racist since the latter often marks the position of those who object to anyone taking an active role in opposing racism and apartheid. On those occasions where the term non-racist is used it is to show sensitivity to the historical specificity of the political situation in South Africa, where an essential part of the struggle against apartheid is the need to undermine the perception of a world inevitably structured along racial lines.

12. Following the ANC's statement in October 1991, the emphasis of PAA's activity switched from campaigning for/monitoring of the policy on sanctions to reconstruction and development projects, the aim of which are to contribute to overcoming the long-term consequences of apartheid. For example, consignments of books donated by the BPS have been sent — the majority to the University of Fort Hare in Ciskei. Transportation of the books was financed by the remainder of subscriptions from PAA members, together with substantial donations from the Canon Collins Educational Trust of South Africa and HEART (see Bledin, 1991). PAA is no longer operating, but individual members remain involved in solidarity work within other ANC/AAM structures which engage in solidarity projects with the region of southern Africa.

13. This would be timely since key clauses in the Universal Declaration of Human Rights themselves are under threat of erosion, and are therefore in need of expressions of popular support.

14. Seidel (1988) makes a similar point about the need for an 'elaborated' understanding of the meaning of human rights, which does not amount to a populist version of anti-racism.

15. The messages conveyed by two other sets of articles on issues connected with South Africa similarly give little cause for optimism. The first set concerned the acceptance of psychological evidence in mitigation at South African murder trials (November, 1991). Coleman seemed personally outraged by a response to his original article by Reicher for suggesting that there was an ideological and political dimension to the Court's decision because the evidence depoliticized the action of the crowd, and for arguing that psychologists take responsibility for the social consequences of psychological research. Little awareness of the social and political practice of psychology is expressed in comments by the writer of the original article here. The second set had at its centre a statement by a spokesperson for the Psychology Association of South Africa. This (i) sought to distance the situation of psychology in South Africa from that in the rest of Africa; (ii) made no mention of the impact of apartheid on that Society's functioning; and (iii) contained the clearly racist assertion that black people frequently found it difficult to cope with rapid change (Raubenhaimer, 1993). Fortunately, each of these claims/oversights were rebutted/addressed in the reply by Foster et al. (1993). However, it has been noted that one possible reading of the message of both articles presented together is that racism is a problem that exists 'elsewhere' (Howitt, 1993; see also Davies, 1993). More optimistically, the first signs of a developing institutional reflexivity by the BPS may have begun to appear given a willingness to publish articles on racism in a British journal (Howitt and Owusu-Bempah, 1990), calling for a clear anti-racist policy (Husband, 1992), and on the limits of a Eurocentric psychology in Africa (Akin-Ogundeji, 1991).

REFERENCES

Adorno, T. W., Frenkel-Brunswick, E., Levinson, D. J. and Sanford, R. N. (1950) *The Authoritarian Personality*. New York: Harper and Row.

Aitkenhead, M. (1988) 'Institutions and Moral Dilemmas: An Essay on Impossible Thoughts', *Social Psychology Section Newsletter* (Spring): 43–55.

Akin-Ogundeji, O. (1991) 'Asserting Psychology in South Africa', *Psychologist* 4 (3): 20–4.

Allport, G. (1954) *The Nature of Prejudice*. Reading, MA: Addison-Wesley.

Antaki, C. et al. (1990) letter to the *Psychologist* 3 (7): 316.

Barker, (1981) *The New Racism*. London: Junction Books.

Baron-Cohen, S., Bledin, K. and Pickles, C. (1988) 'Links Between Psychology in Britain and South Africa', letter to the *Psychologist* 1 (12): 488–99.

Berkowitz, L. (1962) *Aggression: A Social Psychological Analysis*. New York: McGraw Hill.

Bhavnani, K-K. (1988) 'Empowerment and Social Research: Some Comments', *Text* 8 (1–2): 41–50.

Bhavnani, K-K. (1990) 'What's Power Got To Do With It? Empowerment and Social Research', in I. Parker and J. Shotter (eds) *Deconstructing Social Psychology*, pp. 141–52. London: Routledge.

Billig, M. (1978) 'The New Social Psychology and "Fascism" ', *European Journal of Social Psychology* 7 (4): 393–432.

Billig, M. (1985) 'Prejudice, Categorisation and Particularisation: From a Perceptual to a Rhetorical Approach', *European Journal of Social Psychology* 15: 79–103.

Billig, M. (1988) 'The Notion of "Prejudice": Some Rhetorical and Ideological Aspects', *Text* 8 (1–2): 91–110.

Bledin, K. (1991) 'The BPS and Psychologists Against Apartheid', letter to the *Psychologist* 4 (11): 510.

Brah, A. (1992) 'Difference, Diversity and Differentiation', in J. Donald and A. Rattansi (eds) *'Race', Culture and Difference*. London: Sage.

Breakwell, G. and Davey, G. (1990) 'Rushton: Race Differences: the Honorary Editors' Reply', *Psychologist* 3(7): 318.

Brotherton, C. et al. (1987) 'Links Between Psychology in Britain and South Africa', letter to the *Bulletin of the British Psychological Society* 40: 27–8.

Burman, E. (1990) 'Introduction', in E. Burman (ed.) *Feminists and Psychological Practice*, pp. 1–13. London: Sage.

Coleman, A. (1991) 'Psychological Evidence in South African Murder Trials', *Psychologist* 4 (11): 482–91; plus his reply to Reicher 'Are there theories at the bottom of his jargon?'

Collins, P. H. (1986) 'The Emerging Theory and Pedagogy of Black Women's Studies', *Feminist Issues* 6: 3–17.

Condor, S. (1988) ' "Race stereotypes" and racist discourse', *Text* 8 (1–2): 69–89.

Cook, J. A. and Fonow, M. M. (1986) 'Knowledge and Women's Interests: Issues of Epistemology and Methodology in Feminist Sociological Research', *Sociological Inquiry* 56: 2–29.

Currie, D. (1988) 'Re-thinking What We Do and How We Do It: A Study of Reproductive Decisions', *Canadian Review of Sociology and Anthropology* 25 (2): 231–53.

Davies, S. (1993) 'Psychology in Agony: The South African Experience', letter to the *Psychologist* 6 (6): 249.

Donald, J. and Rattansi, A. eds (1992) *'Race', Culture and Difference*. London: Sage.

Duelli-Klein, R. (1983) 'How To Do What We Want To Do: Thoughts about Feminist Methodology', in G. Bowles and R. Duelli-Klein (eds) *Theories of Women's Studies*, pp. 88–104. London: Routledge.

Essed, P. (1988) 'Understanding Verbal Accounts of Racism: Politics and Heuristics of Reality Constructions', *Text* 8 (1–2): 5–40.

Essed, P. (1991) *Understanding Everyday Racism*. London: Sage.

Fatkmilehin, I. et al. (1990) letter to the *Psychologist* 3 (10): 451–2.

Fiske, S. and Taylor, S. (1984) *Social Cognition*. New York: Random House.

Flax, J. (1987) 'Postmodernism and Gender Relations in Feminist Theory', *Signs* 12 (4): 621–43.

Flynn, J. R. (1990) 'Explanation, Evaluation and a Rejoinder to Rushton', *Psychologist* 3 (5): 199–200.

Foster, D., Lionel, N. and Dawes, A. (1993) 'Reply to Raubenheimer', *Psychologist* 6 (4): 172–4.

Gorelick, S. (1991) 'Contradictions of Feminist Methodology', *Gender and Society* 5 (4): 459–77.

Griffin, C. (1986) 'Qualitative Methods and Female Experience', in S. Wilkinson (ed.) *Feminist Social Psychology*, pp. 173–91. Milton Keynes: Open University Press.

Hamilton, D. ed. (1981) *Cognitive Processes in Stereotyping and Intergroup Behaviour*. Hillsdale, NJ: Erlbaum.

Harding, S. (1986) *The Science Question in Feminism*. Milton Keynes: Open University Press.

Harding, S. (1991) *Whose Science? Whose Knowledge? Thinking From Women's Lives*. Milton Keynes: Open University Press.

Harrison, G. (1974) 'A Bias in the Social Psychology of Prejudice', in P. Armistead (ed.) *Reconstructing Social Psychology*, pp. 189–203. Harmondsworth: Penguin.

Hartsock, N. (1983) 'The Feminist Standpoint: Developing the Ground for a Specifically Feminist Historical Materialism', in S. Harding and M. B. Hintikka (eds) *Discovering Reality*, pp. 282–310. Dordrecht: Reidel.

Henriques, J. (1984) 'Social Psychology and the Politics of Racism', in J. Henriques, W. Hollway, C. Urwin, C. Venn and V. Walkerdine (eds) *Changing the Subject: Psychology, Social Regulation and Subjectivity*, pp. 60–90. London: Methuen.

Henwood, K. L. (1993) 'Women and Later Life: The Discursive Construction of Identities Within Family Relationships', *Journal of Ageing Studies* 7(3): 303–19.

Henwood, K. L., Pereira, C., Bloom, L., Baron-Cohen, S., Bledin, K. and Pickles, C. (1989) 'Moral and Legal Issues in the South African Boycott', letter to the *Psychologist* 2 (8): 329.

Henwood, K. L. and Coughlan, G. (1993) 'The Construction of "Closeness" in Mother Daughter Relationships Across the Lifespan', in N. Coupland and J. Nussbaum (eds) *Discourse and Lifespan Identity* pp. 191–214. London: Sage.

Henwood, K. L. and Pidgeon, N. F. (1992a) 'Qualitative Research and Psychological Theorising', *British Journal of Psychology* 83: 97–111.

Henwood, K. L. and Pidgeon, N. F., (1992b) 'Grounded Analysis and Psychological Research', paper presented at the Annual London Conference of the British Psychological Society, December.

Henwood, K. L. and Pidgeon, N. F. (1993a) 'Remaking the Link: Qualitative Research and Feminist Standpoint Theory', manuscript submitted for publication in *Feminism & Psychology*.

Henwood, K. L. and Pidgeon, N. F. (1993b) 'Grounded Analysis, Subjectivity and Social Psychology', paper presented at the Annual Social Section Conference of the British Psychological Society, Jesus College Oxford, September.

Hogg, M. and Abrams, D. (1988) *Social Identifications*. London: Routledge.

Hollway, W. (1989) *Subjectivity and Method in Psychology: Gender, Meaning and Science*. London: Sage.

hooks, bell (1981) *Ain't I a Woman: Black Women and Feminism*. Boston: South End Press.

Howitt, D. (1990) letter to the *Psychologist* 3 (10): 452–3.

Howitt, D. (1991) 'Internalised Ideologies: Racism and Psychology', in D. Howitt (ed.) *Concerning Psychology: Psychology Applied to Social Issues*, pp. 95–119. Milton Keynes: Open University Press.

Howitt, D. (1993) 'Racist Psychology: Where?', letter to the *Psychologist* 6(5): 202–3.

Howitt, D. and Owusu-Bempah, J. (1990) 'Racism in a British Journal?', *Psychologist* 3 (9): 396–400.

Husband, C. (1984) 'Working Notes on Social Identification Theory — Potential Limitations and Possibilities', ESRC funded workshops on Social Identity Theory and Race Relations, University of Bristol, 1983–4.

Husband, C. (1986) 'The Concepts of Attitude and Prejudice in the Mystification of Racism', paper presented at the British Psychological Society Social Section Conference, University of Sussex, September.

Husband, C. (1992) 'A Policy Against Racism', *Psychologist* 5 (9); 414–17.

Kimble, J. and Unterhalter, E. (1983) ' "We Opened the Road for You, You Must Go Forward": ANC Women's Struggles, 1912–1982', *Feminist Review* 12: 11–35.

Kitzinger, C. (1990) 'Resisting the Discipline', in E. Burman (ed.) *Feminists and Psychological Practice*, pp. 119–36. London: Sage.

Kitzinger, C., Wilkinson, S. and Perkins, R. eds (1992) *Heterosexuality*, Special Issue of *Feminism & Psychology* 2 (3).

Knorr-Cetina, K. (1981) *The Manufacture of Knowledge*. Oxford: Pergamon.

Lea et al. (1990) letter to the *Psychologist* 3 (7): 316–17.

Lorde, A. (1984) *Sister Outsider*. New York: Crossing Press.

Mackie, D. and Hamilton, D. eds (1993) *Affect, Cognition and Stereotyping: Interactive Processes in Group Perception*. New York: Academic.

Markova, I. (1988a) 'South Africa and the Academic Boycott', *Social Psychology Section Newsletter* (Spring): 1–6.

Markova, I. (1988b) 'On Material and Spiritual Goods: Reply to Steve Reicher', *Social Psychology Section Newsletter* (Spring): 20–2.

McArthur, L. (1982) 'Judging a Book by its Cover: A Cognitive Analysis of the Relationships Between Physical Appearance and Stereotyping', in A. Hastorf and A. Isen (eds) *Cognitive Social Psychology*, pp. 149–211. New York: Elsevier.

McCullough, M. (1991) 'Rushton and Racism', letter to the *Psychologist* 4 (1): 21.

Michael, M. (1991) 'Intergroup Theory and Deconstruction', in I. Parker and J. Shotter (eds) *Deconstructing Social Psychology*, pp. 170–82. London: Routledge.

Miller, (1982) *In the Eye of the Beholder: Contemporary Issues in Stereotyping*. New York: Praeger.

Newman, C. (1989) 'A Resolution on Apartheid', *Psychologist* 2 (8): 328.

Nielsen, J. M. (1990) 'Introduction', in J. M. Nielsen (ed) *Feminist Research Methods*, pp. 1–37. Boulder, CO: Westview Press.

Parker, I. (1989) *The Crisis in Modern Social Psychology and How to End It*. London: Routledge.

Parker, I. (1991) *Discourse Dynamics*. London: Routledge.

Parker, I. and Shotter, J. (1990) *Deconstructing Social Psychology*. London: Routledge.

Phoenix, A. (1990) 'Social Research in the Context of Feminist Psychology', in E. Burman (ed.) *Feminists and Psychological Practice*, pp. 89–103. London: Sage.

Potter, J. and Wetherell, M. (1987) *Discourse and Social Psychology*. London: Sage.

Raubenhaimer, I. (1993) 'Psychology in South Africa', *Psychologist* 6 (4): 169–71.

Reicher, S. (1984) 'St Pauls: A Study in the Limits of Crowd Behaviour', *European Journal of Social Psychology* 14: 1–21.

Reicher, S. (1986) 'Contact, Action and Racialisation: Some British Evidence', in M. Hewstone and R. Brown (eds) *Contact and Conflict in Intergroup Encounters*, pp. 152–68. Oxford: Basil Blackwell.

Reicher, S. (1988a) 'Psychology and Apartheid', *Social Psychology Section Newsletter* (Spring): 7–19.

Reicher, S. (1988b) 'Reply to Markova', *Social Psychology Section Newsletter* (Spring): 23–9.

Reicher, S. (1991) 'Politics of Crowd Psychology', *Psychologist* 4 (11): 487–91; plus his reply to Coleman and Luitingh 'The Logic of Psychology, Not the Intentions of the Psychologist' 495.

Rushton, J. P. (1990) 'Race Differences, r/k Theory, and a Reply to Flynn', *Psychologist* 3 (5): 195–8.

Seidel, G. (1988) 'Verbal Strategies of the Collaborators: A Discursive Analysis of the July 1986 European Parliamentary Debate on South African Sanctions', *Text* 8 (1–2): 111–27.

Smith, D. (1974) *The Everyday World as Problematic: A Feminist Sociology*. Milton Keynes: Open University Press.

Stanley, L. and Wise, S. (1983) *Breaking Out: Feminist Consciousness and Feminist Research*. London: Routledge.

Stanley, L. and Wise, S. (1990) 'Method, Methodology and Epistemology in Feminist Research Processes', in L. Stanley (ed.) *Feminist Praxis*, pp. 20–60. London: Routledge.

Tajfel, H. (1969) 'Cognitive Aspects of Prejudice', *Journal of Social Issues* 25: 79–97.

Tajfel, H. (1978a) 'Intergroup Behaviour: Individualistic Perspectives', in H. Tajfel and C. Fraser (eds) *Introducing Social Psychology*, pp. 401–22. Harmondsworth: Penguin.

Tajfel, H. (1978b) 'The Social Psychology of Minorities', Minority Rights Group Report No. 38. London: Minority Rights Group.

Tajfel, H. and Turner, J. (1979) 'An Integrative Theory of Intergroup Conflict', in W. G. Austin and S. Worchel (eds) *The Social Psychology of Intergroup Relations*, pp. 33–47. Monterey, CA: Brooks Cole.

Taylor, S. (1981) 'A Categorization Approach to Stereotyping', in D. Hamilton (ed.) *Cognitive Processes in Stereotyping and Intergroup Behaviour*, pp. 83–114. Hillsdale, NJ: Erlbaum.

Turner, J. and Oakes, P. (1986) 'The Significance of the Social Identity Concept for Social Psychology with Reference to Individualism, Interactionism and Social Influence', *British Journal of Social Psychology* 25: 237–52.

Unger, R. (1982) 'Advocacy Versus Scholarship Revisited: Issues in the Psychology of Women', *Psychology of Women Quarterly* 7 (1): 5–17.

Ussher, J. (1990) 'Choosing Psychology or Not Throwing the Baby Out with the Bath Water', in E. Burman (ed.) *Feminists and Psychological Practice*, pp. 47–61. London: Sage.

van Dijk, T. (1984) *Communicating Racism: Ethnic Prejudice in Thought and Talk*. London: Sage.

van Dijk, T. (1992) 'Discourse and the Denial of Racism', *Discourse and Society* 3 (1): 87–118.

Wetherell, M. (1986) 'Linguistic Repertoires and Literary Criticism: New Directions for a Social Psychology of Gender', in S. Wilkinson (ed.) *Feminist Social Psychology*, pp. 77–95. Milton Keynes: Open University Press.

Wetherell, M. and Potter, J. (1992) *Mapping the Language of Racism*. Hemel Hempstead: Harvester Wheatsheaf.

Widdicombe, S. (1992) 'Subjectivity, Power and the Practice of Psychology', *Theory and Psychology* 2 (4): 487–99.

Williams, J. (1984) 'Gender and Intergroup Behaviour: Towards an Integration', *British Journal of Social Psychology* 23: 311–16.

Karen HENWOOD is a feminist social psychologist. In the mid to late 1980s she became involved in the campaign of solidarity with the struggle against apartheid in South Africa, and through this activity became aware of the tenuous nature of resistance to racism within the discipline. She lectures at Brunel University and is a member of the joint AAM/ANC Health Committee based in London. ADDRESS: Department of Human Sciences, Brunel University, Uxbridge, Middlesex UB8 3PH, UK.

Corinne SQUIRE

Empowering Women? The *Oprah Winfrey Show*

The Oprah Winfrey Show, *the most-watched US daytime talk show, aims to empower women. This article examines the show's representations of gender and how images of 'race', sexuality and class cross-cut them. It considers the show's status as television psychology. It explores the show's translation of aspects of black feminism to television, and discusses the social implications of its 'super-real' representations.*

Winfrey: Listen ... obviously I come from a very biased point of view here.

Female guest: Because you're a woman.

Winfrey: Yes. Well, and because I — what we try to do — we do program these shows to empower women (*Oprah Winfrey Show*, 1989b).

INTRODUCTION

Every weekday in the USA, 20 million people watch the *Oprah Winfrey Show*, making it the most-watched daytime talk programme. Snaring an unassailable 35 percent of the audience, it acts as a lead-in for local stations' lucrative early evening news programmes (McClellan, 1993; Boemer, 1987). The show has become a common source of information and opinions about relationships, psychopathology and gender. It is a cultural icon, signifying at the same time lurid dilemmas, emotional intensity, fame and black women's success. It is even a well-known chronological marker, as in 'I worked so hard I was done in time for *Oprah*', or, 'I did my shopping so quick I was home by *Oprah*'.

Winfrey, the first African-American woman to host a national talk show[1] is also well known for her television specials on self-esteem and child abuse, for her role as Sophia in the film *The Color Purple*, as an advocate for abused children and as a philanthropist supporting programmes for poor black youth. The tabloids chronicle her fluctuating weight and self-esteem and her longstanding

Feminism & Psychology © 1994 SAGE (London, Thousand Oaks and New Delhi), Vol. 4(1): 63–79.

relationship with a businessman, Stedman Graham. She is one of the richest women in the world, with a yearly income of around $40 million, $16 million more than Madonna (Goodman, 1991). In 1989 she was voted the second most-admired woman in the USA — after Nancy Reagan. The Oprah phenomenon is interesting in itself but this essay will restrict itself to considering Oprah, 'day-time queen' (Guider, 1987), in the context of the show.

In this article, I will treat the television programme as a polysemous, difficult but readable text; examine its compliance with and departure from television conventions; investigate its framing by broader 'texts' of social power and history; and see it as suffused with the intensity and fragmentariness of subjectivity. While psychologists are increasingly taking on such modes of analysis, psychological studies of television generally use more traditional methods, like content analysis or the micro-analysis of speech and non-verbal communication. An exception is Valerie Walkerdine's 'Video Replay' (1989) which provides an exemplary reading of the criss-crossed narratives of gender and class that inhabit our subjective responses to the small screen.

Like other daytime talk shows, *Oprah* aims to entertain, inform and encourage communication about difficult issues. It is a kind of popular psychology, lacing advice and catharsis with comedy and melodrama. But the show also tries, Winfrey says, to empower women: to be a televisual feminism. Not only the host but many guests and the majority of the studio and watching audiences are women, and most episodes address female-identified topics: relationships, communication, physical appearance. Host, guests and the studio audience also spend a lot of time in animated, messy discussions of injustices that are at the centre of much contemporary feminist campaigning, like job discrimination, male violence and sexual abuse.

While Winfrey often says the show transcends 'race', it features black guests and issues of concern to black people in the USA more than comparable shows and focuses particularly on black women's perspectives. Since the 1980s such perspectives have had a major impact on US feminism as black women activists and writers make their voices heard within the largely US women's movement (see, for instance, Butler, 1990; de Lauretis, 1986; Hill Collins, 1990; hooks, 1981, 1989; Moraga and Anzaldua, 1981; Spelman, 1990; Spivak, 1988). Differences in class and sexuality between women, which are also concerns of contemporary feminism (Lorde, 1984; Rich, 1986) have only a small place on the *Oprah* show however. Edginess characterizes *Oprah's* occasional mentions of lesbian and gay sexuality, and class is rarely explicitly discussed.

I am going to explore the show's diverse and intricate representations of gender, 'race', sexuality, class and subjectivity, and how the nature of television affects these representations. In the process I aim to develop an account of *Oprah*'s relationship to feminism. I am adopting a very general definition of feminism here, assuming that it is concerned, first, to understand gender relationships as fully as possible, in their interrelationships with other social differences, with history, with subjectivity and with different representational media like television; and second, that it tries to make gender relations and relation-ships between women less oppressive (Coward, 1983). Does *Oprah*, much watched by women, and a secular authority on gender issues, speak to these feminist concerns? I shall argue that it does and that its most interesting contri-butions are first, a feminism generalized from black women's histories and writ-ing, and second, its super-realism — an unsettling combination of emotional and empirical excess that puts common assumptions about gendered subjectivities in doubt.

ANALYSING *OPRAH*

Western feminists were slow to pay attention to television, despite its dominant position in their culture. Television representations of gender seemed dauntingly conventional in the face of feminists' limited power to effect change. Left analy-ses of the media as ideological control also contributed to feminist dismissals of television as shallow, repetitive and emotionally manipulative. Since the 1970s, however, a number of feminists have treated the pleasures and powers of televi-sion seriously, recognizing that they must pay attention to this engrossing cul-tural form if they are to address the realities and fantasies of gender with which we all live (Kaplan, 1987). Such analyses have to balance an awareness of femi-nist elements in television messages and in audience understanding of them, with a recognition of television's traditionalism and of the ways in which the television message and the power relations of television consumption constrain viewer interpretations (Brunsdon, 1989; Morris, 1988; Nightingale, 1990). Recent analyses of film and television by black writers and by theorists of queer representations start from this complexity, taking it for granted and then com-pounding it (Bad Object-Choices, 1991; Dent, 1992; Doty, 1992; Julien and Mercer, 1988).

The article draws on a regular monitoring of the *Oprah Winfrey Show* from late 1988 to mid 1993 but its core is an analysis of episodes shown during two weeks in May 1990. Throughout the study, the contents of the show have been fairly constant. Episodes split evenly between 'self-help' topics — obsessions, disobedient children and destructive relationships — and an 'all others' category which includes shows on appearance (cosmetic surgery, dieting, people who think they are ugly) and physical, mental or behavioral abnormality (disabling allergies, multiple personality, women who murder their children) and, more rarely, shows on social issues (buying a house, education, poverty), 'cute' shows ('Alaskan men', people who can't throw anything away) and celebrity inter-views (Joan Rivers, Barbara Bush). The show's form, too, is consistent. Winfrey introduces each episode by reading an outline of the day's topic to camera, talks to guests, solicits a few questions from the audience, brings in some expert opin-ions, and then alternates guests', experts' and audience members' comments while she roams around the audience with a mike in the style Phil Donahue brought to talk-show prominence. The representations of gender, 'race', sexuality, class and subjectivity with which I am concerned are also highly consistent across shows. I shall go through each of these as elements in a sequential manner, but the intersections should soon become apparent.

REPRESENTATIONS OF GENDER ON *OPRAH*

Sometimes the *Oprah* show seems simply to endorse traditional notions of femaleness. In the woman-dominated world of daytime television, it appears, the predominantly female audience watches the mainly female casts of the early afternoon soap operas endlessly play out relationship dilemmas — and then listens to a female talk-show host, her many female guests and her largely female studio audience discuss how to improve your looks, marriage and parenting. The advertisements in the breaks, like most advertisements and indeed most programming (Bretl and Cantor, 1988; Davis, 1990), show women in traditional roles, worrying about their weight and their children. While the show encourages women to speak frankly about their lives, including their sexualities, the conventional limits apply. In one episode Winfrey assured a woman who had employed a male surrogate sex therapist to teach her to reach orgasm that she could be 'explicit'. 'Well, he started by using his finger inside me, very gently. I felt a contraction ...', the woman said, and was abruptly cut off by a commercial. During the break Winfrey said, 'I didn't mean *that* explicit' (King, 1987: 126). Conventionally, the show uses women to conjure prohibited pleasures; their transgressive, cathartic confessions become the apotheosis of television's voyeurism (Ellis, 1982).

Winfrey touches audience members a lot, cries and laughs, and they touch, laugh and cry back. These exchanges signify an empathy that is traditionally feminine, but also feminist in its insistence on the 'personal', and that is largely free of the inflections of authority and sexuality mixed in with male hosts' touching.

The show also presents feminist arguments about women's lower economic and social status, men's difficulties in close relationships, women's difficulties in combining paid work and parenting, the suppression of women's sexuality and men's physical and sexual abuse. Moreover, since television representations often have more than one meaning, even the show's apparently conservative representations of gender can support feminist readings. The show's representations of the female body for instance are not simply incitements to female self-hatred. In one notorious episode Winfrey hauled onstage 67 pounds of lard — the amount of weight she had lost; since then she has forsworn dieting. Today, the show routinely notes the oppressiveness and irrelevance of dominant images of the female body, explores how preoccupations with food and weight cloak depression and feelings of low self-worth and acknowledges the comforting, social and sensual nature of eating and one episode focused exclusively on discrimination against fat people. Winfrey's own size acts as a reminder of how women's bigness can be a form of power, perhaps especially when they are black women in a field dominated by white men. As Gracie Mae Still, the narrator of Alice Walker's '1955' put it, 'fat like I is looks distinguished. You see me coming and know somebody's *there*!' (1982: 13).

The show sometimes considers motherhood with conventional reverence, but also treats it as a matter of hard work or discusses it in a more flexible way, as when Maya Angelou calls Winfrey her 'daughter–friend' (*Oprah Winfrey Show*, 1993). It has also problematized motherhood, as in an episode on maternal child abuse.

The show's feminism is most explicit, however, in its often-declared commitment to empowering women. This term has multiple meanings, indicating variously an interest in women's political, economic and educational advancement; in women getting help for personal and relationship problems; and most generally, in women perceiving a range of individual and social choices as open to them and deciding among them. Each meaning implies a different version of feminism. The first suggests a public, the second a personal focus for feminism and the last founds feminist politics in psychological wellbeing. Nevertheless the show's representations of empowerment all assume a commonality between women that allows the representations to make the category 'women' their unproblematic center. Feminism must use this category to ground its analyses and claims, but the category always has a social and historical context that gives it a specific meaning (Riley, 1988; Spelman, 1990). *Oprah*, however, represents women as sharing emotional and social qualities — communication skills, for instance — regardless of the differences between women. The show's aim is to empower this shared womanhood.

The dominant presence of women on the show is underwritten by a complementary male presence. The show continually solicits men's opinions, runs episodes on men as lovers and parents, and raises and counters the suggestion that *Oprah* is 'anti-men'. The show's 'woman-centred' talk is always, silently, about men, for gender is a relationship: one term evokes the other.

The complementariness of *Oprah*'s representations of gender raises an important question about its relationship to feminism. Might women's disempowerment, against which the show defines itself, nevertheless be its most powerful message? A narrative of empowerment structures each episode but the show's repeated accounts of victimization often seem to overwhelm them. After the daily success story of women getting their lives in order, you know that tomorrow you will start off once more with the harrowing experiences of women whose lives have been taken from them by abuse, illness or poverty. Feminism has to describe structures of male power in order to resist them and to this degree it is complicit with them. But on the *Oprah Winfrey Show*, self-consciously complicit description often seems to collapse into a fruitless reiteration of stories of personal suffering. Domestic violence, child abuse and eating disorders support regular episodes, each claiming to bring to light a horrible and hitherto secret oppression, each by this claim implicitly reinstating the horror and prohibitions around the topic; for talking about a forbidden subject may maintain as much as disperse a taboo. *Oprah*'s current emphasis on health and exercise at the expense of diets, for example, is undercut by a conventional subtext of the female body as subject to control (Bordo, 1989; Coward, 1989), and by the frequency with which diets are mentioned, only to be dismissed.

The show's complementary meanings have some promising feminist implications as well. The show often presents women as objects of beauty: in makeover episodes, for instance; or on the daily credits, shot when Winfrey was near her thinnest, had a Revlon modelling contract and could operate as a powerful screen player in the cultural and psychic masquerade of femininity (Heath, 1985). The credits show Winfrey in a series of slowed, staggered close-ups and medium close-ups, listening sympathetically to guests, laughing, swinging her hair, bouncing across the screen. Beginning with Laura Mulvey, feminist film theorists have argued that such representations of femininity put the spectator in a complementarily masculine position of pleasure and desire (Mulvey, 1975, 1981). *Oprah*'s predominantly female studio and viewing audience is thus set up to look at the feminine object, Winfrey, from a patriarchal position: as men. The audience may either adopt this masculine spectatorship or abdicate spectatorship for an identification with the femininity on screen (see also de Lauretis, 1991; Doane, 1987). Such work suggests that *Oprah* offers women a variety of psychic investments, so its feminism will not be a simple matter of women watching women but will filter through the multiple subjectivities of spectatorship.

If we view *Oprah*'s multiple representations of gender in a context wider than the show, their relationship to feminism often starts to seem closer. Despite the limits the show sets on what can be said, for instance, and its tendency to present talk as a cure-all, its stress on 'explicit' speech seems oppositional in the broader context of US pro-censorship campaigns, especially since explicit talk on *Oprah* is often talk about a common censorship target, female sexuality. The show's representations of men also appear more resistant if they are read against the power relationships generally obtaining between women and men. Episodes shift from description to prescription, from problems with men or men's problems, to women's solutions. Even if a similar move will be made all over again in the very next episode, the move cuts against the cultural grain. Viewed historically, too, *Oprah*'s repeated and apparently unchanging considerations of some sensational topics may indicate not just unsated voyeurism or stalled feminism but a series of historically distinct concerns. A show about rape survivors, for example, means something different after the Palm Beach case, in which William Smith, a nephew of Edward Kennedy, was acquitted of raping a lower middle class white woman, than it does after the Central Park case, in which black youths were convicted of beating and raping a white woman stockbroker who was running in the park.

'RACE' AND RACISM

Henry Louis Gates (1989) describes how, in the 1950s, his family would rush to see African Americans on television, and how concerned they were that the performers be good. More African Americans are on television now but blacks are still underrepresented and appear mainly as a set of sitcom and drama cliches or as news anchors. The concern of people of color about their television representation remains strong (Fife, 1987; Grey, 1989; Ziegler and White, 1990). Shows like *Oprah* generate big expectations and concomitant criticism. *Oprah* has been said to absolve white guilt by presenting a rags-to-riches black, unthreatening female, who hugs whites in the audience more than people of color. The show has also been accused of being negative about African-American men, having few minorities on the production team, and giving racist white organizations airtime rather than confronting more subtle and pervasive racisms. Winfrey ridicules calls for her to be more black, asking, 'How black do you have to be?' (King, 1987: 187). The demand that she 'represent' African Americans is indeed a sign of her token status on television. As Isaac Julien and Kobena Mercer have written of film, the notion that one instance 'could "speak for" an entire community of interests reinforces the perceived secondariness of that community' (1989: 4).

The *Oprah* show is, in any case, permeated with 'race' as much as it is with gender. Winfrey's own Chicago-based production company, the first owned by an African American, makes it. This, together with her ratings, gives her Cosby-like powers — to determine topics and how to treat them, for instance — that black people rarely have in television. The show itself consistently addresses racism, explicitly, by calling for equal opportunities and recruiting people of color for the production team and, implicitly, by challenging casual instances of racism. In an episode on interracial relationships, Winfrey ironizes a white male guest's history of dating only black women, saying, 'It's that melanin that got you … that melanin count just overwhelmed him'. *Oprah* avoids overt racial politics but towards the end this episode featured audience members' political analyses of interracial relationships:

> *Female audience member:* …the reason people are taking it so terribly is that we are part of a racist society period, and that has to change for anything to change.
>
> *Female guest:* That's right (*Oprah Winfrey Show*, 1989a).

Less overtly, the show often features visual representations of racial difference without verbal comment, a silence that may be the result of television's caution about 'race' but that may work, as Kum-Kum Bhavnani (1990) has described, as anti-racist empowerment. In one segment of the '1991 Follow-up Show' (*Oprah Winfrey Show*, 1992), for instance, an African-American family, identified simply as a 'family' living in a project, got a 'dream house'. Two other segments showed dramatic reunions between adopted children and birth parents. In both cases children of mixed parentage met previously unknown white or black parents, while 'race' went unmentioned. These silences allowed racial differences to appear but refused them legitimacy in the narratives. In the silences, the cultural mythology of a de-raced all-American 'family' achieved a tactical defeat of other more clearly racist mythologies of black welfare mothers and tragic mulatto children.

The show's representations of black America are also telling. It regularly features successful African-American business people, professionals and entertainers, generating a picture of black culture and achievement rare in mainstream media. After a long absence, rappers now appear on the show occasionally; there are indeed parallels between *Oprah*'s woman-empowering aims and those some women rappers express (Rose, 1990). The show regularly considers issues that are important and controversial among blacks: education, self-esteem, class tensions, conflicts between black women and men over black women's alleged disrespectful and money-grabbing, 'ain't nothing going on but the rent' approach to black men and black men's claimed irresponsibility, black discrimination against dark-skinned black people, interracial adoption and relationships, and black hair and skin care. Black-oriented advertisements and public service announcements are more frequent than on most other network shows. More generally, Winfrey's and her black guests' stories of their lives combine with the show's references to black struggles, especially those of strong black women, to provide a perpetually renewed and reformulated television history of African America, not as comprehensive as those produced during Black History Month, but there all year round.

Winfrey sometimes talks black American, usually to make a joke. Television conventionally allows such language for comedic purposes but it remains language infrequently heard outside sitcoms, dramas and documentary representations of inner cities. Winfrey even induces similar speech in others. Once, trailing one of her specials on the early evening news after her show, she talked with the black newsreader Roz Abrams, and the somewhat formal Abrams called her 'girlfriend'. For a hallucinatorily brief moment black women's acquaintanceship and talk displaced the bland chumminess and linguistics common in such exchanges.

Occasionally Winfrey addresses whites in the studio audience to explain some aspect of black life. This move homogenizes both the life and the audience, and can seem to offer a quasi-anthropological supplement to talk shows' usual peeping-tom pleasures. But it gives a public voice to marginalized phenomena and acknowledges an ignorance and distance that usually goes unspoken, while Winfrey's blunt pedagogy circumvents voyeurism.

Finally, black feminism seems, as much as woman-centered feminism, to define the show. This black feminism recognizes the different history of patriarchy among African Americans (Gaines, 1988), writes the history of black women's resistance in the anti-slavery and civil rights movements and in every family and celebrates the strength and creativity of black women (Walker, 1983). Winfrey often invokes the film *The Color Purple*, the writing of Gloria Naylor (1982) and the work of Maya Angelou (1970), whose account of growing up in the black South she says describes her own life and whom she calls her mentor (*Oprah Winfrey Show*, 1993). Men's abuse, which Patricia Hill Collins (1990: 185) says needs to be the object of black feminist analysis, implicitly receives this attention through the host's and black audience members' repeated engagements with it. Angelou and Walker are often said to ignore the history and problematic of black masculinity, and in the process collude with white racism. *Oprah* is subject to similar criticisms but tackles the issues by presenting positive images of African American fatherhood and male mentoring. Winfrey still Signifies on black men though, as Gloria-Jean Masciarotte (1991), citing Gates (1988) citing Hurston, says; and other African American women on the show do the same. This Signifyin(g) is, as Gates says, both a verbal game and a serious cultural engagement. A black woman in the audience raised a laugh when she admonished a black male guest, a Lothario vacillating between two white women, one with dark, one with light hair, 'She over there on the light side, she over there on the dark side, you in the middle on the *grey* side' (*Oprah Winfrey Show*, 1992). The show itself also Signifies, in Gates's broad sense of textual revision, on the texts of African American women writers, rewriting them in a different medium and for a larger racially diverse audience. For many of the white and black viewers of *Oprah,* the show's enduring canon of these writers — along the more variable set of female self-help gurus and high-achieving women who guest — must constitute the dominant cultural representation of feminism.

SEXUALITIES

In common with the rest of television, the *Oprah Winfrey Show* is heterosexist. Openly lesbian or gay guests appear rarely, the show carefully establishes the heterosexuality of well-known guests, and when it addresses homosexuality directly it tends either to problematize it or to mainstream it as a human issue, distanced from sex and politics (Gross, 1989). Bisexuality is a special problem. In an episode presented jointly with the hunt-the-criminal programme *America's Most Wanted*, a man's bisexuality became the emblem of his ability to elude the criminal justice system: 'The problem with John Hawkins is he's a very good-looking guy, he's a very good con, and he's bisexual, so he has the ability to basically adapt into any community or any type of social structure', said a police officer (reshown on *Oprah Winfrey Show*, 1992).

Sometimes *Oprah* gives screen time to camp men who function briefly and conventionally as jesters. More of a challenge to dominant assumptions about sexuality is the show's marking of differences within heterosexuality, for instance the line it draws between abusive and non-abusive heterosexual relationships. This acknowledgement of plural heterosexualities coexists with the show's more traditional representations of sexual relationships between women and men either as always involving the same desires and social patterns, as in episodes along the lines of 'Save Your Marriage' and 'Best Husband Contest' or as infinitely various, as in 'Men Who Married Their Divorced Wives' and 'Women Who Married Their Stepsons'. Finally, the show's overwhelmingly female spectacle and spectatorship might conceivably be read as a kind of televisual lesbianism but the link between female spectatorship, sexuality and sexual politics is very unclear (de Lauretis, 1991; Stacey, 1988).

CLASS

Despite a late-1980s' burst of class-conscious sitcoms, television is not very interested in class relationships. On *Oprah* though the all-American narrative of Winfrey's progress from poverty to wealth is often invoked, and her riches legitimized as the rightful reward of her struggle for a piece of the pie. The wealth is frequently represented as exuberant consumption by references to Winfrey's restaurant, her condo, her farm and her furs. In a study of women's reactions to *Dynasty*, Andrea Press (1990) writes that working class women have a particular affinity with such representations; the *Oprah* show's periodic ditchings of gritty emotion in favour of glitz may then be a part of its success. But the show represents Winfrey's good works and her dispensations of wealth to the poor too. Taken together, these representations turn wealth into something new, strange and full of responsibilities. The show also refers often and unromantically to poverty, in episodes on project life for instance, and points up class differences in values and lifestyles. At the start of a show on 'Stressed-out Dads', Winfrey showed two clips from *thirtysomething* of yuppie fathers caring for their children and then said, laughing and sarcastic, 'I know that happens in y'all's house every night' (*Oprah Winfrey Show*, 1990b).

The show may present Winfrey as a de-raced all-American success story but it gives a strong presence to middle class African Americans and pays attention to the responsibilities and close historical relationships middle class blacks have with and for poorer blacks, especially young people. Many issues debated between black women and men on the show involve class: the averred paucity of suitable black men available to educated black women; these women's alleged prejudices about ordinary working black men, and whether black women or men, especially those in the middle class, should have interracial relationships. No other networked shows give these topics the acrimonious airings they get on *Oprah*; the other daytime talk shows seem unable to see their contentiousness. *Oprah* is indeed at times better able to recognize the shifting and intersecting agendas of class, gender and 'race' than is much feminist theory.

OPRAH AS PSYCHOLOGY

Alongside the show's investment in social relationships runs a much more explicit preoccupation with psychological issues and explanations. The daytime talk show is a psychological genre (Carbaugh, 1988). Most *Oprah* episodes focus on overtly psychological phenomena like 'obsessions' and 'negotiation skills', psychologists are the show's commonest 'expert' guests, Winfrey's interventions and those of audience members are mostly directed at clarifying experiences and emotions, and interpersonal communication is presented as a cathartic and enabling solution to social as well as personal problems. The show gives almost all the problems it addresses, even those like unemployment, some psychological content, usually in terms of 'feelings'. Each episode's narrative moves towards psychological closure: people end up 'feeling' better because they have 'expressed themselves' or 'started to think about what they really want'. Winfrey's psychological democracy, her representation as a person just like the audience members, is also very powerful. Showing an extreme version of the usual perception of television as the mass medium closest to interpersonal communication (Ellis, 1982; Pfau, 1990), women in *Oprah*'s audience frequently preface their contributions by telling Winfrey how much they like her and the show, and how they feel they know her almost as a friend (Waldron, 1987: 182).

The ubiquity of psychological discourse on *Oprah* is important to recognize at a time when psychology has wide-ranging social power in the overdeveloped world, and in view of the female-identified and often feminist-approved status of explanations in 'personal' terms. Psychologism has been indicted as the failing of talk shows generally. Aaron Fogel (1986) describes the genre as a collective psychological reaction to Puritanism, and Giuseppe Minnini (1989) characterizes it as pure ego, a 'talk-showman'[sic] holding forth in a way that does not allow dialogue, let alone productive engagement with issues. Less moralistically, it could be argued that *Oprah*'s psychologism sometimes drowns out its, at times, more complicated representations of power relationships. In an episode on obsessional jealousy, one woman's account of how her youth had facilitated her husband's manipulation of her was invalidated and replaced by Winfrey's, a psychologist's and audience members' declarations that people can only do things to you if you let them.

The show mirrors psychologists' professional confidence in their ability to improve things with a relentless optimism that leaves little room for persistent problems or imperfect solutions. Psychologists do not however have an easy ride on the show. They are often drowned out by audience members' and Winfrey's own floods of psychological pronouncements and Winfrey jokes about these appropriations of expertise. The show steers its audience towards self-help groups or books written by its guest rather than towards professional help. In an episode that featured women living with men who would not marry them, first the audience, and then Winfrey made restrained fun of the guest psychologists' zeal:

Psychologist 1: ... counseling would really be appropriate (audience laughter starts) for a couple who seems to be, stuck, no, I'm talking about together, and together with a counselor establishing an agenda for themselves as a couple ...

Winfrey: All therapists want everybody to go to counseling, yeah (laughs)

Psychologist 2: Oprah it helps ... it helps a lot.

Winfrey: Oh I know it does, I know it helps a lot (*Oprah Winfrey Show*, 1990a).

Antiprofessionalism is a common stance in the USA but *Oprah*'s lay psychology has other connotations too. Its emphasis on getting people to communicate is part of a utopian picture of a viewing community and a world in which everyone knows they are not alone. Often the stress on communication recalls a religious commitment to testifying (see also Masciarotte, 1991), and this convergence of talk show with worship (Fogel, 1986) takes on a specific resonance in *Oprah* from the history of black churches as places where African American women's voices could be raised and heard. The show's persistent focus on self-esteem ties into an implicit liberal democratic politics of rights, responsibilities and choice, and, through the non-specific spirituality the show attaches to self-worth, to New Ageism. *Oprah*'s optimism about psychological improvement is associated with beliefs in religious redemption and in social progress, for which redemption is itself a metaphor. Andrea Stuart (1988; see also Bobo, 1988) has suggested that black women watching *The Color Purple* read its happy ending not within the film narrative, where it seems inconsistent and sentimental, but within broader religious, social and historical narratives where it offers an important antidote to hopelessness. Perhaps *Oprah*'s daily psychological resolutions of dramatic suffering support a similar reading.

An individual woman may be represented on *Oprah* as shaped by social forces like racism and male violence but also as fully and only responsible for her own actions. An odd melange can result, of growth psychology, religious devotion, political analysis and personal hubris. An emblematic example on *Oprah* itself was Angelou's presentation of herself and her work. Describing her composition of a poem for Clinton's inauguration, she said she was not nervous: all she had to do was 'get centered' and write. No false humility was required: after all, 'I come from the Creator trailing wisps of glory'. And telling of her own overcoming of abuse, poverty and racism she recalled the key realization: 'God loves *me*. Oprah, Oprah, the skies opened up. I can do *anything*' (*Oprah Winfrey Show*, 1993). Winfrey looked deeply touched, they clasped hands and the show broke for commercials. The show's loose concatenations of ideas are easy to deride but they build up a complicated picture of psychological, as well as social and historical relationships, relationships which the show does not try to resolve. Some might see the ambiguities as disabling and claim television audiences cannot cope with them. But I think it is productive for a talk show to display, as *Oprah* does, the contradictions that traverse our subjectivities, rather than to opt for social determinist explanations of problems, victimologies that allow subjectivity no clear place or to invoke an unproblematic human agency as the general solution, as talk shows usually do. *Oprah*'s infusion by black feminism seems to be what generates this complexity.

OPRAH, TELEVISION AND SUPER-REALISM

Oprah's reflexivity about being television calls attention to how the characteristics of television, and of the daytime talk show in particular, shape it. More than most television (see Ellis, 1982), the daytime talk show is a casual form, not watched continuously. To compensate, it is made eye-catching, with clear, immediate images and plenty of camera movement and cutting to offset the slowness of talk. Daytime viewers may be attending to things other than television or just passing through a room where the television is on, so the shows favor soundbites: punchy questions; short, clear encapsulations of arguments and feelings; brief passages of incoherent speech, tears or silence to signal deep emotion; bursts of laughter and applause, snatches of theme music bracketing breaks and the programme itself, and enticing cliffhanger trails before each break: 'when we get back, are strong-thinking, decisive women a threat to you men?' (*Oprah Winfrey Show*, 1989b). These characteristics produce a currency of rapid, intense, simple and repetitive aural and visual representations, from the six-note sequence that means *Oprah*, to the screwed-up, crying faces of incest survivors asked 'How did it feel?' These fragmented representations are always breaking up the coherence and continuity of the talk show's narrative of psychological improvement.

It might be said of *Oprah*, as is often argued of talk shows and television in general, that its dispersed, atomistic representations do not disturb but only support the cultural consensus (Ellis, 1982; Fogel, 1986; Miller, 1990; Minnini, 1989). From this perspective, *Oprah* is too frivolous to be feminist. Some feminists have, however, interpreted television representations that reach *Oprah*'s level of disruption as carnivalesque or melodramatic challenges to television's conventional representations of gender (Ang, 1985; Brown, 1990; Deming, 1990). I am going to argue that *Oprah*'s televisual characteristics produce rather a *super-realism* that has some modest feminist value.

Daytime talk shows like *Oprah* try to reach a realist truth by interleaving information and entertainment, and deploying narratives of psychological growth to pull this 'infotainment' together. Sometimes, they do not manage the integration and super-realism, a realism torn out of shape by excesses of emotion or empiricism, disrupts the explanatory framework. On *Oprah*, this disruption happens in one of two ways. First, super-realism may take over when a 'psychological' truth recurs so often on the show that it begins to shed its individual psychological character and starts to look more like a social, political or religious fact. The narratives of sexual abuse on *Oprah*, for example, very similar and endlessly repeated, seem to go beyond psychological understanding to become facts about gender relationships that demand explanation in other, social terms. It is the televisual superficiality and facility of the show that allows this super-real excess to register.

Oprah's second type of super-realism appears when the emotions in the show get so intense that the show forgoes any claim to provide information and simply displays an extreme effect — accessible to psychoanalytic interpretation, perhaps, but not to the kinds of psychological explanations most of us are familiar with and use. For instance, when the show featured an abused woman with 92 personalities, it could not provide a coherent account of her subjectivity. Abuse started to seem utterly idiosyncratic and affectively overwhelming. Again, this registering of excess relied on the show's super-real televisual character: on snappy formulations of monstrous feelings and quick moves to commercial breaks ('back in a moment') that left the unspeakable and the unimagineable resounding around American living rooms.

I would argue that *Oprah* owes its cultural effects largely to its super-realist emotional and empirical excesses, which rework or Signify on television and culture, something talk shows' more conventional psychological explanations are unlikely to do. Its contribution to US debates about the education of black children or the relationships between black women and black men comes not so much from its explicit consideration of these debates as from their unannounced, unasked for and unmarked recurrence within the show, so frequently and pervasively that they become super-real facts, uncontainable within the show's psychological narratives.

Henry Louis Gates (1989) wrote that he hopes 'blacks will stop looking to tv for (their) social liberation'. Feminists of color and white feminists rarely look to television for social liberation. But television can achieve what feminist writing finds difficult: *Oprah*'s interwoven explorations of 'race', class and gender and its popularization of aspects of black feminist thought are examples. And feminists may discover something about how to deal with the complex connections between subjectivity, gender and other social relationships from the suspension of the *Oprah Winfrey Show* between fluff and gravity; psychology, social analysis and emotions; realism and super-realism; and from their own difficulties in addressing this mixture.

NOTES

I would like to thank Ann Phoenix, Kum-Kum Bhavnani, Chris Griffin and an unnamed reviewer for their helpful comments and encouragement.

1. Another African-American woman, the comedian Marsha Warfield, has had a half-hour networked morning show, and Montel Williams, the 'male Oprah', has an hour long morning show on CBS. A new crop of *Oprah* challengers, several with African-American hosts, appeared in 1993 (Freeman, 1992). The earliest African-American

talk-show host was Ellis Haizlip who, in the late 1960s and early 1970s, fronted *Soul*, 'a live performance/talk show inspired by the burgeoning cultural nationalist movement' (Jones, 1991).

REFERENCES

Ang, I. (1985) *Watching Dallas: Soap Opera and the Melodramatic Imagination*. London: Methuen.

Angelou, M. (1970) *I Know Why The Caged Bird Sings*. New York: Random House.

Bad Object-Choices ed. (1991) *How Do I Look? Queer Film and Video*. Seattle: Bay Press.

Bhavnani, K-K. (1990) 'What's Power Got To Do With It?', in I. Parker and J. Shotter (eds) *Deconstructing Social Psychology*. London: Routledge.

Bobo, J. (1988) '*The Color Purple:* Black Women as Cultural Readers', in D. Pribram (ed.) *Female Spectators Looking at Film and Television*. London: Verso.

Boemer, M. (1987) 'Correlating Lead-in Show Ratings with Local Television News Ratings', *Journal of Broadcasting and Electronic Media* 31: 89–94.

Bordo, S. (1989) 'Reading the Slender Body', in M. Jacobus, E. Foxkeller and S. Shuttleworth (eds) *Body/Politics*. New York: Routledge.

Bretl, D. and Cantor, J. (1988) 'The Portrayal of Men and Women in US Television Commercials: A Recent Content Analysis and Trends over 15 years', *Sex Roles* 18: 595–609.

Brown, M. E. (1990) 'Motley Moments: Soap Operas, Carnival, Gossip and the Power of the Utterance', in M. E. Brown (ed.) *Television and Women's Culture: The Politics of the Popular*. London: Sage.

Brunsdon, C. (1989) 'Text and Audience', in E. Seiter, H. Borchers, G. Kreutsner and E. Warth (eds) *Remote Control*. New York: Routledge.

Butler, J. (1990) *Gender Trouble*. New York: Routledge.

Carbaugh, D. (1988) *Talking American: Cultural Discourses on Donahue*. Norwood, NJ: Ablex.

Coward, R. (1983) *Patriarchal Precedents*. London: Routledge and Kegan Paul.

Coward, R. (1989) *The Whole Truth*. London: Faber and Faber.

Davis, D. (1990) 'Portrayals of Women in Prime-time Network Television: Some Demographic Characteristics', *Sex Roles* 23: 325–32.

de Lauretis, T. ed. (1986) *Feminist Studies/Critical Studies*. Bloomington, IN: Indiana University Press.

de Lauretis, T. (1991) 'Film and the Visible', in Bad Object-Choices (ed.) *How Do I Look? Queer Film and Video*. Seattle: Bay Press.

Deming, C. (1990) 'For Television-centred Television Criticism: Lessons from Feminism', in M. E. Brown (ed.) *Television and Women's Culture: The Politics of the Popular*. London: Sage.

Dent, G. ed. (1992) *Black Popular Culture*. Seattle, WA: Bay Press.

Doane, M. A. (1987) *The Desire to Desire*. Bloomington, IN: Indiana University Press.

Doty, A. (1992) *Making Things Perfectly Queer*. Minneapolis, MN: University of Minnesota Press.

Ellis, J. (1982) *Visible Fictions*. London: Routledge and Kegan Paul.

Fife, M. (1987) 'Promoting Racial Diversity in US Broadcasting: Federal Policies Versus Social Realities', *Media, Culture and Society* 9: 481–505.

Fogel, A. (1986) 'Talk Shows: On Reading Television', in S. Donadio, S. Railton and S. Ormond (eds) *Emerson and His Legacy*. Carbondale, IL: Southern Illinois University Press.

Freeman, M. (1992) 'Can We Talk? New for 1993', *Broadcasting and Cable* (December): 14.

Gaines, J. (1988). 'White Privilege and Looking Relations: Race and Gender in Feminist Film Theory', Last Special Issue on 'Race', *Screen* 29: 12–27.

Gates, H. L. (1988). *The Signifying Monkey*. New York: Oxford University Press.

Gates, H. L. (1989) 'TV's Black World Turns — But Stays Unreal', *New York Times* (Nov.): 12.

Goodman, F. (1991) 'Madonna and Oprah: the Companies They Keep', *Working Women*. 16: 52–5.

Grey, H. (1989) 'Television, Black Americans, and the American Dream', *Critical Studies in Mass Communication* 6: 376–86.

Gross, L. (1989) 'Out of the Mainstream: Sexual Minorities and the Mass Media', in E. Seiter, H. Borchers, G. Kretscner and E. Warth (eds) *Remote Control*. New York: Routledge.

Guider, E. (1987) 'Katz Advises How to Handle Daytime Queen', *Variety* (July): 8.

Harrison, B. (1989) 'The Importance of Being Oprah', *New York Times Magazine* (June): 11.

Heath, S. (1985) 'Joan Riviere and the Masquerade', in V. Burgin, J. Donald and C. Kaplan (eds) *Formations of Fantasy*. London: Methuen.

Hill Collins, P. (1990) *Black Feminist Thought*. Cambridge, MA: Unwin Hyman.

hooks, b. (1981) *Ain't I A Woman? Black Women and Feminism*. Boston: South End Press.

hooks, b. (1989) *Talking Back: Thinking Feminist, Thinking Black*. Boston: South End Press.

Jones, L. (1991) 'Hot Buttered "Soul"', *Village Voice* (March): 12.

Julien, I. and Mercer, K. (1988) 'Introduction: De Margin and De Center', Last 'Special Issue' on 'Race', *Screen* 29(4): 2–10.

Kaplan, E. A. (1987) 'Feminism Criticism and Television', in R. Allen (ed.) *Channels of Discourse*. Chapel Hill, NC: University of North Carolina Press.

King, N. (1987) *Everybody Loves Oprah*. New York: Morrow.

Lorde, A. (1984) *Sister Outsider: Essays and Speeches*. Trumansburg, NY: Crossing Press.

Masciarotte, G-J. (1991) 'C'mon Girl: Oprah Winfrey and the Discourse of Feminine Talk', *Genders* 11: 81–110.

McClellan, S. (1993) 'Freshman "Deep Space Nine" Records Stellar Sweep Debut', *Broadcasting and Cable* (April): 24–6.

Miller, M. C. (1990) *Boxed In: The Culture of Television*. Evanston, IL: Northwestern University Press.

Minnini, G. (1989) 'Genres de discourse et types de dialogue: Le "Talk-show"', in E. Weigand and F. Hundnurscher (eds) *Dialoganalyse* II. Tubingen: Niemeyer.

Moraga, C. and Anzaldua, G. (1981) *This Bridge Called My Back*. Watertown, MA: Persephone Press.

Morris, M. (1988) 'Banality in Cultural Studies', *Block* 14: 15–26.

Mulvey, L. (1975) 'Visual Pleasure and Narrative Cinema', *Screen* 16: 6–18.

Mulvey, L. (1981) 'Afterthoughts on "Visual Pleasure and Narrative Cinema" Inspired by "Duel in the Sun"', *Framework* 15/16/17: 12–5.

Naylor, G. (1982) *The Women of Brewster Place*. New York: Viking.

Nightingale, V. (1990) 'Women as Audiences', in M. E. Brown (ed.) *Television and Women's Culture: The Politics of the Popular*. London: Sage.

Oprah Winfrey Show (1989a) 'Blacks and Whites Dating', New York: Journal Graphics, 1 March.

Oprah Winfrey Show (1989b) 'Home Fights', New York: Journal Graphics, 25 April.

Oprah Winfrey Show (1990a) 'A Mother's Plea: Marry My Daughter', 23 May, author's transcript.

Oprah Winfrey Show (1990b) 'Stressed-Out Dads' 30 May, author's transcript.

Oprah Winfrey Show (1992) '1991 Follow-up Show', 8 January, Channel 4, Britain, author's transcript.

Oprah Winfrey Show (1993) 'Maya Angelou Interview', 13 July, author's transcript.

Pfau, M. (1990) 'A Channel Approach to Television Influence', *Journal of Broadcasting and Electronic Media* 34: 195–214.

Press, A. (1990) 'Class, Gender and the Female Viewer: Women's Responses to *Dynasty*', in M. E. Brown (ed.) *Television and Women's Culture: The Politics of the Popular*. London: Sage.

Rich, A. (1986) 'Compulsory Heterosexuality and Lesbian Existence', in *Blood, Bread and Poetry*. New York: Norton.

Riley, D. (1988) *Am I That Name? Feminism and the Category of 'Women' in History*. Minneapolis, MN: University of Minnesota Press.

Rose, T. (1990). 'Never Trust a Big Butt and a Smile', *camera obscura* 23: 109–32.

Spelman, E. (1990) *Inessential Woman*. London: Women's Press.

Spivak, G. (1988) *In Other Worlds*. New York: Routledge, Chapman and Hall.

Stacey, J. (1988) 'Desperately Seeking Difference', in L. Gamman and M. Marshment (eds) *The Female Gaze*. London: Women's Press.

Stuart, A. (1988) '"The Color Purple": in Defence of Happy Endings', in L. Gamman and M. Marshment (eds) *The Female Gaze*. London: Women's Press.

Waldron, R. (1987) *Oprah!* New York: St Martin's Press.

Walker, A. (1982) *You Can't Keep A Good Woman Down*. London: Women's Press.

Walker, A. (1983) *In Search of Our Mothers' Gardens*. New York: Harcourt Brace Jovanovich.

Walkerdine, V. (1989) 'Video Replay', in V. Burgin (ed.) *Formations of Pleasure*. London: Methuen.

Ziegler, D. and White, A. (1990) 'Women and Minorities on Network Television News: An Examination of Correspondents and Newsmakers', *Journal of Broadcasting and Electronic Media* 34: 215–23.

Corinne SQUIRE teaches psychology at Brunel University. She is the author of *Significant Differences: Feminism in Psychology* (Routledge, 1989) and has edited a book on *Women and AIDS* (Sage, 1993). ADDRESS for correspondence: Department of Human Sciences, Brunel University, Uxbridge, Middlesex UB8 3PH, UK.

Nora RÄTHZEL

Harmonious 'Heimat' and Disturbing 'Ausländer'[1]

This article aims to set an agenda for further research into the following issues: which concepts of 'homeland' ('Heimat') lead to anxieties about those defined as 'foreigners' ('Ausländer') and which ones are able to include the 'newcomers'? How do these concepts relate to people's ability to intervene into contradictory social structures? In order to do this, it presents some results from a study which explores concepts of 'Heimat' and 'Ausländer' held by the ethnic majority. Statements made by the sample of middle-class women and men in Switzerland and Germany suggest that the holding of harmonious images of Heimat tends to be associated with perceiving 'Ausländer' as the source of social conflicts. However, the inability to appropriate even an imaginary space seems to be related to an inability to open up to new experiences as neighbourhoods change.

When young people in Germany started to attack the homes of asylum seekers with the encouragement of 'ordinary people', politicians from all parties condemned them but, in the same breath, all (except for the Greens and the Communists) added that one had to understand that 'people feel threatened by the presence of so many foreigners'. What lies behind such suggestions is a specific concept of 'cultural identity'. It is thought of as something stable, connected with the place in which one lives in such a way that this place must never change. If it does, so it is said, people lose their orientation and start to attack those whom they see as responsible for this change.

This view is often underpinned by the notion that there is a 'threshold of tolerance' for 'strangers'; that the entry of 'too many foreigners' breaches that threshold and hence makes negative reaction likely and understandable. One could dismiss this concept by arguing that it is derived from studies of animals and therefore not theoretically sound. The problem is that it seems to convince many people. Therefore it is important to understand why this kind of argument is so convincing to so many and why many people feel that it articulates exactly what they feel 'deep in their hearts'.

Feminism & Psychology © 1994 SAGE (London, Thousand Oaks and New Delhi), Vol. 4(1): 81–98.

The issue of how the appeal to a psychosocial construct, German cultural identity, can be used to justify (or even mobilize) political action is one of the most pressing political, psychological and sociological concerns of the late 20th century. This issue, together with the understanding of how gender is inserted into nationalist discourses, is also important to feminism if it is to achieve the goal of liberating all women. It is for reasons such as this that the examination of the ways in which people experience and construct 'home' ('Heimat') and 'others' ('Ausländer') is an important one.[2]

My approach is informed mainly by theories developed within Cultural Studies and current German Critical Psychology.

CULTURAL IDENTITY AND THE COLLECTIVE CONTROL OVER THE CONDITIONS OF LIFE

In cultural studies identity is not imposed on individuals by socialization (as assumed in theories subscribing to the threshold of tolerance) but they actively construct their identities within a given social framework. Consequently, identities are not seen as stable, static and fixed for a lifetime but flexible, ever changing (Hall, 1990; Rutherford, 1990; Cohen, 1992). Moreover, it is argued, people do not have just one identity but diverse, even conflicting identities (Rutherford, 1990). While the importance of cultural identities is stressed it is also argued that one has to avoid the danger of essentializing them; treating them as if they have a fixed, determined essence (see the interview with June Jordan in Rutherford, 1990 and Nash, 1993).

The central concept of German 'Critical Psychology': 'Teilhabe an der Kontrolle der Lebensbedingungen' (collective control of the conditions of life) and Handlungsfähigkeit (capacity or ability to act (Holzkamp, 1983)). The specificity of human beings, it is argued, lies in the fact that they produce their life conditions instead of adjusting to them. The biological basis for this is their ability to learn. This is one answer to the debate about whether individuals are determined by their genes or by their 'environment'. The biological determination, Holzkamp-Osterkamp (1973) argues, is precisely that human beings are scarcely determined biologically, they can (which means they have to) learn anything that is necessary for them to conduct their lives. By the same token this means that they are not determined by environment either. They learn how to deal with the structures with which they are confronted (Holzkamp-Osterkamp, 1973). They always have choice, though within the limits of the social and historical situations in which they live. Therefore, from the point of view of critical psychology there can be no natural threshold of tolerance.

Cultural studies and critical psychology are in agreement that individuals are active. They differ in their emphasis on individuals' need collectively to control their conditions of life. These differences can best be seen if both positions are simplified. In cultural studies we find the concept of empowerment. However, I think that this is often restricted to the flowering of identities that give people strength, some security and the possibility of building some space for themselves where they can flee from the alienations of social structures. The relationship of those identities to social conditions as a whole is often not mentioned and if so, then only superficially mentioned (Rutherford, 1990: 25).

But critical psychology in turn dismisses the cultural aspects of life. There is no concept of cultural identity as such. As the majority of individuals in societies structured through domination are not in control of the conditions of their lives, they have only two ways in which to gain power: they can gain control at the expense of others (through sexism, racism, elitism) which means that they subordinate themselves to the dominant structures and groups; or they can take up the struggle for collective control over social space, which implies postponing their immediate short-term interests in favour of their long-term interests, which do not stand in opposition to the interests of other dominated groups.

I believe that this somewhat heroic view is exactly one cultural studies wants to stand against and was partly developed to oppose. But it might be, that the baby was thrown out with the bath water — perhaps because the water became so muddy that the baby became invisible. An example may serve to make this point clearer.

In his illuminating essay 'Home Rules', for instance, Cohen (1993) quotes Edward Upward, who, after joining the Communist party in the 1930s, distanced himself from his earlier writings and instead wrote a story 'Journey to the Border' in which the hero is saved from the brink of madness by discovering dialectic materialism and the world of class struggle. Upward urges the hero to 'move out of the region of thinking and feeling altogether, to cross over the frontier into effective action' (Cohen, 1993: 59).

Articulated in such an absolutist way it seems reasonable to distance oneself from Upward's injunction to his hero. Yet, I would argue that there is something worthwhile in this quotation. Political action to change social structures is important in order to 'empower' individuals, hopefully, to improve their living conditions. However, they are also a central source of what may be called 'identity'. It would be useful to combine the concepts produced by cultural studies and by critical psychology in order both to keep the notions of active individuals making political interventions and of cultural and other identities. The following is an attempt, though by no means a complete one, to combine cultural studies and German critical psychology in order to work towards an understanding of the ways in which the concepts of 'Heimat' and 'Ausländer' articulate with the identities of some German and German-speaking Swiss people, many of whom have some commitment to anti-racist ideas.

'HEIMAT' AND 'AUSLÄNDER' IN EVERYDAY THINKING

I want to use the German words, 'Heimat' and 'Ausländer', throughout the text instead of their nearest English equivalents, home and foreigners, which do not give the full meaning of those notions. The term Heimat lies between the home in which one lives and the country. It merges (verdichtet) both meanings. At a specific conjuncture and for specific groups Heimat can indicate a region (there is the German tradition of Länder, late nation-building), a village, a city, a community or, as in fascism, the whole nation-state whose citizens are defined by descent. The Heimat movement (Heimatbewegung) developed in the 19th century in the course of industrialization. It concentrated on nature, folk costumes, music and so on. In the first 20 years of the Federal Republic, the term was hardly used, because of its fascist connotations. Since the beginning of the 1970s but especially since the beginning of the 1980s, the term has regained respectability. This came, according to Bredow and Foltin (1981), partly as a reaction against the 'emotionless' politics of 'sixty-eight'. (For the German construction of Heimat see the empirically detailed and theoretically thorough study done by Applegate (1990).)

The term Heimat is also relevant in the German-speaking part of Switzerland. It is very much connected to nature and landscape. And as the Swiss character was constructed through attachment to the 'soil', partly in opposition to the German construction of 'through blood', Heimat is a prime symbol of the nation.

As for the term 'Ausländer', it is more exclusionary than the terms 'foreigners' or 'strangers'. Aus means 'over' (the game is over) or is short for 'outside'. So 'Ausländer' is literally a person who is or belongs outside the country. As far as I can trace it, the term became common with Fichte in his famous 'Speech to the German nation'. Fichte was one of the main articulators of German national identity in opposition to the French occupation. 'Ausländerei' was meant as an accusation of having affinities to the French, that is with ideas from the French revolution. I use 'Ausländer' in quotation marks to suggest that the population of migrant origin in Germany cannot be seen as not belonging to the country.

The material I am going to analyse comes from seminars I held in German towns and in German-speaking towns in Switzerland. People in a variety of institutions and in grass-roots initiatives asked me to do one- or two-day seminars on racism. At the beginning of those seminars I asked people to write down and/or draw their associations with, for example, 'Heimat', 'Ausländer' and 'Germany'.

In this article I am looking only at answers given to the words 'Heimat' and 'Ausländer' and (with one exception) I consider only those answers where I asked the participants to note their gender on the papers. In total I have been discussing images of Heimat and 'Ausländer' with about 70 participants in different seminars. This article deals mainly with the findings from the following three groups:

1. A grass-roots collective in a middle-sized town in West Germany, in the Ruhrgebiet. This is a traditional coal area, which has suffered many pit closures during the last 20 years and will have to face some more in the future.

The members of this collective fought (as they told me) a relatively isolated struggle against racism. The majority, young people between 18 and 25, saw themselves as an alternative, autonomous group. The event they invited me to was a one-day meeting on the issue of racism. In the afternoon I ran a workshop entitled 'Heimat and Racism' attended by eleven women and six men. I do not know their professions but most of them will have been students.

2. A class of students studying to become social workers in a specific educational institution, that combined social work with cultural activities like sculpture and film. Part of their study included working in social institutions. I was invited to do the seminar by their teachers, who wanted to include the issue of racism in the curriculum. The school was in a German-speaking town in Switzerland. The members of the class were between 20 and 30 years of age. There were thirteen women and six men. As I understood from discussions between the sessions many of them were also engaged in anti-racist activities, all of them thought of themselves as being anti-racists. The seminar lasted two days.

3. A left wing Jewish group who had invited me to support them in discussing what they called their 'double-position' as the objects of racism, who, in spite of this, could themselves behave in racist ways. Eleven women and three men between the ages of 30 and 45 attended the seminar for one and a half days. They were teachers, surgeons, social workers, psychotherapists and students. All but one lived in the German-speaking part of Switzerland.

As the seminar in the Swiss school was the most extensive I am going to focus my discussions on the findings there and bring in the other two groups only where the results differ markedly.

The nature of the study was such that it could not be in-depth. The purpose of meeting with participants was in order to run a seminar and time was limited. In addition, responses had to be sought anonymously in order to respect confidentiality in the seminar situation. This is why in general I cannot relate the answers to specific individuals. (Whenever I do identify specific people in the article it is because during discussions some participants chose to explain what they had written.)

Nevertheless, I think that the findings have some value for a theory of the subject. Certainly, the people I spoke with lived under very different conditions. But the concepts they chose in order to express themselves came from a limited amount of 'raw material'. The answers given show the variability and the overlap between individual constructions.

The participants had some characteristics in common: All of them were intellectuals and used to developing their opinions by reading and discussing theoretical accounts. All were involved in left and/or anti-racist politics. All now belonged to the middle-class (whatever their class origins). All but three members of the first and all of second group belonged to the ethnic majority of the countries in which their seminars took place (Germany and Switzerland). When I speak of the women or the men, I mean those in my sample. Although I try to draw some tentative general conclusions, as to gender differences and differences between minorities and majorities in Western European societies, these findings need to be compared with similar investigations under different social and historical conditions.

One might ask why a study concerned with racism focuses exclusively on people who consider themselves to be anti-racists. First, because I think that anti-racists and racists do not live in entirely different universes. The study may be able to provide some general evidence about the source of attitudes which reject and marginalize 'Others'. Second, one might also find some elements that serve to develop 'anti-racist identities'.

The first part of the article will deal only with images of Heimat since these seemed to form the basis for images of 'Ausländer'. However, the article concentrates mainly on the *inter-relationship* between images of Heimat and images of 'Ausländer'. I have structured the associations made by the participants according to what I think are central spheres of human life: space, activities, social relationships/communication, feelings and sensual needs. The sections concerned with conflicts emerged out of the major differences respondents constructed between images of Heimat and of 'Ausländer'.

HEIMAT — A HARMONIOUS PLACE OF PASSIVE ENJOYMENT

From the questionnaires it is clear, that when thinking of Heimat, one of the images that entered women's minds most frequently was place, particularly the landscape: either a specific river, lake or mountain; or mountains, trees, woods and wind in general. Most of these features are in the country where women live. But there are also distant landscapes that become Heimat: a volcano, the sea, an island with palm-trees or the Arizona desert. The counterpart to those vast and empty places where women feel at home is their house, their flat or bedroom. Only very few women think of public places when they think of Heimat: a cafe, a restaurant, a square.

How does Haug's and Hauser's (1991) argument that women have no place relate to these findings? For Haug and Hauser the 'placelessness' (Ortslosigkeit) of women means that they have no place where they can find refuge, since both 'home' and the public space are uninhabitable.

Certainly it is not in public spaces that the women in the seminars feel at home. But why did women depict the community flat or the individual room as Heimat? Why was the landscape, the lake, the desert, an image of home? Does this emphasis on places where 'I have the freedom to be myself', as one woman put it, imply that women are appropriating new places in a new way? This could be one side of the coin. But there are reasons to doubt this. Many of the places women mentioned as Heimat are associated with leisure activities. So where is women's non-leisure time spent? Half of the women wrote the term 'work' into their pictures but without giving their employment any specific location.

WOMEN'S DREAMS

Heimat appears as paradise on earth: in the middle of an untouched landscape one enjoys the sweet smell of flowers, a gentle wind, the roaring of the river and the fresh taste of bread and cheese. From time to time one returns to the cosy house where music and a nice book are waiting. Somewhere, helpful friends and an understanding and loving family stand ready to provide an atmosphere of warmth, acceptance and belonging. These feelings are the ones most frequently mentioned.

This harmony can only be conceived of by radical deletions: landscapes are emptied of living beings, rooms and houses are free of people who want to see a different television programme, are disturbed by the music one wants to hear or are in fact themselves listening to music that ruins one's nerves. Yet, feminist research has long exposed the falsity of the claim that 'family' is a warm and cosy place, where one is understood and accepted (Barrett and McIntosh, 1982).

The participants in the Swiss school were themselves puzzled by the image they had of Heimat and family. They initially suggested that Heimat was apparently nothing they currently experienced but something they had known as children. But then they recalled that childhood had not been like that either and that therefore their image of Heimat was illusory.

This harmonious image of Heimat may also be read as an expression of what women lack: a landscape that is not polluted, friends who accept them, a family that can provide safety, the possibility to be what they want to be. The drawings may be seen as expressing women's dreams, not their experiences. The retrospective dream of what a childhood could have been instead of a memory of what it really was like.

If this is true, can we criticize those images? Can we criticize dreams? This might seem an odd thing to do but if dreams and utopias have some influence on the way we act (in that we may try to make our dreams come true) then such criticisms are important. For if our dreams do not contain the elements which are necessary for living, then those elements are not available for inclusion in transformative practices. One woman wrote: 'Heimat is the site of self-determination.' If dreams of self-determination encompass very few spheres of life, they cannot even be seen as an imaginary appropriation of the world but rather as a retreat from it.

MEN'S REALITIES

If public space is the place for men, why is it that they do not locate themselves there? Men hardly drew or mentioned any places. One young man drew smog, a plant, an island with palm trees but only to explain later that these were the places, where he had not found a home. The only place where he could feel at home was his inner self, symbolized by a heart. There was only one other man, who drew a place, the lake he likes to walk around. All other men arranged words and symbols on their paper, mentioning home once and once places where holidays were spent.

But the men also mentioned conflicts more often, their images were less harmonious than the women's. We can divide the men who mentioned conflicts into two groups: those for whom Heimat meant both comfort and anxiety, belonging and isolation, trust and separation; and those for whom it meant only conflicts. The latter criticized the political and economic system and saw themselves as removed from Heimat. Not feeling at home because of the conflicts there may seem more realistic than dreaming of a cosy place without conflicts. But this detachment from Heimat also indicated a harmonious image of Heimat. It is because Heimat is imagined as harmonious but is not experienced as a cosy place that it is rejected altogether.

THE HEIMAT OF THE 'OTHER'

In the Swiss school group there were two non-Swiss people: a German woman and a Turkish man. Both wrote virtually the same sentence: 'Heimat is the place where I am accepted and loved by people.' I wondered if this was a spurious finding but during the seminar with the Jewish group this finding was confirmed as systematic for the members of minority groups in the sample. More than two-thirds of the participants did not mention any place in Heimat. Nobody mentioned activities or sensuality. Three did relate Heimat to place but only by writing briefly: 'Nature — whatever that might mean', 'nature and landscape'. (Unfortunately, this was the group that I did not ask to record their gender, so I cannot go into more detail on this, but only three of the fourteen group members were men.) All but one thought of Heimat as 'being understood', 'feeling accepted and safe'.

It seems as if for ethnic minorities/migrants the mechanism of suppressing the reality of social relationships in order to construct a harmonious place of Heimat does not work. This may be because of the impossibility of separating the 'private' and the so-called 'public' spheres. Racism and anti-semitism do not occur just in public spaces, are not only part of social structures but of the 'private sphere' as well. In order to construct a harmonious image of Heimat, any trace of real experiences must be erased.

One might argue that the same could be said in relation to women in general. Patriarchy operates in the private as well as the public field. Although this is true, there seems to be a way in which women, who are seen as belonging to the nation, can find ways of psychologically appropriating space and remembering certain moments of pleasure which constitute a sense of belonging. These possibilities seem far less available to members of minority groups.

But this is not the whole story. I also asked the Swiss Jewish group to write down their associations with Switzerland. All but one had some good things to say about the country. All except one stated, that, in spite of all problems, they considered Switzerland the place where they felt at home. The degree of ambivalence varied but there was no total rejection of, or indifference to, their country.

It is striking that, although they felt excluded from it, their images of Heimat were even more unanimously harmonious than for the participants of the other seminars. In this context one woman picked up the idea of Heimat as an imaginary place, as a dream. The term produced a yearning for something unattainable. The descriptions of Heimat can, in this case, be read as a reaction to the experience of exclusion. First, the romantic vision of Heimat is accepted. Second, it is accepted that the term is only meant for those whom the dominant powers and 'common sense' understandings define as belonging to the nation. Those who do not belong can merely claim to feel at home but are not allowed to use the emphatic term Heimat that evokes the idea of roots, of having been there forever. Thus, it is not the definition of the term Heimat that is questioned, but the right of 'minorities' to use it. On the other hand, rejection, anti-semitism, threat and persecution are and were real experiences in Switzerland. Is it possible or even desirable to claim such a place as Heimat?

The focus on acceptance into the community and being understood as the main condition for Heimat can be read in different ways. On the one hand, it is a liberation from dependence on a particular place or environment. On the other hand, it indicates the need for acceptance and therefore dependence on other people. In the discussion, some participants confirmed this dependency and the problems it produced in social relationships. Some felt that the claim to a place as Heimat, the appropriation of a place as one's own, might be one way to develop a more autonomous security. These contradictions, of dependency and autonomy, in the ways Heimat is imagined raise questions about whether it is possible to produce social relationships that are less contingent on mere acceptance but rely more on creating common ground (both as physical space and as common interests).

COMPARISONS BETWEEN IMAGES OF 'AUSLÄNDER' AND IMAGES OF HEIMAT

In the comparisons that follow I am not treating the images as either racist or not racist. I consider this question as secondary to the one I am interested in here, which is to find out the meaning of those images for the people who articulate them. The question of how such images hinder or facilitate the construction of a more democratic and anti-racist society is a pressing one.

In almost all respects the images of 'Ausländer' were the counter images of Heimat. That is especially true for feelings: angst and threat are the feelings mentioned most often in association with 'Ausländer'. Next comes the failure to understand, misunderstanding, mistrust, rejection and aggression. Others are more uncertain, they feel distance, envy and powerlessness — those are the negative feelings, but there is also curiosity, fascination and admiration.

In analysing angst expressed by women, Haug and Hauser (1991) identify a mechanism by which women construct themselves as persons dominated by anxieties. They fear public spaces, because they have no place there. But, since women are constructed as weak and hysterical if they express fears of public domains, many women internalize the conflicts they feel and construct themselves as fearful individuals rather than public places as threatening. Against this background we might consider women's angst in relation to 'Ausländer' as a way out of this dilemma. For the angst towards strangers is a socially accepted one. Every day politicians express their understanding of it. Scholars in television programmes, their voices loaded with concern and importance, explain how anxiety towards strangers is a biological characteristic of the human species.

But many women also mentioned positive associations with 'Ausländer'. To get a better picture it might be useful to examine these associations more closely.

SENSUALITY AND THE BODY

Sensuality in Heimat was connected to food, the typical food of the area, the enjoyment of wind, landscapes and once the smell of lime trees (although neither men nor women mentioned such elements very often). With the word 'Ausländer' there is an explosion of sensual elements, especially for women. Food is mentioned, especially the smell of 'exotic food', but also music and dancing. 'Ausländer' are associated with 'colour', with different (dark) colour of skin, eyes and hair. They are said to dress differently. These images are certainly not new. The ways in which they are articulated make them components of the stereotype of the 'happy native'. If we compare them with the absence of such descriptions in relation to Heimat, it is possible to draw some tentative conclusions: the highlighting of dress and physical features in relation to 'Ausländer' but not to Heimat point to the fact that features of the dominant culture, as with the dominant sex, are understood as the norm and thus do not require to be made explicit but can be taken for granted. Anything differing from the 'norm' becomes visible as different and, as a result, is commented on. In this case, the cultural practices of the Swiss are central to the conceptions of self held by many of the Swiss respondents but are not discussed.

'AUSLÄNDER', A THREAT TO SUBORDINATION

It is in this context, that theories about the 'natural character' of 'xenophobia' have been formulated (Eibl-Eibelsfeld, 1989). It is 'natural', so it is argued, to be scared of 'strangers' because, by their very difference from 'us', they question the most intimate and apparently 'natural' forms of living. But it would be naive to accept that physical features of the body, let alone eating and dress habits are natural. From Foucault's (1977) writing we know that the body is a means to secure 'horizontal discipline' in space. In addition, we do not have to be feminists to know that our bodies are not just 'ourselves' but a site of strategies of sexualization and 'normalization' (Haug, 1987).

Since women learn to build their identities around their bodies (Räthzel, 1987), one way of transforming their subordination to their bodies into autonomy is to live self-normalization as rebellion. Instead of wearing the 'normal' clothes and hair, appearance can be used as a signifier of some counter-culture or just of a very 'individual' personality. In spite of the pleasure this can produce and the fact that it is apparently an act of resistance, this praxis stays within the boundaries of the dominant rule, as long as it centres identity around the body. To be confronted with different ways of dealing with the body diminishes the differences visible within the dominant culture. New and different personal and individual styles of representation can suddenly be seen as 'normal'.

My thesis is, therefore, that the anxieties about, and aggression towards, 'Ausländer' are not really caused by the fact that they are a threat to our sense of belonging and our sense of Heimat. Those images of 'Ausländer' are threatening, because they make our taken-for-granted 'identities' visible as specific 'identities' and deprive them of their assumed naturalness, which, as Bauman (1993) suggests, is vital to their functioning. Once we start thinking about them, becoming aware of them, we cannot feel 'at home' any more. Not, because our homes are changing (although this is also true) but because we start to realize that behaviours we consider to be deeply intimate are social products and hence open to challenge. More than that, they are the result of a process of normalization from above and from below; of 'formation of the self' in which we have actively surrendered to disciplinary strategies as in the example of sexualization of the female body. A faint suspicion about the degree to which we have subordinated ourselves to structures of domination might, therefore, be the rational source of 'irrational' anxieties towards 'Ausländer'.

'AUSLÄNDER' AND SOCIAL STRUCTURES

In one respect all men and women in the sample agree about 'Ausländer', they see them as related to conflicts. The range of conflicts covers almost every sphere of life: personal problems of communication; social conflicts like drug dealing and prostitution; social structures like patriarchy and capitalism; and political and economic conflicts of which 'Ausländer' are the objects such as racism, exploitation and lack of citizenship. Going further to world problems as a whole, these conflicts include: flight, wars, dictatorships, poverty, famine. It seems as if everything that has been repressed in the image of Heimat is emptied into the image of 'Ausländer'.

In Heimat, society did not exist. In thinking of 'Ausländer' not only the society, in which people live but the whole world comes into the frame. On the one hand, the notion of 'Ausländer' opens up the closed and empty world of Heimat. The potentially positive feelings connected with 'Ausländer', like curiosity, the challenge to learn something new stand in opposition to the positive feelings regarding Heimat, like security, understanding and being understood. But they also stand in opposition to the negative feelings in relation to Heimat, which were anxiety and isolation.

One might say, then, that the extent to which Heimat is constructed as a place of harmony and light, parallels the extent to which individuals see their alienation not as a result of living in a society structured through dominance and exploitation but as originating from 'outside', being caused by 'Ausländer'. The threat represented by 'Ausländer' might be the suspicion that, in order to gain Heimat as a safe place, one has to confront its internal contradictions.

But this is only the general picture from the majority of the sample. In the following section I would like to compare specific reactions from the German grass-roots group and the Swiss school group and to analyse some of the more unusual accounts produced to show other articulations.

POLITICS, HEIMAT AND 'AUSLÄNDER'

The most striking difference between the German group and the Swiss school group is the few images of 'Ausländer' the former has. There are no specific descriptions, almost nothing is mentioned in relation to sensuality and nothing at all in relation to activities. This may be partly due to the little time there was for the study. But leaving this aside, why were so few descriptions of 'Ausländer' produced?

One could interpret this as a positive sign. These young people, who are active in defending refugees, do not subscribe to the general sterotypes of the 'happy native' or the 'dangerous, patriarchal drug dealer'. But there are some doubts as to such an optimistic conclusion. First, the main tendency of the results does not differ from the Swiss group: 'Ausländer' are mainly connected with conflicts, Heimat with positive feelings and harmony. Second, where there is something like a specification of 'Ausländer' the women, for instance, write 'different': different culture, language, traditions, habits, history. There is never any similarity. Third, all the participants (except for one woman in each group) constructed an absolute separation between everything that is connected to 'Ausländer' and everything that is connected to Heimat.

The conflicts mentioned in Heimat have nothing to do with the conflicts mentioned in relation to 'Ausländer': racism, the lack of citizenship, the rejection of refugees, the tightening of immigration laws in both countries. All these conflicts mentioned in relation to 'Ausländer' do not seem to occur in the participants' Heimat. Although they are concerned with them; although some focused their political activities around them, they still seem to happen somewhere 'out there', where one does not belong.

Therefore, the almost non-existent image of 'Ausländer' in the German group is not something one can feel terribly comfortable with. It seems to indicate a political awareness not to reproduce either the negative or the positive stereotypes — which is, of course, a step forward. The problem, however, is that there seems to be nothing to replace these stereotypes. One could speculate that the stereotypes are still there but are suppressed in order for respondents to consider themselves 'politically correct'.

'AUSLÄNDER' AS NEIGHBOURS — TWO WOMEN

Two women wrote that 'Ausländer' are their neighbours. The woman in the German group, let us call her Anna, wrote: 'Thinking of the word "Ausländer" I suddenly realize, that all my neighbours are "Ausländer" and that I almost don't notice that any more. Yet, in the media they are always something abstract and always depicted in the role of victims.' This was the only participant who made a clear distinction between her own experiences and media images. It was also the only time that somebody explicitly stated that 'Ausländer' have become a normal part of life, neither a source of specific conflicts nor of specific 'enrichment'. Under Heimat Anna wrote:

> Heimat is my social and professional environment and, very important, the history connected with it, in this case the Ruhrpott. But Heimat does not depend on a certain place. It is there, where I can actively take part in shaping the conditions of life. The basis for this are people whose thinking I can understand at least partly.

As we find no special conflicts with 'Ausländer' we find no special harmony in Heimat. The image is centred around Anna's opportunities to make interventions. It is connected to a specific place and its history but not reduced to it. There is the necessity of understanding people, but this is not totalized as in the majority of other people's statements, where to understand and to be understood is linked to being accepted and is central to the concept of Heimat.

Time was too short for me to find out much about Anna. Nevertheless, I think that, in her short account, there are important themes which point to something beyond the flexibility of 'identity'. These are: breaking down the boundaries that separate Heimat and 'Ausländer'; an emphasis on collective control over life conditions; and the appropriation of space without being appropriated by it.

The woman in the Swiss school group who wrote that 'Ausländer' are her neighbours, let us call her Berta, felt threatened by her Turkish neighbours. She was not sure if the man, in touching her arm, was not showing disrespect since he kept 'his own wife' isolated from others. She felt that his wife did regard her as sloppy, because of the way she lived. She wrote further: 'It is all very nice to say that "Ausländer" are an enrichment, but I do not feel enriched at all when the cafes in my neighbourhood, which used to be mainly women's cafes, are transformed into meeting points for men only.'

Again, I know too little about her to be able to draw any definite conclusions. But I would like to try to develop some speculations that could be the starting point for further investigations. As Haug and Hauser (1991) suggest, women do not internalize society's rules in the way an 'ideological subject' or an 'autonomous subject'[3] is supposed to do. Instead, they position others as wards to control them. For example, they may consider that their neighbours, the milk-man and other people are watching them and be in a constant state of anxiety that they will be found to be 'out of order'. Therefore, according to Haug and Hauser (1991), women are never really integrated into society.

Berta positions her Turkish neighbours as wards. But this gives the situation a certain twist. On one level, she feels probably the same anxieties as the women described by Haug and Hauser. But on another level she can construct the wards as those who really do not fit into society. This relieves the burden from her shoulders and puts it on theirs. Foreign women are, according to Berta, striptease dancers or prostitutes; the men gamble in the streets or do not work at all; too many of them live in one flat; they hide their children and grandparents; and they dress much too skimpily in winter.

In seeing 'Ausländer' as out of order and at the same time as not belonging to society, Berta may be able to experience her outsider status at least partly as integration. While she herself may not entirely be an insider because she is a woman and left wing, her identification of others, who belong even less, may well provide some sort of positive identification for her.

The image Berta has of Heimat and of 'Ausländer' shows her as positioned within different conflicts. She feels excluded by 'Ausländer' from the cafes she used to enjoy. In addition, the city council has also diminished the public spaces she used to see as hers by taking away the Kanzlei. The Kanzlei was originally a factory which was squatted and transformed into a political and cultural centre for the left wing, alternative scene. It was closed down by the city council shortly before our seminar took place.

The contradiction in Berta's attitude towards life is that, on the one hand, she goes into public spaces (she is one of the two women mentioning public places in Heimat), she is interested in new experiences, she organizes her life autonomously around friends and neighbours. As with Anna, her image of Heimat does not explicitly include safety and security but a variety of activities. But unlike Anna, those activities are only leisure activities. It seems to be pre-cisely Berta's openness, her readiness to experience Heimat as an open space inhabited by people but in which she plays no active part, that makes her more vulnerable and thus more ready to see 'Ausländer' as a threat.

To avoid misunderstanding: in speaking about her constructions I do not want to dismiss Berta's experiences as having no basis in reality. The question is how to deal with the conflicts which can occur when different lifestyles clash, especially when they include contradictory structures of domination. For on the one side, we find gender relationships working against Berta but, on the other side, ethnic relationships work against those men and neighbours she sees as a threat. Berta's reaction is retreat, a feeling of disempowerment and, as a result, strong resentments against those whom she then sees not only as occupying her cafes but as transforming the whole of society into something dangerous and uncontrollable.

The question that arises, that is not dealt with in anti-racist movements, is how to negotiate solutions with which the different groups can live. It is not enough to denounce resentments as morally inappropriate, much less to announce that one has to understand the anxieties of the majority population. In my opinion strategies that centre around a collective, active appropriation of space are necessary. Those strategies would have to break down the separation of spheres as a precondition to finding solutions which take the different structures of domination and their interdependency into account. Just as an example: Berta could take the friends she likes to have supper with at home into the cafes and invite her Turkish neighbours to some of those suppers.

ONCE AGAIN: MEN'S REALITIES — AND THEIR IMAGES OF 'AUSLÄNDER'

In concluding this section I want to return to the men, who did not feel 'at home' because of the political conflicts they perceived there. I have already pointed out that this attitude is the other side of an image of a harmonious Heimat. But what are the images of 'Ausländer' that go with such an attitude?

I must say that I have never subscribed to the idea that women were somehow the better human beings and men underdeveloped, selfish creatures, incapable of caring for others. But the image of Heimat and 'Ausländer' of the majority of men in this sample is rather scary. The only non-negative thing they could say about 'Ausländer' was that they felt curious about them and admired them. In relation to those of women, the majority of men's images were much more negative and resentful — despite the fact that their images of Heimat were not as harmonious. Perhaps this points to the fact, that having no place where one can feel at home, no anchorage in Heimat, does not generate feelings of solidarity towards those regarded as not belonging either. A good example of this is the one man who sees his inner self as the only place of Heimat. Concerning 'Ausländer' he writes: 'They want to live here, but they don't want to adjust to our norms.'

To have no dreams at all, not even reduced ones, seems to diminish the likelihood that outsiders will be accepted and to create even more anxieties. Maybe this is one of the reasons why men articulate more angst than women with regard to 'Ausländer'.

SOME FINAL REMARKS

The absence of pleasurable associations in most men's images of Heimat and their overemphases on political conflicts, reminds me of a story told by Bertolt Brecht (1967) and called 'Tu Wants to Learn Fighting and Learns Sitting':

> A student comes to Me-ti and says: I want to participate in the class struggle. How shall I fight? The old man laughs and asks: Do you sit well? I don't know, says Tu astonished, how else should I sit? Me-ti explains to him. But, says Tu impatiently, I did not come to learn sitting. I know, said Me-ti, patiently, you want to fight, but in order to do so, you must sit well, because just now we are sitting and sitting we want to learn. Tu says, if you always try to take the most comfortable position and try to make the best of a given situation, in short, if you always search for pleasure, how can you fight? Me-ti says: If you don't strive for pleasure, if you don't want to make the best of a situation and take the best position, why should you want to fight? (Brecht, 1967: 576).

The examples in this article can provide a specific reading of the slogan: The personal is political. It is not that *any* personal reflection is already political but that the way in which we deal with the so-called personal has an impact on our political strategies. In addition, the way we live the personal and even our dreams are determined by political attitudes. The very concept of the personal as something separated from the political is itself a political construction. This early insight of the feminist movement should be revived for further investigations into the relationship between the 'private' and the 'public'.

To return to the beginning: a potentially useful theoretical perspective on this work lies not merely in the multiplicity and flexibility of identities; not only in learning to live with differences; but in learning how to negotiate contradictions. It is precisely the multiplicity of 'identities' and the boundaries between them that allow for what I would call 'defensive practices of identification' as in Berta's case.

The feeling of being subjected to social change can produce the desire to operate control only in the restricted sphere of the 'private'. This kind of retreat which implies constructing very specific identities must be further investigated as a possible source of idealization (in this case of Heimat) and of demonization (in this case of 'Ausländer'). The separation of domains is a way of gaining feelings of control (reduction of complexity) but if those areas remain separate, control is only possible at the expense of losing one's grip on the whole set of interdependencies. Since every human being constructs a Weltanschauung and needs to 'know' how the world functions, one way of explaining conflicts and retaining a harmonious place of self-determination is to see conflicts as a result of 'alien forces'.

The attempt to reintegrate the separated areas of society and of the individual's different identities is a necessary specification of the too abstract concept of a flexible and ever changing identity. As Anna Wulf, the central character in

Doris Lessing's *The Golden Notebook* says: 'I'll pack away the blue notebook with the others. I'll pack away the four notebooks. I'll start a new notebook, all of myself in one book' (p. 528). There is, of course, never a guarantee that a more 'whole' self will appear and, in the book, this attempt at reintegration initially leads to breakdown. Yet, it is a chance worth taking.

NOTES

1. I am extremely grateful to Ann Phoenix who encouraged me to write this article in the first place and then provided very helpful comments on the first version. I also want to express my gratitude to Kum-Kum Bhavnani, Susan Condor and Gail Lewis who put so much work into providing me with very detailed and useful comments. All the errors and weaknesses are my own responsibility. Finally, I want to thank all the participants of my seminars who so openly stated and discussed their views.
2. This work is part of a project that aims to compare the ways in which people construct their homes in relation to nation and 'other' in Hamburg, London and Marseille. The project is undertaken together with Phil Cohen and Max Silverman.
3. 'Ideological subject' is a term used in the tradition of Althusser (1977). The subject subordinates itself to the structures of domination, but constructs itself as autonomous, as acting by free will and independently. This ideological subject is often conceptualized as the positive outcome of the process of socialization, seen as really autonomous. (See Mead, 1993 and Erikson, 1973.)

REFERENCES

Althusser, L. (1977) *Ideologie und Ideologische Staatsapparate*. Hamburg/West Berlin: VSA.
Applegate, C. (1990) *A Nation of Provincials. The German Idea of Heimat*. Berkeley, Los Angeles, Oxford: University of California Press.
Barrett, M. and McIntosh, M. (1982) *The Anti-Social Family*. London: Verso.
Bauman, Z. (1993) 'Das Urteil von Nürnberg hat keinen Bestand. Rassismus, Antirassismus und moralischer Fortschritt', *Das Argument 200: Brauchen wir einen neuen Antifaschismus?* July/August.
Brecht, B. (1967) *Gesammelte Werke*, Vol. 12. Frankfurt am Main: Suhrkamp.
Bredow, W.v. and Foltin, H.-F. (1981) *Zwiespältige Fluchten. Zur Renaissance des Heimatgefühls*. Berlin/Bonn: J.H.W. Dietz.
Cohen, P. (1992) 'Wandernde Identitäten', in R. Leiprecht (ed.) *Unter Anderen. Rassismus und Jugendarbeit*, pp. 77–92. Duisburg: DISS.
Cohen, P. (1993) 'Home Rules. Some Reflections on Racism and Nationalism in Everyday Life', The New Ethnicities Unit, University of East London.
Eibl-Eibelsfeld, I. (1989) 'Fremdenfurcht und Reaktion auf Außenseiter', in Klaus Stadtler (ed.) *Lust am Forschen. Ein Lesebuch zu den Naturwissenschaften*. München: Piper.
Erikson, E. H. (1973) *Identität und Lebenszyklus*. Frankfurt am Main: Suhrkamp.
Foucault, M. (1977) *Überwachen und Strafen. Dje Geburt des Gefängnisses*. Frankfurt am Main: Suhrkamp.

Hall, S. (1990) 'Cultural Identity and Diaspora', in J. Rutherford (ed.) *Identity, Community, Culture, Difference*, pp. 222–37. London: Lawrence & Wishart.

Haug, F. ed. (1987) *Female Sexualization. A Collective Work of Memory*. London: Verso.

Haug, F. and Hauser, A. eds (1991) 'Die andere Angst,' *Argument-Sonderband* 184. Berlin/Hamburg (will be published in English by Verso).

Haug, W. F. (1986) 'Die Faschisierung des bürgerlichen Subjekts', *Argument-Sonderband* 80. Berlin.

Holzkamp, K. (1983) *Grundlegung der Psychologie*. Frankfurt am Main, New York: Campus.

Holzkamp, K. (1993) 'Lernen', *Subjektwissenschaftliche Grundlegung*. Frankfurt am Main, New York: Campus.

Holzkamp-Osterkamp, U. (1973) *Motivationsforschung 1 und 2*. Frankfurt am Main, New York: Campus.

Jordan, J. (1990) in J. Rutherford et al. (ed.) *Pratibha Parmar: Black Feminism: the Politics of Articulation*, pp. 101–26. London: Laurence & Wishart.

Lessing, D. (1982) *Das Goldene Notizbuch*. Fischer Taschenbuch.

Mead, G. H. (1993) *Geist, Identität und Gesellschaft*. Frankfurt am Main, New York: Campus.

Nash, C. (1993) 'Remapping and Renaming: New Cartographies of Identity, Gender and Landscape in Ireland', *Feminist Review* 44:39–57.

Räthzel, N. (1987) 'Women and Bodies', in F. Haug (ed.) *Female Sexualization. A Collective Work of Memory*. London: Verso.

Rutherford, J. ed. (1990) *Identity, Community, Culture, Difference*. London: Lawrence & Wishart.

Nora RÄTHZEL works at the Institut für Migrations- und Rassismusforschung in Hamburg. She has published widely on issues of racism in Germany and the construction of the German nation. She is a member of the Editorial Board of the journal *Das Argument*.

Philomena ESSED

Contradictory Positions, Ambivalent Perceptions:
A Case Study of a Black Woman Entrepreneur

This article addresses black neo-conservatism and the contradictory position of the black middle class in the matrix of domination systems. The empirical basis consists of an open-ended interview with an African-American business woman, an entrepreneur, about her personal success and her role in relation to the black community. The main focus of the article provides an analysis of the arguments she presents to explain problems of race, class, gender and social inequality in society. The resulting picture of beliefs and opinions about inequality and black progress appears to be more complex than a single label like conservatism can account for.

INTRODUCTION

Today many (feminist) scholars share the point of view that race, gender and class are interlocking systems the joint workings of which structure the experience of men and women of all racial-ethnic backgrounds (Bottomley et al., 1991). There is a rich and growing body of historical and theoretical studies which deal with this 'holy trinity'.[1] The significance of seeing race, class and gender as interlocking systems of oppression is not so much to claim that this matrix of domination is the *most* fundamental one but to foster a paradigmatic shift of thinking inclusively about different relationships of dominance.

Black women are not a monolithic group.[2] Therefore, one cannot simplistically speak of a black women's point of view on issues of oppression and resistance. Hemmons (1980) found (among a large percentage of black women an acceptance of 'liberal' perceptions on women's liberation (about 45 percent).) The numbers did not differ by class. With respect to 'racial liberalism', she found, however, that its advocates among black women were predominantly from a middle class background (83 percent). One pitfall of survey studies has to do with the

Feminism & Psychology © 1994 SAGE (London, Thousand Oaks and New Delhi), Vol. 4(1): 99–118.

fact that the thinking processes of black women remain invisible behind the abstract and anonymous class categories and ideological typifications used.

Gathering facts and measuring how often certain racial, gender or class patterns occur is relevant but not sufficient for understanding the specifics of personal biographies and belief systems individuals adhere to in order to account for their experiences. Further, a top down approach fails to account for the willingness of some victims to collude in their victimization (Hill Collins, 1990). Finally, structural determinism does not provide insight into possible contradictions, for example, in the experiences of middle class black women who may reproduce dominance along one axis (e.g. in class terms) and resist oppression at other levels (e.g. through opposition against racism).

Given these and other criticisms of 'race, class and gender' theories various attempts have been made to integrate the study of macro and micro levels of domination into one methodological framework. Here, I mention three complementary approaches: a black feminist epistemological approach (Hill Collins, 1990), a racism analysis approach (Essed, 1990a, 1991) and a woman-centred approach (Bell et al., 1993). Hill Collins' (1990) explanation of 'multiple levels of domination' highlights the need for black feminist theory to emphasize simultaneously three levels as sites of domination and potential resistance — the systemic level of social institutions, the community level and the personal biography. Essed's (1991) concept of 'everyday racism' crosses the boundaries between structural and interactional approaches to racism by linking the details of micro experiences to the structural and ideological context in which they are shaped. Bell et al. (1993) present the 'woman's life context model'[3] as a framework for understanding all levels of a (black) woman's life: from early life experiences to career development and the private world of family, spirituality and so on. Although from different angles, all three approaches stress the importance of contextual forces of gender, race-ethnicity, sociopolitical history and class in shaping the personal biographies of black women. Moreover, all three approaches consider the concrete experience an essential criterion of meaning.

The analysis of experiences may expose coherence and contradictions in values, emotions, motivations, goals and choices one would not otherwise discover in all their complexity.[4] In view of the multiple locations black women have in the social matrix, this article addresses the accounts of an individual black woman pursuing personal and collective interests. The focus is not on everyday discourse or ideology but on subjectivity, on the *lived experience* (Ellis and Flaherty, 1992) of human ties based on racial, gender, ethnic and class factors and on the physical, political, economic, historical and social context of that experience. In this respect the notion of multiple subjectivity is often used (e.g. Hollway, 1989), but, I prefer to speak of *multiple identifications* in order to emphasize that subjectivities are not static but always in the process of being constructed in relation to perceived material, political or social interest. The acknowledgement of the multiple roles of women enables them to identify with ideas, beliefs, goals or opinions embedded in different, maybe even conflicting, ideological systems.

I will present a case study of the meanings one specific black woman attaches to her multiple locations and experiences in the matrix of dominance. She is an entrepreneur, a real estate broker, a profession which is rare among black women. Not surprisingly, studies about black women entrepreneurs are equally rare although some attention has been paid to the career developments of black women in management (e.g. Fernandez, 1981; Fullbright, 1986; Nkomo, 1989; Bell et al., 1993). These works argue that black women are structurally disadvantaged in various ways. The climb to the top is hampered by glass ceilings, as it is by the lack of role models which can encourage early exposure to a business environment. Black women also generally lack the necessary corporate sponsors who usually facilitate acculturation and mobility in the organization. The obstacles created by the lack of sponsors and role models are further reinforced by the systemic discrimination black women are confronted with in everyday interaction, communication and decision-making processes in organizations.

The case study focuses on accounts of the gender and racial dimensions of a career life, the strategies developed to manage these aspects and perceptions of self as a black, female, middle class professional in relation to other social groups.

Information was gathered through an in-depth interview which constituted one among a series of interviews with US and Dutch black women, professionals and students, in the context of a project on everyday racism (Essed, 1991). The interviews had an informal nature, resembling ordinary conversations. In various related subprojects I worked out different epistemological questions including the explanation of the method and methodology of the use of accounts (Essed, 1988) and the political–ideological context of the reproduction of knowledge of racism in everyday life (Essed, 1990b). The embedded nature of the macro and the micro was at the heart of all of these projects. The point was made that, from a macro point of view, the massive and systemic reproduction of belief systems which legitimate certain dominant group positions, predisposes individuals to internalize these ideas, whether or not they themselves occupy these dominant positions. From a micro point of view, however, individuals do not necessarily and unthinkingly accept 'dominant' ideologies. Moreover, the cognitive domain of individuals is a fundamental area where new and critical knowledge can generate change. One can think of the efforts of 'thinkers' and/or intellectuals to rearticulate a group standpoint in the struggle against domination but also of those who put innovative ideas into practice (Essed and Helwig, 1992). The study of individual motivation and sense-making in the process of resistance against confining race and gender boundaries is still, however, largely unexplored.

Some comments are also in order about the methodological implications of a case study approach. In mainstream social sciences there is a tendency to over-value large-scale studies. It is true that statistical sampling is important, for example, in order to establish correlations or cause–effect relationships. However, sampling seldom provides us with the tools to understand the complexity of structure, processes, motivations, ambivalences and experiences. To give an example, it has been stated repeatedly that many black women claim their racial identity to be much more salient than either class or gender identity (Stasiulis, 1987; King, 1989). It has remained implicit, however, in terms of which choices, emotions, practices, identifications or arguments the primacy of the racial cause structures the course of an individual black woman's life.

Further, by using 'case study' I do not mean to imply the narrow sense of studying the unique situation of an individual but rather the intensive study of a *selected example* in order to illustrate the phenomenon of multiple locations and identifications. The intensive study of an insight-stimulating example (Selltiz et al., 1976) may evoke new ideas and insights that are usually overlooked. The aim is to understand rather than to find methods of justification and verification (Code, 1989).

The study of a selected example is useful as a methodology for the analysis of multiple sites and dimensions of oppression and resistance, because different structural axes and levels of domination all come together in the personal biography.[5] Implications are that even a single case, if described in a language 'by means of which you can really grasp the interaction between various parts of the system and the important characteristics of the system' (Normann in Gummesson, 1991: 78) can make it possible to reach a fundamental understanding of structural and phenomenological processes rather than of mere generalizations about the frequency of certain practices.

The black woman entrepreneur who provides this selected example told me the long story of her career, of how she built up her enterprise. At the time of the interview she had just signed her biggest contract so far. Her story is interesting because it illuminates many of the contradictions of the position of a black middle class woman whose upward mobility is rooted in the Civil Rights era. Economically, she has a privileged position compared to the majority of blacks but her career history illustrates that even blacks with high education experience discrimination in the labor market. She breaks through sex role constraints by pursuing the, for a woman, unusual career of real estate broker. In business she resists discrimination in many situations but, as a wife and as a mother of sons, she has also to deal with the specific forms of racial discrimination against the black man. She is compassionate about racial solidarity, yet she does not identify with the cause of economically deprived black women such as welfare mothers. Relationships between these different, at times, contradictory forces can be exposed through the analyses of the arguments the woman uses in order to account for her experiences with race, class, gender and social inequality in society.

THE NEW BLACK MIDDLE CLASS

In the 1990s black working women are less a unified group than 30 years ago, when they were commonly excluded from traditional white women's work such as clerical jobs and the better paying manufacturing and professional jobs (Jones, 1985; Hine, 1989). Due to the struggle for Civil Rights and the subsequent US policies of affirmative action in the 1960s and 1970s, a small black middle class has developed. Various studies have addressed the increasing gap between the black middle class and the impoverished majority of blacks (Wilson, 1987) but hardly any attention has been paid to black middle class women's experiences of self in relation to lower class blacks.

Investigations of the black middle class in the USA are notoriously difficult and have appeared in various publications (Frazier, 1957; Muraskin, 1975; Landry, 1987; Boston, 1988). For the purpose of this article, a descriptive rather than a conceptual use of the notion of class is made. One can make a distinction between four principal professions in the black middle class: politicians, clergymen, educators and entrepreneurs (Marable, 1983). Entrepreneurs can be seen as the key element in the black bourgeoisie because they are likely to believe strongly in the idea that any aspiring black can 'make it' in the existing social system. They only need to develop the right attitude.

The history of institutionalized racism and the involvement of black political, clerical, intellectual and economic leaders in the struggle for Civil Rights makes the role of black entrepreneurs more complicated than that of the white business 'elite'. It seems likely that many of those involved in black business enterprise would like to perceive themselves as positive models for the black masses. This is probably more so for members of the 'new' bourgeoisie many of whom directly benefited from the affirmative-action programs. Instead of dealing with this problem in a theoretical way, the question is redefined as an empirical problem: does a black woman entrepreneur explain race-ethnicity, gender and class inequality in a way that both reinforces a positive self-image vis-a-vis the black community and supports her business interest?

INTRODUCING THE CASE STUDY

The empirical basis of this article consists of the story of Carol L., a 39-year-old real estate broker.[6] The complete story as she told it to me consists of many pages of which only those covering the accounts of her career life in relation to family and community are used here. Let me first, however, give some background information about her specific biography.

Carol L. comes from an immigrant family. The story of how they left Grenada in order to 'try their luck' in the USA, is probably not very different from other families who migrated from the Caribbean to the USA, during the 1950s.[7] When she was 11 years old her father, a carpenter, went to the USA in order to become an architect. He got a job in Ohio and two years later he sent for his wife and their two children. Carol remembers their first period in the USA as one of 'suffering together'. The winters were long, the summers short. Moreover, 'trying to get an architectural degree, with a family, as a black man in the 1950s in (name of city) was just like impossible'. But, she also has memories of 'good times'. There was a small community of Caribbeans[8] and her father was the president of the local club. Carol remembers an 'international atmosphere' in the house where it seems that they were 'always putting up [students] from Africa'. In school, where most of the black children were from the South, Carol got teased and, sometimes, beaten up because of her accent, which was considered 'too proper'. The reverse held true, however, for the teachers: 'They all loved me ... I was constantly promoted ... because of my accent.'

Determined to have their own children attend college the parents planned years in advance. They decided that it was better to move to a state where you could go to the state universities 'for free' if you were a resident. They went to California, where Carol L. has stayed ever since.

Carol L. only started to identify with US blacks when she entered college in the late 1960s and 'Black people all of a sudden began to realize that other black people existed other than in America.' She received her BA in psychology with honors from Stanford and was accepted at Harvard Law School. She left Harvard when she fell in love with a man she 'could respect more than anything else'. Against her family's expectations he was not a Caribbean but a US black. To their further dismay he happened to be a musician without a college degree and without a job. Soon after their marriage she gets pregnant with their first child. The next five years are a challenge to their marriage. He gets into college but she herself feels hampered by the heavy load of children, mothering and a husband who 'does not want' her 'to work'. Things start to change for the better, however, when he finishes his college 'very well'. In the meantime she obtains her real estate license. After leaving Law School for the sake of her marriage she definitely decides she 'will not quit real estate', whatever her husband has to say about it.

She started with very little capital, gradually making more money throughout the years. Her recent million dollar contract illustrates the difference between being marginal and having joined the black bourgeoisie. The project involved the development of a center for sports and leisure activities attractively located just outside a big city with a substantial black population.

PERCEPTIONS OF SOCIAL IDENTIFICATION AND GROUP DIFFERENTIATION

There are various criteria to categorize social groups. Here, I focus on three criteria, namely race-ethnicity, gender and class, by which Carol. L. defines her own position vis-a-vis other blacks.

In order to qualify Carol L.'s specific explanations of the impact of race, ethnicity, gender and class factors on her career life I make a distinction between conservative and radical explanations (Eisenstein, 1984; Sowell, 1987; Young, 1990). Rather than embarking on a philosophical discussion of radicalism and conservatism I focus on the following general characteristics of argumentation prevalent in these different systems of thinking about race, gender and economic inequality. Conservative patterns of argumentation tend to reduce structural factors to cultural factors, and cultural factors to individual factors. Thus, in explaining racial inequality a conservative is likely to make a distinction between supportive or deficient cultural backgrounds and to overemphasize the role of personal aspirations. Radical views on race relations see race conflict and racism as the primary determinant of social inequality (Omi and Winant, 1986; Hacker, 1992).

RACE/ETHNICITY

The 1980s have shown all over the US resurgent racism and conservatism in mainstream politics (Boston, 1988; Marable, 1992; Pinkney, 1984). Among those who are or have become more tolerant of social and economic inequality are representatives of the new black middle class. Neo-conservative ideas on race contend that racial discrimination has declined significantly and that, therefore, color can no longer be seen as the basis of differential successes in society (Eisenstein, 1984; Boston, 1988). This, however, does not hold true for Carol L. She acknowledges that race continues to be an ever-present part of black and white American way of life.

She is quite explicit about the racism she experienced during her own career. Carol L. (and her husband) went through a long struggle against discrimination before the City agreed to support her project. She perceives these experiences largely as racial discrimination but does not exclude the role of gender altogether. The racism she encounters is shaped by the economic conditions facing a small entrepreneur who seeks support from the City to develop a big project. For almost 8 years the City refuses to negotiate with her about the funding of her project. Because of this she loses a lot of her own money. When exclusion fails, the City introduces another strategy to impede her project. Patronizingly, the City gives Carol L. a loan without allowing her the autonomy to spend it. Aware of 'normal' procedures as they apply to whites she contrasts her own experience to those of whites in a similar situation (see Essed, 1988, 1991), without, however, making a gender distinction. She argues that the factor of race operates to the advantage of white (male) entrepreneurs. She explains:

> Most of these developers, when they negotiate with the City, give an estimate. Two or three years later costs might turn out to be three times as much, but that is no big thing. We had to prove beyond any reasonable doubt that the project was feasible, so far as to get all the contracts, we had to have it 60 percent leased before we got this financing. We had to have the numbers firm and tied down on how much it would cost to build.

The racist idea is that white (male) developers 'honestly earn' their money whereas black developers only want to make 'a fast buck'.

> Our project is called 'Desert Lake', which is a name my husband picked because of things as rare as a lake in this dry area. But they changed it to 'Desert Snake' at the City before they gave us that money. They said that they tried to characterize us as carpetbaggers with this 'Desert Snake', people who just picked the property up to make a quick profit.

Further Carol L. defines black and white relationships as a fundamental conflict over the control of economic resources. Despite the salience of racism she strongly believes in personal initiative and argues that investments in black property and skills are the key to black progress in society:

> I first felt that integration was the key and then I began to see that it was draining the skills and energies of the blacks from the ghetto into the white community, draining all of the best from the ghetto into the white community.

The acknowledgement that racism continues to be a structural obstacle to black progress is not quite consistent, however, with her belief in personal initiative as the motor for success. This dissonance in beliefs (structural racism versus aspirations get you anywhere) is reduced with the argument that racism only impedes progress when you lack aspirations.

> Most blacks take discrimination laying down. [They] do not aspire to be more than gardeners, secretaries.

From this argumentation we can infer that she combines a structuralist approach to race relationships (primacy of race conflict) with the culturalist explanation that blacks lack sufficient cultural and personal motivation to achieve. This view is also strongly endorsed by scholars such as Sowell (1983) and Steele (1990), whose ideas on racial issues are generally considered to be neo-conservative.

Similar contradictory perceptions can be found in her explanations of the impact of ethnicity on black progress. As the daughter of an immigrant worker from Grenada, Carol L. does not have an ordinary black American background. She recognizes the different impact of racism in the lives of US blacks versus Caribbean immigrants:

> I had lived in America long enough to perceive that black people from any other country than America got better treatment by American whites ... I would notice as a little girl that Mom and Dad would get their accent very British and very proper in certain circumstances and they would be let in and there were many incidents during the late 60s that prove that. People went down to the South and put a headband on their head and wore a gown and pretended they were talking Swahili and could be served at a lunch counter [whereas] if they were just old Joe from down the street, they could not have been served. So it works that way today.

Her reaction to this situation transcends ethnic boundaries within the black community. She refuses to identify herself in front of whites as an immigrant from the Caribbean. She identifies with the cause of American blacks and she never talks with a Caribbean accent in public situations.

However, when Carol L. discusses why Caribbean immigrants have been treated differently in the American system, her argumentation takes another direction. She downplays the impact of racism and highlights cultural and personality factors in explaining what she considers the success of West-Indians:

> Most immigrant people came here willing to do dirt labor like any immigrant is willing to do and knowing full well that they could go ahead and hoard that money away and rise above ... The attitude in the head causes the attitude in the home. An immigrant child is told you must study, you must learn. But, I know from my husband that he was one of the first in his family to graduate from high school. They had no expectations of him to go to college. They did not wish him to or tell him to and he went to Catholic schools that would not even let him take college prep classes. He was taking shop and typing, when other people were taking the college prep courses. So, the orientation is what gets you there.

The above accounts illustrate an interesting combination of empathy with, and simultaneously, disassociation from US blacks. Whilst expressing solidarity when she rejects privileged treatment as a Caribbean, she nevertheless identifies (to a certain extent) with the 'superior attitude of the West Indians' (Cruse, 1967: 436) towards US blacks.

GENDER

For the purpose of the analysis, feminist views,[9] if included in the accounts of Carol L., can be perceived as indicative of a 'radical' view on gender. 'Conservative' views on gender are, however, not necessarily indicative of 'anti-feminism'. As Klatch (1987: 10) pointed out:

> ... the preservation of traditional gender roles is at the very core of the social conservative woman's activism. In contrast, the laissez-faire conservative woman acts in defense of her self-interest in the market place, not to protect her interest as a woman [in a traditional role] in the family.

We will see that through the experience of *race* Carol L. holds contradictory views on gender. As a *black* woman she strongly supports the traditional view of the *man* as head of the family. Yet, in order to succeed at the market place she had to challenge and change traditional gender roles within her own family.

Gender does not only structure the life of women but also of men. Let us picture, for the sake of the argument, a mainstream white business man. He is probably married. His wife may or may not have her own career. But she is no doubt in charge of the largest proportion of the household work. The man is likely to be the main income provider. They have two sons who, so the parents hope, will be working for the company so that it will remain in the family after the father dies.

Carol L. is also married and she also has two sons but gender structures her life quite differently. It is inherently interwoven, as we will see, with racial issues.

In order to understand the (racially structured) impact of gender on the career of Carol L. it is relevant to address briefly the impact of racism on the social construction of gender (Carby, 1982; Parmar, 1982; Wallace, 1978). Both black women and black men are confronted with racist perceptions of black gender roles, such as the stereotype of the domineering black woman and that of the absent black father. Similarly, the stereotype of black women as sexually promiscuous and the black rapist stigma are different sides of the same phenomenon, which I have called gendered racism (Essed, 1991).

The concept of gendered racism highlights the interrelationship between gender and race factors. Some contend, however, that in relation to *white* society race, rather than gender, is the primary source of the oppression (Stasiulis, 1987). Thus, in various studies it has been found that black women have been socialized historically to be very loyal to the black family (Joseph and Lewis, 1981), in particular to the black male, and to protect the black male (Betters-Reed and More, 1992). This can also be evidenced in the story of Carol L. Her perceptions of gender are complex and center around her concern about the decline of the black family (Hare and Hare, 1984). She points to the issue of gendered racism, when she criticizes the criminalization of black *men* and the high occurrence of police violence against black *men*.

Unlike the earlier mentioned mainstream white business man who already pictures his sons following in his footsteps, Carol L. does not as naturally take it for granted that her sons will outlive her:

> The incidence of violent deaths among black men is something like 40 to 50 percent higher than any other group. And so I worry about that, I worry about my boys being shot and beat up and hurt. ... Two are small, but the other one is 11. I keep telling him you cannot act like the little blonde boy down the street ... because I know one day if he is caught in a group of boys running away from a liquor store and the alarm is going off that it has been robbed, the police are going to aim at him. And I have to get him to accept the responsibility for that, even though it is not his fault.

In addition, she criticizes the pathological image of black men as fathers:

> In this culture about the lowest form of life is considered the black male. He is given no credit for anything, I mean unless he can shoot the ball through the hoop, or knock people down on the football field. If he could sing and dance maybe, but even then the point is that you expect a black man to be trifling no good, leave his wife, not support his kids, it is expected.

Interestingly, with respect to black men, Carol L. emphasizes their structural positioning in the race conflict. Placing the problem of gender-related racism in the wider context of patriarchal relations, she asserts that whites control blacks through the control of black women:

> The color structure is not as threatened by the women. If the white organization has a black woman and a black man side by side in the same position and one of them is to be promoted, if you look at the statistics, they'll more often promote the woman than the man, and the reason is simple. If the woman is the breadwinner and the woman is the head of the family, you've got the people in control. You start letting the men in and you're going to have a power group to deal with. But women are more easily controlled.

The view that race conflict is a war over power which rages throughout the existing patriarchal relations is supported by others as well (e.g. Cock, 1992). Some statistics on the US labor market confirm that the declining employment opportunities discouraged labor force participation in particular for African-American men (Amott and Matthaei, 1991). Others maintain, however, that black women have remained at the bottom of professional occupations (Sokoloff, 1992).

Carol L., therefore, considers the white fear of black men a structural condition against the background of which she explains her personal experiences. She took a hard line in her negotiations with the city, and she feels that she could only afford to do so because she is a woman:

> [The thing is] I was not a threat ... But had those same words been coming out of my husband's mouth, it would have been war. So I was able to get away with saying all of the things we wanted to say.

Carol L. is also deeply concerned about the marginalization of black men and the pressures put upon the black family (Wilkinson and Taylor, 1977; Cheatham and Stewart, 1990). When it comes to black women, however, she hardly acknowledges the persistent struggles of black women, who, located at the center of class, race and gender oppression, continue to organize on issues affecting the survival of the black community, including reproductive rights, housing, education, health issues, union organizing and police brutality (Amott and Matthaei, 1991; Brand, 1991; Harley and Terborg-Penn, 1978; Davis, 1981; Steady, 1985).

This apparent absence of any identification with the black woman's cause may have to do with her specific position in the race, gender and class spectrum. Unlike many other middle class women Carol L. is the main income provider of the family. Unlike many other black or white women she is engaged in a (white) male dominated profession. It took her courage to get into this position. Let us compare her situation, again, to the mainstream white male entrepreneur. His position in the gender system makes it unlikely that he will ever be challenged for the fact that he, rather than his wife, runs the company. The gender impact is quite different, however, for Carol L. and her husband. Both of them have been challenged and/or ridiculed by friends and family for the fact that Carol is in charge of business and that her husband takes more responsibility for running the household than men usually do. Interestingly, while not accepting nuclear family practices on a personal level, she emphasizes their importance on a social level. This may be inferred from the fierceness she expresses at the marginalization of black men as fathers and as head of the family.

Nevertheless, Carol L. is not blind to the gender oppression she had to overcome in her own marriage. She and her husband went through the classical struggle about taking care of household and children, in the end resulting in role switching with her husband:

> So we went through a rocky 2 years there. He went to a marriage counselor [who] got him to understand that I . . . was not going to change any more in order to suit him so he stopped his chauvinism just a little bit and we switched roles because I was really ambitious and was going for the brokers and was out there all the time and he was not earning that kind of money. He stayed at home, he took care of the kids, he cooked the dinners, I mean he became a house husband . . . And it really was a dramatic change. I think it is because he loved me and he did not want to lose me . . . In the meantime, of course, everybody had something to say . . . you know, why don't you go out and make more money and, [why do you] let her do that.

There are contradictions between Carol L.'s rejection of female-headed households and her own experience, namely that she herself has become the financial head of the family. Her resulting cognitive ambivalence is reduced when she emphatically distances herself from the image of the lower class female-headed family. After having said that she did not 'throw out' her husband when times got rough, Carol L. subsequently overlooks the various structural explanations for the increasing number of black female-headed households, such as the economic decline, high unemployment rates, the fact that welfare policies often work financially against the unity of the family and the shortage of men in the black community (Amott and Matthaei, 1991; Jackson, 1991). Instead, she blames lower class black attitudes for the decline of the family:

> A lot of times I think black women are as responsible for it [absence of the father] as the society, because the first hint of trouble they kick him out. You know, the first thing that goes wrong, then they go: 'I can get on welfare, I do not need you'.

To conclude, Carol L.'s statements about gender in the black community are ambivalent. She is critical of the economic marginalization of black men as a mechanism of white control over blacks but at the same time she puts the blame for the social marginalization of black men largely on lower income black women.

CLASS

Carol L. uses three criteria, namely income, attitude or lifestyle and status, with which she differentiates herself from both the lower class and traditional middle class blacks. According to Carol L., their income makes her family part of the 'top 10 percent of blacks who are allowed to go to college':

> The condition of black people in America is really dreadful, it is really awful. There is 10 percent that can break loose and join the yuppies any day they want. People like me and my husband had an opportunity to go to college and do all of that, but there are still hundreds and hundreds of kids, born in the ghetto in welfare, mother on welfare, grandfather on welfare.

On the basis of the factors of attitude, race-consciousness and status, Carol L. differentiates between different representatives of the middle class, namely those who have race loyalty and those who only take advantage of other blacks. Having been involved in the Civil Rights Movement of the 1960s, she feels an obligation to the community to make her goals reach further than having a 'little BMW and a nice house', as she puts it herself. In other words, Carol L. perceives herself financially and educationally as part of a black privileged group (the top 10 percent) but she does not consider herself part of what she considers the black elite of the city. Those are members of the old black middle class. In this category are self-employed people such as doctors, lawyers and directors. During the segregation era there emerged from the old black middle class a stratum whose race consciousness took a reactionary direction. Their race–class consciousness centers on factors such as club or fraternity membership, family background and skin color. Carol L. strongly rejects their mentality and practices:

> We were not part of the black elite because we've only been here 12 years and the black people in this town are more conservative about origins than the whites. You do not count if you're a first generation ... You have to have been born here. Or your parents have to have been born here.

Her dislike for the black aristocracy and representatives of traditional black business is particularly evident when she criticizes their lack of support when she had to negotiate with the City. Carol L. and her husband got support from 'some prominent individuals' in organizing a lobby to exert pressure on the City to finance the project. However, she did not get very far because she and her husband did not

> ... take the time to kiss all the appropriate asses, ... and we had not gone through prominents.

Carol L. believes that representatives of this black elite associate with white entrepreneurs and turn themselves against members of their own race:

> His [white developer who got a grant] daddy owns property free and clear ... It
> is again a private club and the fair haired people, the people that are part of the
> club — and not just whites ... We know that our enemies include certain black
> people who will look bad as soon as our 'Anchor' project is finished because
> they were some of the ones pulling down the big administrative bread on that
> 35 million dollar project that has recently been proved such a failure.

Acting upon the principle that blacks should invest in black business and tal-
ent Carol L. hires a black architect. His race loyalty appears, however, to be dis-
appointing: He 'rips them off': 'We thought that he would be interested and
really protect us.'

Carol L. sees this as another proof that representatives of the established elite
cannot be trusted. She points out that she was in a vulnerable position. Anybody,
including another black man, could take advantage of the fact that she was hampered by bureaucracy in making 'quick and fast deals':

> He took advantage of us, strictly again because of the welfare mentality [of the
> city]. They gave us this 200,000 dollars but they did not give it to us directly,
> they gave it to a pass through agency because they could not trust us, right?

Whereas Carol L. takes a radical stand when she criticizes other representatives of the black middle class for lacking race loyalty, her opinions about the
causal factors of black poverty are rather conservative. She believes in individual initiative and action. She equates 'American blacks' with the poor.
According to Carol L. the lifestyles of poor blacks keep them locked in conditions of poverty without opportunities to advance their position: 'No one expects
them to learn, they do not expect it either'. On the surface, Carol L.'s beliefs
about the attitudes and lifestyles of low income blacks appear not to be different
from white racist prejudices about blacks. However, her cognitions about 'poor
blacks' cannot be interpreted in terms of a belief system of racial or ethnic differences between herself and 'blacks'. Her belief system does not attribute the
lifestyles to race or ethnicity but to their attitudes toward life in conditions of
poverty. Carol L. perceives herself as different from 'poor blacks' because she
has a higher income and level of education which she says could only be
achieved with an attitude of high aspirations geared toward upward mobility,
despite debilitating forces of racism. Therefore, her beliefs about 'blacks' (passive, no aspirations, unable to keep up a proper family life) must be interpreted
as class bias.

In her discussion of race, class and gender issues, Carol L. uses three main
value criteria on the basis of which she either identifies with or criticizes other
social groups. Repeatedly, she presents as positive values the pursuit of (1) high
aspirations, (2) respect for marriage and (3) race consciousness. The first two
values are consistent with conservative ideas (emphasis on individual initiative,
the 'naturalness' of male authority in family life) while the third value, the idea
of racial solidarity, is rooted in a radical view of society (primacy of race

conflict). Conversely, Carol L. perceives as negative values (1) low aspirations, (2) the decline of male authority in black family life and (3) disloyalty to blacks.

BLACK SOLIDARITY: CLASS INTEREST FORMULATED AS RACIAL INTEREST

The idea of personal change as a primary condition for social change has consequences for the way Carol L. experiences her role in the struggle against black poverty. She places a premium on individual responsibility and individual action: blacks with property must make investments for the benefit of the black community, and blacks without any property need to acquire more aspirations. Carol L. tries to live up to these ideals. She consistently emphasizes her allegiance to the black community and the symbolic meaning of their project for the community:

> They have been taking bets for all these years to see whether we could make it and we became a symbol for the community and we knew that.

Carol L. presents the project as a joint interest of her family and the black community which makes her class interest compatible with her idea of racial solidarity across class boundaries. From her side, Carol L. tries to give individual support to black families in poor financial conditions. She believes that taking care of them will help them to break the cycle of poverty.

> My husband and I try in whatever small way we can. We know one couple right now, he is black and she is Korean, and they've got 3 little boys and a girl all under the age of 6, on welfare, and we are trying to help them break out of the cycle because he is doing what his daddy did and she cannot write English or Korean. And if nobody gets in there and helps, those little kids will be repeating the same thing.

CONCLUDING DISCUSSION

In an article on the West Indian immigrant tradition of radicalism Forsythe (1976: 329) points out that 'the majority of West Indian [immigrants] ... embrace a racial radicalism ... because of their experiences as blacks'. Only 20 percent, however, embrace racial radicalism in conjunction with economic radicalism. The case study is in line with these findings but it revealed much more. Through the analysis of her accounts it was shown *how* Carol L. constructs social reality in a way that both reinforces her positive self image vis-a-vis the black community (racial radicalism) and supports the continuity of her enterprise (economic conservatism). Carol L.'s class position clearly has an impact on her perceptions of social change. Basically, she envisions social change in the context of the existing economic system. For that purpose she redefines class interest in terms of racial solidarity. Acting as a role-model for lower class blacks is consistent with her belief that cultural and attitudinal deficiency are to blame for conditions of poverty.

Does this make Carol L. a conservative? Hopefully, this article has shown that reductionism in terms of only one of the locations a black woman has in the matrix of dominance is over-simplified. It appears that radical views (primacy of race conflict) and more conservative ones (the lower class black female to blame for the marginalization of the male in the black family) can be simultaneously present in the perceptions one individual has of race, class and gender relations. Carol L. explicitly defines herself as a product of the struggles of the 1960s and she feels that she has an obligation to 'the black race'. She appears radical when she defines racial inequality as an economic war between races. Further, accepting a structural approach she adamantly relates gender and race in her view that white control of the black race operates through the marginalization of black men as financially and socially significant members of family and community life. However, her ideas to solve the problem are conservative: largely ignoring the multiple oppression of the majority of black women, she adheres to the rehabilitation of male patriarchal authority in the black family.

With this case study I have argued that theorizing the structural context as shaping the experiences of black women is relevant but not enough. Through the analysis of accounts, specific nuances of the experience of race, ethnicity, gender and class can be made explicit. Carol L.'s experience of (Caribbean) ethnicity qualified her views on race in the US and on US blacks. Race had an impact on Carol L.'s perceptions of gender, and the experience of (Caribbean) ethnicity and class structured her perceptions of working class black women. The notion of class, in its turn, was experienced in relation to race and in terms of its different dimensions: income, attitude or lifestyle and status.

It may be concluded that difficult as it is to try to understand the meaning of personal perceptions, a one-case study approach challenges us to be specific about real-life experiences in explanations of the meaning and impact of race, class and gender. Black women occupy different positions according to their role as women, as black women, as income providers, as wives or as mothers. The conditions of these different roles may be contradictory or problematic to combine in a consistent way, as is evident in the experience of Carol L. A case study such as this one forces us, as researchers, to break through the anonymity of race-ethnicity, class and gender categories in order to discover the lived feelings, intentions, ambivalences, emotions, arguments and explanations of black women about the relations between self, social group and society.

NOTES

1. See e.g. Albrecht and Brewer, 1990; Andersen and Collins, 1992; Braxton and McLaughlin, 1990; Davis, 1981, 1989; Giddings, 1986; Hill Collins, 1990; hooks,

1981, 1989, 1992; Jones, 1985; Loewenberg and Bogin, 1976; Malson et al., 1988; Noble, 1978; Rothenberg, 1988; White, 1985.

2. Compare, for instance, Rollin's study on black domestic women (Rollins, 1985) to the study of women of color in management (Bell et al., 1993).

3. Bell et al. mention that this model was originally developed in Bell (1986).

4. The problem of tensions between different ideological themes in everyday discourse has been addressed in several social psychological studies. Some have challenged the idea that ideology is a unified system of ideas stressing, instead, the dilemmatic nature of ideology (Billig et al., 1988; Billig, 1991). These studies emphasize the significance of focusing on the 'thinking individual' in order to understand relationships between the individual and society, opinions and ideology. While agreeing with the need to expose the 'thinking' of individuals I have reservations with respect to the perception of ideology as unstructured and unsystematic.

5. For further illustration see, for example, Essed (1991) where one complete chapter deals with a one-case study (the story of Rosa N).

6. For reasons of anonymity names and some background information have been changed.

7. There seems to be a remarkable lack of recent comprehensive studies on the experience of Caribbean immigrants in the USA (Regis and Lashley, 1992). A notable exception is Sutton and Chaney (1987).

8. Carol L. uses the term of 'West Indians' instead of Caribbean.

9. For the sake of the argumentation I use here the notion of 'feminist views', but I am aware of the problem involved with this notion when in fact referring to a complex of associated belief systems which overlap at some points and differ at others.

REFERENCES

Albrecht, L. and Brewer, R. eds (1990) *'Bridges of Power': Women's Multicultural Alliances*. Philadelphia, PA: New Society.

Amott, T. and Matthaei, J. (1991) *Race, Gender, and Work*. Boston, MA: South End Press.

Andersen, M. and Collins, P. (1992) *Race, Class, and Gender*. Belmont, CA: Wadsworth.

Bell, E. (1986) 'The Power Within: Bicultural Life Structures and Stress Among Black Women', unpublished doctoral dissertation, Case Western Reserve University.

Bell, E., Denton, T. and Nkomo, S. (1993) 'Women of Color in Management: Towards an Inclusive Analysis' in E. Fagenson (ed.) *Women in Management*, pp. 105–30. Newbury Park: Sage.

Betters-Reed, B. L. and More, L. L. (1992) 'Managing Diversity: Focussing of Women and the Whitewash Dilemma', in U. Sekaran and F. T. Leong (eds) *Womanpower, Managing in Times of Demographic Turbulence*, pp. 31–58. Newbury Park: Sage.

Billig. M. (1991) *Ideology and Opinions*. London: Sage.

Billig, M., Condor, S., Edwards, D., Cane, M., Middleton, D. and Radley, A. (1988) *Ideological Dilemmas*. London: Sage.

Boston, T. (1988) *Race, Class, and Conservatism*. Boston: Unwin Hyman.

Bottomley, G., de Lepervanche, M. and Martin, J. eds (1991) *Intersexions*. North Sydney: Allen and Unwin.

Brand, D. (1991) *No Burden to Carry*. Toronto: Women's Press.

Braxton, J. M and McLaughlin, A. N. eds (1990) *Wild Women in the Whirlwind: Afra-American Culture and The Contemporary Literary Renaissance*. London: Serpent's Tail.

Carby, H. V. (1982) 'White Woman Listen? Black Feminism and the Boundaries of Sisterhood', in Centre for Contemporary Cultural Studies (eds) *The Empire Strikes Back*, pp. 212–35. London: Hutchinson.

Cheatham, H. and Stewart, J. eds (1990) *Black Families.* New Brunswick, NJ: Transaction.

Cock, J. (1992) *Women and War in South Africa*. London: Open Letters.

Code, L. (1989) 'Experience, Knowledge, and Responsibility', in A. Gary and M. Pearsall (eds) *Women, Knowledge, and Reality*, pp. 157–72. Boston: Unwin Hyman.

Cruse, H. (1967) *The Crisis of the Negro Intellectual*. New York: Quill (reprint 1984).

Davis, A. (1981) *Women, Race and Class*. New York: Random House.

Davis, A. (1989) *Women, Culture, and Politics*. New York: Random House.

Eisenstein, Z. R. (1984). *Feminism and Sexual Equality*. New York: Monthly Review.

Ellis, C. and Flaherty, M. eds (1992) *Investigating Subjectivity*. Newbury Park, CA: Sage.

Essed, Ph. (1988) 'Understanding Verbal Accounts of Racism', *Text*, 8 (1): 5–40.

Essed. Ph. (1990a) *Everyday Racism: Reports from Women in Two Cultures*. Claremont, CA: Hunter House.

Essed, Ph. (1990b) 'Black Women's Perceptions of Contemporary Racism in the Netherlands', *International Journal of Group Tensions* 20 (2): 123–43.

Essed, Ph. (1991) *Understanding Everyday Racism: An Interdisciplinary Theory*. Newbury Park, CA: Sage.

Essed, Ph. and Helwig, L. (1992) *Bij voorbeeld: multicultureel beleid in de praktijk (Multi-cultural Policy in Practice)*. Amsterdam: FNV.

Fernandez, J. P. (1981) *Racism and Sexism in Corporate Life*. Lexington, MA: Lexington Books.

Forsythe, D. (1976) 'West Indian Radicalism in America: An Assessment of Ideologies', in F. Henry (ed.) *Ethnicity in the Americas*, pp.301–32. The Hague: Mouton.

Frazier, F. E. (1957) *Black Bourgeoisie*. New York: Collier (reprint 1962).

Fullbright, K. (1986) 'The Myth of Double-Advantage: Black Female Managers', in M. C. Simms and J. Malveaux (eds) *Slipping Through the Cracks: The Status of Black Women*, pp. 33–45. New Brunswick, NJ: Transaction Books.

Giddings, P. (1986) *When and Where I Enter. The Impact of Black Women on Race and Sex in America*. Toronto: Bantam (reprint 1985).

Gummesson, E. (1991) *Qualitative Methods in Management Research*. Newbury Park, CA: Sage.

Hacker, A. (1992) *Two Nations*. New York: Charles Scribner's Sons.

Hare, N. and Hare, J. (1984) *The Endangered Black Family*. San Francisco, CA: Black Think Tank.

Harley, S. and Terborg-Penn, R. eds (1978) *The Afro-American Woman*. Port Washington, NY: National University Publications/Kennikat Press.

Hemmons, W. (1980) 'The Women's Liberation Movement: Understanding Black Women's Attitudes', in L. Rodgers-Rose, (ed.) *The Black Woman*, pp. 285–99. Beverly Hills: Sage.

Hill Collins, P. (1990). *Black Feminist Thought*. Boston: Unwin Hyman.

Hine, D. C. (1989) *Black Women in White*. Bloomington, IN: Indiana University Press.

Hollway, W. (1989) *Subjectivity and Method in Psychology*. London: Sage.

hooks, b. (1981) *Ain't I a Woman? Black Women and Feminism*. Boston, MA: South End Press.

hooks, b. (1989) *Talking Back: Thinking Feminist — Thinking Black*. London: Sheba Feminist Publishers.

hooks, b. (1992) *Black Looks. Race and Representation*. Boston, MA: South End Press.

Jackson, J. ed. (1991) *Life in Black America*. Newbury Park, CA: Sage.

Jones, J. (1985) *Labor of Love, Labor of Sorrow*. New York: Basic Books.

Joseph, G. L. and Lewis, J. (1981) *Common Differences*. New York: Anchor.

King, D. (1989) 'Multiple Jeopardy, Multiple Consciousness: The Context of A Black Feminist Ideology', in M. Malson et al. (eds). *Feminist Theory in Practice and Process*, pp. 75–105. Chicago: University of Chicago Press.

Klatch, R. (1987) *Women of the New Right*. Philadelphia, PA: Temple University Press.

Landry, B. (1987) *The New Black Middle Class*. Berkeley: University of California Press.

Loewenberg, J. and Bogin, R. (1976) *Black Women in Nineteenth-Century American Life*. University Park: Pennsylvania State University Press.

Malson, M., Mudimbe-Boyi, E., O'Barr, J. and Wyer, M. eds (1988) *Black Women in America*. Chicago: Chicago University Press.

Marable, M. (1983) *How Capitalism Underdeveloped Black America*. Boston: South End.

Marable, M. (1992) *The Crisis of Color and Democracy*. Monroe, ME: Common Courage Press.

Muraskin, W. A. (1975) *Middle-Class Blacks in White Society*. Berkeley: University of California Press.

Nkomo, S. (1989) 'Race and Sex: The Forgotten Case of the Black Female Manager', in S. Rose and L. Larwood (eds) *Women's Careers: Pathways and Pitfalls*, pp. 133–50. New York: Preager, rev. edn.

Noble, J. (1978) *Beautiful, Also, Are the Souls of My Black Sisters. A History of Black Women in America*. Englewood Cliffs, NJ: Prentice-Hall.

Omi, M. and Winant, H. (1986) *Racial Formation in the United States*. New York: Routledge and Kegan Paul.

Parmar, P. (1982) 'Gender, Race and Class. Asian Women in Resistance', in Centre for Contemporary Cultural Studies (eds) *The Empire Strikes Back*. London: Hutchinson.

Pinkney, A. (1984). *The Myth of Black Progress*. Cambridge: Cambridge University Press.

Regis, H. and Lashley, L. (1992) 'The Editorial Dimensions of the Connections of Caribbean Immigrants to Their Referents', *Journal of Black Studies* 22 (3) 380–91.

Rollins, J. (1985) *Between Women: Domestics and their Employers*. Philadelphia, PA: Temple University Press.

Rothenberg, P. (1988) *Racism and Sexism*. New York: St Martin's Press.

Selltiz, C., Wrightsman, L. S. and Cook, S. W. (1976) *Research Methods in Social Relations*. New York: Holt, Rinehart and Winston.

Sokoloff, N. (1992) *Black and White Women in the Professions*. New York: Routledge.

Sowell, T. (1983) *The Economics and Politics of Race*. New York: Quill.

Sowell, T. (1987) *A Conflict of Visions*. New York: Quill.

Stasiulis, D. (1987) 'Rainbow Feminism: Perspectives on Minority Women in Canada', *RFR/DRF*, 16(1): 5–9.

Steady, F. C. ed. (1985) *The Black Woman Cross-Culturally*. Cambridge, MA: Schenkman Books.

Steele, S. (1990) *The Content of Our Character*. New York: St Martin's Press.

Sutton, C. and Chaney, E. eds (1987) *Caribbean Life in New York: Sociocultural Dimensions*. New York: Center for Migration Studies.

Wallace, M. (1978) *Black Macho and the Myth of the Superwoman*. London: Calder (reprint 1979).

White, D. G. (1985) *Ar'n't I a Woman?* New York: Norton.

Wilkinson, D. Y. and Taylor, R. L. eds (1977) *The Black Male in America*. Chicago: Nelson-Hall.

Wilson, W. J. (1987) *The Truly Disadvantaged*. Chicago: Chicago University Press.

Young, I. M. (1990) *Justice and the Politics of Difference*. Princeton, NJ: Princeton University Press.

Dr Philomena ESSED is at the University of Amsterdam. She is author of several books, including *Everyday Racism, Reports From Women in Two Cultures* (Hunter House, CA, 1990), *Understanding Everyday Racism: An Inter-disciplinary Theory* (Sage, 1991) and *Diversiteit (Diversity: Women, Color and Culture* in press, Ambo, 1993). ADDRESS: University of Amsterdam, Institute for Development Research Amsterdam (InDRA), Plantage Muidergracht 12, 1018 TV Amsterdam.

Anne WOOLLETT, Harriette MARSHALL,
Paula NICOLSON and Neelam DOSANJH

Asian Women's Ethnic Identity: The Impact of Gender and Context in the Accounts of Women Bringing Up Children in East London

This study examines the ways in which a group of women of Asian origin or descent define and discuss aspects of ethnicity and ethnic identity. Thirty-two Asian women of different religious and cultural backgrounds who were bringing up young children in East London were interviewed by an Asian psychologist. As part of a more extensive interview about childbirth, child care and child rearing, women were asked about their ethnic identity. Their accounts indicate that their constructions of ethnicity and ethnic identity are fluid and changing, taking account of gender, developmental changes associated with motherhood and the context of their lives as mothers of young children. Analysis of their accounts is used to argue that ethnicity and ethnic identity are not homogeneous categories, that they operate across gender and, therefore, greater consideration needs to be given in developmental psychology to the complexity and variations in women's representations of ethnicity.

INTRODUCTION

Studies of ethnic identity have examined the ways in which people from a number of communities construct their identities and relate to the majority cultures of the countries in which they live. Most research has assumed that ethnic identity and individuals' adjustments to the wider culture can be conceptualized and measured in a global way (Berry et al., 1986). The suggestion has been made that the move from one ethnic identity to another entails a single cultural change or alteration rather than continuous fluid changes. The implication is that the individual has to make an 'either/or' decision about whether or not to retain their original cultural values and traditions.

Feminism & Psychology © 1994 SAGE (London, Thousand Oaks and New Delhi),
Vol. 4(1): 119–132.

As Phinney (1990) argues in a recent review, the measures of acculturation used by investigators vary considerably. These include measures of self-identification, such as sense of belonging, pride and sense of satisfaction in one's own culture, and participation in ethnic group activities such as speaking the language of and having contact with one's own culture and shared religious practices. The variety of measures used by researchers suggest the complex range of factors people employ in constructing their ethnic identity and the need to recognize that ethnic identity is not an entity but a complex of processes (Weinreich, 1988). This recognition raises problems for attempts to measure and categorize individuals along simple dimensions. In arguing for the need to engage with the complexity of ethnic identity, Weinreich (1988) points to the importance of viewing ethnic identity as historically constituted. His approach, however, is less concerned with changes in ethnic identity over time. In part this stems from the limited developmental perspective of research on ethnicity and ethnic identity which has focused on a narrow range of people. While the experiences and adjustments of young people as they adopt adult identities have been thoroughly investigated (e.g. Hutnick, 1986; Kitwood, 1983; Sharpe, 1976; Shaw, 1988; Stopes-Roe and Cochrane, 1988), there has been less interest in changes in identity as men and women become parents and bring up children.

The impact of gender on the representation of ethnic identity is not frequently or adequately considered. Studies have tended to problematize the ideas and experiences of women of Asian origin and descent and such work is rarely used to explore and explain diversity or to discuss the implications of such diversity for conceptualizations of gender and ethnicity (Phoenix, 1990a; Rocherson, 1988). This is surprising given the extensive exploration of women's experiences and gender identity by researchers within a feminist tradition (e.g. Boulton, 1983; Gordon, 1990; Griffin, 1985; Marshall and Wetherell, 1989; Phoenix et al., 1991; Westwood and Bhachu, 1988). Increasingly research is recognizing the complexity of women's construction of their ethnic and gender identities and the importance of examining the variability of gender representations as located in specific contexts (Griffin, 1985; Phinney, 1990; Phoenix, 1990b; Stopes-Roe and Cochrane, 1988; Westwood and Bhachu, 1988; Woollett et al., 1991).

This article seeks to increase understanding of the relationship between gender and ethnic identity by examining the representations of ethnic identity, including the impact of gender and gender-related issues, on the ethnic identity of a group of Asian women bringing up children in East London.

METHOD

Thirty-two Asian women living in East London were interviewed. As can be seen from Table 1 the group varied in a number of respects and included Muslim, Hindu and Sikh women who were the mothers of between one and four children, women who had lived in the UK all their lives as well as those who

TABLE 1
Characteristics of Women Interviewed

Age of women	Mean age: 26.4 years	
	Range 18–34 years	
How long married	Mean length of marriage: 6.03 years	
	Range: 2–13 years	
Parity	First	10
	Second	12
	Third	8
	Fourth	2
Religion	Hindu	15
	Muslim	10
	Sikh	7
Husband's occupation	Professional/student	7
	Supervisor/self-employed/skilled	12
	Unskilled	10
	Unemployed	3
Resident in UK	Years living in UK: Mean 12.9 years	
	Range: 1–25 years	
Women born and educated in UK		13
Women came to UK as adults and in UK 10 years plus		4
Women came to UK as adult: in UK 5 to 10 years		10
Women came to UK as adult: in UK less than 5 years		5

had moved to the UK more recently. These characteristics were not necessarily independent of one another: some of the women who had moved more recently to the UK did not speak fluent English unlike those who had been born or educated in the UK (see Table 2) (Woollett and Dosanjh-Matwala, 1990). Interviews were structured around women's experiences of childbirth and their ideas about contraception and family composition, child rearing and child care and about how women saw themselves as Asian women (Woollett et al., 1990, 1991). The interviewer was an Asian woman psychologist fluent in English, Urdu, Punjabi and Hindi. Women were recruited through their GPs and through contacts suggested by the women themselves. Women who had at least one child under the age of two years, who spoke one of the languages in which the interviewer was fluent and were willing to be interviewed in their homes were recruited to the study. The interviews were semi-structured, allowing women to answer questions at their own pace and encouraging them to reflect on and explain their answers to questions. Interviews were tape recorded and transcribed and, where necessary, translated into English.

ANALYSIS AND DISCUSSION

The following analysis is drawn from women's replies to a range of questions about ethnicity and ethnic identity and the ways in which they considered

TABLE 2
Details of Women Interviewed

Number	Parity	Religion	Years Resident in UK	Interview in
1.	3	Sikh	12	Punjabi/English
2	2	Sikh	13	Punjabi
3	3	Hindu	9	Hindi
4	4	Muslim	25	English
5	1	Muslim	Born in UK	English
6	1	Muslim	21	English
7	2	Muslim	3	Urdu
8	2	Hindu	12	Punjabi
9	1	Muslim	Born in UK	English
10	2	Muslim	6	Punjabi
11	1	Hindu	20	Punjabi
12	3	Sikh	8	Punjabi
13	1	Sikh	Born in UK	Punjabi/English
14	1	Muslim	1	Urdu
15	1	Hindu	11	English
16	3	Hindu	9	Hindi
17	3	Hindu	9	Punjabi
18	4	Hindu	10	Punjabi
19	2	Sikh	9	Punjabi
20	2	Hindu	16	English
21	2	Hindu	4	Hindi
22	2	Hindu	7	English
23	1	Hindu	13	English
24	3	Hindu	11	Hindi
25	2	Sikh	4	Punjabi
26	1	Hindu	16	English
27	3	Sikh	5	Punjabi
28	2	Muslim	20	Urdu
29	3	Hindu	10	Hindi
30	2	Hindu	25	English
31	2	Muslim	2	Urdu
32	1	Muslim	25	English

themselves to be similar and dissimilar to other Asian and white women. Throughout the analysis numbers are given after each extract to identify the woman speaking. Additional biographical information about each woman can be found in Table 2. Questions from the interviewer are given in italics and in brackets. Where ... appears in an extract, material has been omitted due to limited space; square brackets are used to indicate additional material supplied by the authors.

WOMEN'S ACCOUNTS OF THEIR ETHNIC IDENTITY: RELIGION, DRESS, FOOD AND SOCIAL RELATIONSHIPS

All the women interviewed identified strongly with their ethnic group. They saw culture as a source of pride and considered it important to remember their ethnic identity. However, their accounts indicate that this is formulated in a variety of ways. Women used a range of terms to characterize themselves. Terms such as 'Asian', 'Indian' and 'Pakistani' were used frequently and others, including 'Punjabi', 'Gujerati', 'Bengali', 'Muslim' and 'Hindu' less often. Women from the majority culture were usually referred to as 'English' and less often as 'British' or 'white'. The following extracts indicate the diversity of terms used in self-characterization and the varied aspects of 'culture' referred to in relation to ethnicity.

1. (*Is being different a good thing?*) I think people should live according to what their culture says. Everyone has that freedom ... but nobody should forget who they are ... people shouldn't leave their culture, like me and other Pakistanis and Indians should try to promote their religion. (7)
2. (*When does being a member of a group become important?*) Being a member of a caste or religion is important all the time, you shouldn't try to forget your history or background. Everybody has something to be proud of. (11)
3. (*When does being a member of a group become important?*) You should not forget what you are. Just because you have come to this country, it doesn't make you English. You should remember where you've come from. It's good to live with other Asians. There are advantages like teaching your children about Punjabi lifestyles. By living with other Asians you remember your culture and religion and that's important to me. (17)
4. There are so many nice things in our culture, like our colourful clothes, food, the way we greet each other and talk to each other. (28)

Culture is used in varying ways in the extracts above: in Extracts 1, 2 and 4 'culture' is inclusive of religion, in Extract 2 there is reference to 'caste' and 'history or background' and in 3 to 'where you come from', while Extract 4 includes mention of 'clothes, food and the way we greet each other'.

When these aspects of culture are examined in more depth, religion can be seen to play a key role in women's conceptualizations of ethnicity. Twenty-two women made reference to religion and religious practices which were used as important ways of defining ethnicity and maintaining a sense of 'who you are'. Extracts 5 and 6 illustrate how religion is drawn upon as a means of gaining and maintaining a positive sense of ethnic identity:

5. (*When does membership of a group become important?*) I like living among Sikhs. Our religion is better than other religions. There are many celebrations and many people can understand our language. (19)
6. (*When does membership of a group become important?*) The religious group is important. Most of my friends and relatives are Muslims who speak Gujerati. I suppose it's important to remember who you are all the time because it will help your children to remember who they are ... they'll learn about Muslims. (31)

Extract 7 discusses the importance of religion but also views beliefs in 'freedom and independence' as central to self-definition.

7. Even though I don't practise my religion as much as I should, I believe in
my religion ... I know all about it and I am very proud of it. But then again I
believe in freedom and independence and things like that. (6)

As this and Extract 8 suggest, even women who see religion as a key aspect of
their ethnic identity argue that upholding religious values and living according
to religious practices are not straightforward because people interpret and practice religion in varying ways.

8. (*Would you say you were more westernized or more Indian?*) I'm westernized to a certain extent but I do believe in my religion even though I don't
practise it as much as I should. I'm half and half you could say. (What half
of you is Muslim?) My beliefs. I believe in a lot of it [religion] as well.
Even though I had a love marriage or whatever I still believe in arranged
marriages because my sister had one and she's very happy. You see our religion I think, people have changed it to suit themselves rather than the religion itself. People get a lot of wrong views over it. It's quite simple, you
know, you speak the truth, certain things like you shouldn't eat pork and
why you shouldn't drink. There are reasons for it, you see and people have
changed it to suit themselves. I haven't rejected it. At first I did when I was
going to school and I used to rebel against it, like why should I do this?
Why should I wear our clothes? All the other girls are going out, but I'm not
allowed to, you know certain things like that. But I've come to terms with it.
(32)

Extract 8 indicates the lack of direct mapping between practice and ethnic identity and the difficulty of measuring acculturation in terms of the degree of prac-
tising/upholding religious values. Religious beliefs often informed other aspects
of ethnic identity such as dress, food and social relationships. Dress was used in
Extracts 9 and 10 as an indicator of 'Indian' identity, with terms such as 'Indian'
or 'simple' and as a means of differentiating themselves from other Asian
women who are characterized as more 'independent' or 'fashionable', as in
Extract 11:

9. (*How Indian or how westernized would you say you were?*) More Indian
because our family has always lived in that style so we do too. We wear
Indian clothes, nothing fashionable. (18)
10. (*How Asian or westernized would you say you were?*) We're completely
Indian. We are just simple. I always wear a saree, maybe sometimes I will
wear a dress or trousers when I have to go out. But I rarely dress like that.
At home I'm always in a saree. (29)
11. (*Do you know anyone who is more westernized?*) My sister. She is very different and looks so different. She's really fashionable and wears dresses.
She's got a short hair cut and that. She is very independent because she lives
on her own. (26)

Yet even with frequent association of dress with ethnic identity, some women
articulated a problem with dress reflecting a woman's ethnic identity in a

straightforward way, as can be seen in Extracts 12 and 13. In Extract 12 wearing a suit (Punjabi suit or salwaar-kameez) or a saree does not necessarily indicate traditional thinking but can be combined with 'forward' thinking and in Extract 13 the woman's choice of clothing is informed by context rather than ethnic identity.

> 12. I think it's what you are as a person and not how you dress. Even if you wear suits you could still be really modern or even a saree every day. I mean my mother she wears sarees but she is very modern. Modern in the sense that she thinks forward. (15)
> 13. (*How Indian or westernized do you think you are?*) We're more Indian because I wear Indian clothes mainly. It's not a must that we always wear Indian clothes. The children are not dressed typically, that they must wear an Indian suit. They wear proper skirts and dresses that are suitable for school. When they come home they wear the suits. (12)

While dress is seen as an important aspect of ethnic identity by almost all the women interviewed in this study, men's choice of clothing was rarely mentioned in the interviews. There was no suggestion that it was an indicator of ethnicity or commitment to their culture. Clothes would appear to have different significance for women as compared with men, and given that most studies have not focused upon women, may explain why dress is rarely used as a measure of ethnic identity in much of the literature.

In a similar way food is rarely examined in studies of ethnicity (Phinney, 1990), although well over half (18) of the women interviewed discussed food in relation to ethnic identity. Extracts 14 and 15 indicate how they referred to food.

> 14. (*Do you know anyone who is more Indian?*) There is this one lady. She's more Indian in that she's never worked. She came from India and just had a baby and she's at home. I think compared with me she is more Indian. She can't speak any English. And dressingwise. I think in cooking too, she won't cook any English food whereas I always give my children whatever they like. I think she is very traditional and backward sort of thing. (22)
> 15. (*How Indian or how westernized would you say you are?*) I think we are more like the Indians, although our children like to live like the English. I think Indian because of our dress. Not food because we eat everything … We have had to become like this because we're living in this country … (*Do you know anyone who is more westernized?*) Yes, my mother-in-law who lives nearby. She can't speak English but she prefers the English lifestyle. She likes the food and tells me to bring the children up in that sort of way. (16)

Food may be a particularly salient aspect of women's rather than men's ethnic identity because women are involved in shopping and preparation of food and because they are more aware of pressures from children to eat food they know about from school or television. Failing to consider dress and food as measures or indicators of ethnic identity underestimates the complexity and richness of ethnicity and ethnic identity by ignoring the gendered aspects of these concepts.

Family and social relationships are referred to by many women but are less frequently used by researchers as a central aspect of ethnicity or ethnic identity. This suggests that they are more salient or relate more closely to the experiences of women than to men. Family and social relationships often provide women with a positive sense of ethnic identity and are discussed in the interviews as contrasting with those of the dominant culture. In Extract 16 a woman whose family and in-laws are in Pakistan indicates her preference to live in an extended family.

> 16. (*Does living on your own make you different?*) Probably, I don't like living on my own. I prefer to live with a family because it's so much better. You can do so many things together and talk about lots of things. I do get lonely living on my own. (10)

Some women obtained a positive sense of their ethnic identity from the practice of arranged marriages. In Extract 17 the practice of arranged marriages is linked to respect for parents and to the maintenance of strong family relationships.

> 17. (*Do you know anyone who is more westernized?*) Yes, there's someone in my husband's family. They have got four girls and two boys. The boys and girls have chosen their own marriage partners ... They don't think about their parents' respect. They think about themselves and they become alone. I think this was bad. They didn't think about their parents' or brothers' and sisters' reputation. They should have considered everybody else. (17)

Therefore, it is not surprising that a sister's love marriage was a source of concern in this extract.

> 18. (*Do you know anyone who is more Asian than you are?*) My sister you could say. Although she's married now she still goes to the temple. (*In any other ways?*) Well I have had an arranged marriage and my sister has had a love marriage, but she is happy and that is the main thing. But she gets on well with the in-laws and everything which is good. (*How did your parents feel about the marriage?*) Well they were against it at first but now they've accepted it and he comes round. (30)

As discussed previously in relation to religion, dress and food, there was considerable variation in the different social arrangements as discussed by the women interviewed. Once again observance of certain family and social arrangements does not automatically indicate particular views towards ethnicity. Extract 19 illustrates the considerable variations in the ways in which arranged marriages operate.

> 19. My thinking is old-fashioned like having arranged marriages, but arranged marriages only in that you're given a choice. There's a lot of misunderstanding amongst the western society about Asians you know, how they're forced into arranged marriages, but that's not the case at all. There are very

strict Muslims or strict religious people who are like that, where daughters don't have a say. But it's all changing now, a lot of people today don't think like that. (4)

To summarize, women's accounts indicate that they identify strongly with their Asian culture and take a variety of factors into account when constructing their ethnic identity. Some of these factors are strongly informed by gender but are rarely examined in research on ethnic identity, rendering women's experiences and gender-related aspects of ethnicity invisible (Phinney, 1990).

CHANGING ETHNIC IDENTITY

There are many instances in the interviews where women discuss the ways in which their ethnic identity has undergone changes. The acculturation model stresses changes over time as people gain experience of the culture into which they have moved and points to the need to consider ethnic identity as continuously evolving. This approach was reflected in the ideas of some women who argued that people who were born in or lived in the UK for many years have adopted the lifestyle of the dominant culture more than those who have recently arrived, as in Extracts 20, 21 and 22.

20. (*Do you know anyone more westernized than yourself?*) There are some that have come here and adopted this culture. They've been here longer than us and their children have been here. So they have adopted what they have seen most. (7)
21. I have a friend who works at the Law Centre. Her lifestyle, the way she talks and dresses is very much like the English because she was born here. (14)
22. (*Do you know anyone more or less westernized than yourself?*) Yes, relatives and friends are more Indian than myself because they are older and their cultural values are deeply rooted and they have not lived here as long as we have. My brother-in-law is very westernized because he was born here and has learned this culture. (3)

However, women also talked about those who did not fit this general rule, pointing to factors such as family pressures which worked against a general process of acculturation through contact with English culture, as in Extracts 23 and 24.

23. She was born in India and then came here. She didn't change at all. She came to the UK when she was 10 years old, she was always behind with the fashion, you know what I mean. (5)
24. (*What about people who have been here for many years and still think like Asians?*) There are people like that. I consider myself to be one of those people. I have been here for so long but still value my culture and religion. I don't want to forget my image or my culture living in a western society. (4)

But the accounts of the women in this study indicate the need to conceptualize changes more developmentally, that is in terms of transitions in their lives as they marry and become mothers and in the ways in which the contexts in which they spend time change as children grow older and go to school. These changing contexts make different demands of women, requiring them to rework their ideas about their ethnic identity.

The ideas and lifestyle of the wider family provide a powerful framework within which women develop and redefine their ethnic identity. Extract 25 discusses the ways in which this interviewee perceives herself to be influenced by people at work, her parents and her in-laws.

> 25. (*How western or Indian do you consider you are?*) Oh it's difficult to say because it depends who you are with, doesn't it? When I'm out working, you think like they do, you have to really. Even when I'm at home because I live with my in-laws she's [mother-in-law] into Indiany things ... but I don't follow all the things. Before marriage I think I was more westernized than I am now because my parents were quite westernized. But I think that after you get married and because I live with my in-laws you abide by their rules. (20)

Children also influence their parents' lifestyle. Extracts 26 and 27 point to the changes for mothers as children get older and Extract 28 reports one child's increasing awareness of ethnic identity.

> 26. (*How Indian or westernized do you think you are?*) We're Indian, we don't meet many English. I think that with children we will have to change a little, we'll have to live a bit more like the English. The children can't do as they please but we can't expect them to live like we've been doing ... My son mixes with anyone, more so with the English. I don't mind that so long as they are well-educated and make themselves good people. (27)
> 27. (*How can you influence children's development?*) Our children learn so much about other cultures and they expect us to learn about them too. They learn so much from school and other people ... My older son knows so much and he asks me questions that I can't sometimes answer ... We will adjust to the way he wants it, like he has started to pick up English words and we will encourage that. (8)
> 28. (*Are your family more Asian?*) My family, yes, are traditional, I send my children to the mosque ... I've lived my life through my religion but I've not practised staunchly. You have to adopt some westernized ways. Take my little one who is five years old, now grown up here and born here ... the eldest one understands more that we're Muslims if they've asked where we're from. Although she was born here she'll say my parents are from Pakistan and I am a Muslim when asked. (4)

Extracts 26–28 illustrate the complexity and fluidity of some women's ethnic identity and the ways in which their ethnic identity is informed by specific contexts or circumstances of their lives. Women continually redefine their ethnic identity in different contexts and settings and they maintain a balance between their own and the dominant culture.

FLUIDITY AND COMPLEXITY

Discussion of ethnicity can be seen to be extremely fluid not only developmentally but also shifting according to different aspects of ethnicity and specific circumstances as illustrated in Extracts 29 and 30. Extract 29 problematizes the dualism between being 'Asian' and being 'westernized' which are discussed in terms of traditional/broad-minded. Being 'traditional' and showing 'respect for elders' and religious beliefs are indicative of a more traditional ethnic identity whereas going out, talking with boys and not being shy are represented as 'broad-minded' with the interviewee directly referring to circumstances as shaping particular self-definitions, 'it depends on the circumstances'. In this respect the flexibility of ethnic identity and the oversimplification of the acculturation model are made explicit.

> 29. (*How Asian or westernized do you think you are?*) In some things I'm more traditional and some things I'm more broad-minded. (*More traditional?*) In family wise might be. Respect for parents, respect for elders and things like that. I believe in our religion, I try to practise it but not really 100 percent. I had an arranged marriage. (*Westernized?*) I'm not shy and I don't mind talking with boys and communicating with anyone. I wouldn't mind going out. So it depends on the circumstances. (6)

Similarly the woman in Extract 30 positions herself in various ways in discussing how, from 'Indian standards', she might be described as westernized, but from her own point of view 'in between'. This extract describes some aspects of different cultures, thus moving away from making an either/or distinction with respect to adopting one set of cultural practices or another as is assumed important in acculturation measures. Further, it is clear that this does not imply any lack of pride in being 'Indian'.

> 30. (*How Indian or westernized do you think you are?*) I think by Indian standards I'm westernized but I think I'm an in-between. I can adjust well to both cultures. I can speak the language pretty well so I can communicate with the elderly. Because I like Indian 'dos' I can mix there as well. The things with the western culture is that I like discos and all that. When I say I'm more westernized according to the Indian culture it's the way I think, in that I don't believe in staying where you are. I think you should [go] forward in life in everything you do. (15)

In Extract 31 the interviewee problematizes a 'westernized/traditional dichotomy'. This is said to depend on specific circumstances: changes in ethnic identity are not simply developmental, taking place over years but relate to more immediate changes in context and to aspects of life concerned with religion, family, older and younger family members.

> 31. (*How western or Indian do you think you are?*) On particular issues I'm more Indian and there are times when I'm more westernized. You know,

religion and that. At times I'm completely Indian, like fasting. I don't give much importance to going to the mandir because none of my family would go. But like, all Gujerati people do, fasting on certain days. Compared with my in-laws I'm more Indian. I'd like to tell my children about it [Indian culture] and maintain it. (*What makes you more westernized?*) In speaking out about what you think about. You know the Indian woman's ways of doing things is 'no matter what family problems there are or whatever you're doing, as women you have to take it'. Personally I'm not like that. I'll say to whoever it is what I think. (22)

Extracts 29–31 raise important issues for acculturation models. While such models entertain certain changes in ethnic identity, by summarizing individuals' relationships with the 'Asian' and 'English' culture on a number of straightforward dimensions, the role of context and the complexity of ethnicity has been neglected. As the examples given here suggest, women's lifestyles and their identification with their culture are often modified by developmental changes following marriage and family and according to the more immediate situation in which they are representing ethnicity.

The concept of acculturation makes the assumption of a certain degree of consistency. When the variation in the representations of ethnic identity is explored, it is not easy to see how a categorization can readily be made for many of these interviewees in terms of straightforward measures of acculturation. The extracts also indicate that such a fluid and contextually informed sense of ethnic identity is not problematic for the women being interviewed. This point is clearly illustrated in Extract 32 where not only complexity in self-definition but also the range of different aspects of identity are discussed including definition as imposed by others.

32. (*In what ways would you say you were westernized?*) I suppose because I don't know any of the Asian ways. The only thing my parents say is going to the temple. But I don't see the point. I don't think I've neglected my religion or culture. I don't know about it ... My mother tells me stories and that about Krishna. I don't know they just sound like fairy stories and not, you know, real stories. I still consider myself as Asian, that can't be changed. It's like all my brothers and sisters they're all born here, the ones after me. When we have arguments they say, 'We're British and I was born there'. So I say 'Well I've been here longer than you'. If they were to walk down the street they would still be called 'Paki'. You can't change your colour, probably the attitude and that. (30)

To summarize: it is important to recognize diversity within the category 'Asian' and in representing ethnicity. Although the women interviewed were similar in age and were all married with young children, they identified a wide range of aspects which informed their ethnic identity and which they used to differentiate themselves from other Asian women.

The accounts of women in this study demonstrate some of the ways in which gender influences Asian women's constructions of their ethnic identity, pointing to a number of ways in which gender has different significance for women and men in informing ethnic identity. This reinforces the argument that research into women's experiences of ethnicity and ethnic identity needs to recognize and make visible gender and gender-related issues.

Representations of identity change over time, informed by life changes related to marriage, having children and as children grow up. They are complex and fluid according to specific circumstances, who people are with and to the meanings for individual women of concepts such as 'traditional' and 'modern'. These changes are not simply due to increasing familiarity with the dominant culture or how long women have been living in the UK and hence raise difficulties for an acculturation model and conceptualizations of ethnic identity which employ simplistic forms of 'ethnic categorization'.

ACKNOWLEDGEMENTS

This study was completed with support of Economic and Social Research Council Grant Number R 000 23 2456.

The authors would like to acknowledge the assistance of Dr S. Sahi, Dr V. D. Desau, Dr A. R. Farrukh, Vimilla Supiah and Ferida Malik, and all the women who gave generously of their time and the helpful comments of two reviewers.

REFERENCES

Berry, J., Trimble, J. and Olmedo, E. (1986) 'Assessment of Acculturation', in W. Lonner, and J. Berry (eds) *Field Methods in Cross-cultural Research*. Newbury Park, CA: Sage.

Boulton, G. M. (1983) *On Being a Mother*. London. Tavistock.

Gordon, T. (1990) *Feminist Mothers*. London: Macmillan.

Griffin, C. (1985) *Typical Girls: Young Girls from School to the Job Market*. London: Routledge.

Hutnick, N. (1986) 'Patterns of Ethnic Minority Identification and Modes of Social Adaptation', *Ethnic and Racial Studies* 9: 150–67.

Kitwood, T. (1983) 'Self-conception Among Young British–Asian Muslims: Confutations of a Stereotype', in G. Breakwell (ed.) *Threatened Identities*. Chichester: Wiley.

Marshall, H. and Wetherell, M. (1989) 'Talking about Career and Gender Identities: A Discourse Analysis Perspective', in D. Baker and S. Skevington (eds) *The Social Identity of Women*. London: Sage.

Phinney, J. S. (1990) 'Ethnic Identity in Adolescents and Adults: Review of Research', *Psychological Bulletin* 108: 499–514.

Phoenix, A. (1990a) 'Black Women and the Maternity Services', in J. Garcia, M. Richards and R. Kilpatrick (eds) *The Politics of Maternity Care*. Oxford: Clarendon Press.

Phoenix, A. (1990b) 'Theories of Gender and Black Families', in T. Lovell (ed.) *British Feminist Thought*. Oxford: Blackwell.

Phoenix, A., Woollett, A. and Lloyd, E. eds (1991) *Motherhood: Meanings, Practices and Ideologies*. London: Sage.

Rocherson, Y. (1988) 'The Asian Mother and Baby Campaign: the Construction of Ethnic Minorities' Health Needs', *Critical Social Policy* 22: 4–23.

Sharpe, S. (1976) *Just Like a Girl: How Girls Learn to be Women*. Harmondsworth: Penguin.

Shaw, A. (1988) *A Pakistani Community in Britain*. Oxford: Basil Blackwell.

Stopes-Roe, M. and Cochrane, R. (1988) 'Marriage in Two Cultures', *British Journal of Social Psychology* 27: 159–69.

Weinreich, P. (1988) 'The Operationalization of Ethnic Identity', in J. W. Berry and R. C. Annis (eds) *Ethnic Psychology: Research and Practice with Immigrants, Refugees, Native Peoples, Ethnic Groups and Sojourners*. Amsterdam: Swets and Zeitlinger.

Westwood, S. and Bhachu, P. eds (1988) *Enterprising Women: Ethnicity, Economy and Gender Relations*. London: Routledge.

Woollett, A. and Dosanjh-Matwala, N. (1990) 'Asian Women's Experiences of Childbirth in East London: The Support of Fathers and Female Relatives', *Journal of Reproductive and Infant Psychology* 8: 11–22.

Woollett, A., Dosanjh-Matwala, N. and Hadlow, J. (1991) 'Reproductive Decision Making: Asian Women's Ideas about Family Size, and the Gender and Spacing of Children', *Journal of Reproductive and Infant Psychology* 9: 237–52.

Anne WOOLLETT is the Acting Head of Department at the Department of Psychology, University of East London. Her publications include: *Motherhood: Meanings, Practices and Ideologies* (co-edited with A. Phoenix and E. Lloyd, Sage, 1991); *Families: A Context for Development* (co-edited with D. White, Brighton: Falmer Press, 1992).

Harriette MARSHALL is the Senior Lecturer at the Department of Psychology, University of East London. Her publications include: 'The Social Construction of Motherhood: An Analysis of Childcare and Parenting Manuals', in A. Phoenix, A. Woollett and E. Lloyd (eds) *Motherhood: Meanings, Practices and Ideologies* (Sage, 1991); and 'Analysing Discourse: Qualitative Research and the Helping Professions', in P. Nicolson and R. Bayne (eds) *Counselling and Psychology for Health Professionals* (Chapman and Hall, 1993).

Paula NICOLSON is a Lecturer at the Department of Psychiatry, University of Sheffield. Her publications include: *Counselling and Psychology for Health Professionals* (co-edited with R. Bayne, Chapman and Hall, 1993); and *The Psychology of Women's Health and Health Care* (co-edited with J. Ussher, Macmillan, 1992).

Neelam DOSANJH is a Clinical Psychologist. Her publications include: Woollett, A., Dosanjh-Matwala, N. and Hadlow, J. (1991) 'Reproductive Decision Making: Asian and Non-Asian Women's Ideas about Family Size, Gender and Spacing of Children', *Journal of Reproductive and Infant Psychology* 9: 237–52; Woollett, A. and Dosanjh-Matwala, N. (1990) 'Asian Women's Experiences on the Postnatal Wards', *Midwifery* 6: 178–84.

L. Mun WONG

Di(s)-secting and Dis(s)-closing 'Whiteness': Two Tales about Psychology

'Whiteness' is di(s)-sected and dis(s)-closed to reveal its privileged position within psychological texts. This allows me to discuss the three ways in which 'whiteness' has surfaced. First, 'whiteness' is absent. Second, 'whiteness' is displaced by synonyms that shift its anxieties on the 'other'. And third, 'whiteness' is discussed as the predominant epistemological backdrop of psychological texts that e-race, make invisible and token the presence of racial minorities. I will use two instances of psychological practice — e-racing theory and the porno-raced method — to discuss how 'whiteness' has manipulated racial minorities to inform, test and construct its own meanings.

INTRODUCTION

In the last decade, we have witnessed an inter/cross disciplinary emergence of the 'new politics of difference' (West, 1990). The burgeoning fields of cultural studies, feminist theory, African-American studies, postcolonialism, and queer theory have collectively forced traditionalists to re-evaluate their current theorizing of class, gender, race, nation and sexuality. These groups that have been historically defined as marginalized, subjugated or oppressed have placed themselves in the foreground of cultural and social analysis. The impetus for the emergence of works by historically marginalized groups is mainly derived from a reaction against the way they have been represented and defined. Hall (1988: 27) remarks:

> The struggle to come into representation was predicated on a critique of the degree of festishisation, objectification and negative figuration which are so much a feature of the representation of the black subject. There was a concern not simply with the absence or marginality of the black experience but with its simplification and its stereotypical character.

Feminism & Psychology © 1994 SAGE (London, Thousand Oaks and New Delhi), Vol. 4(1): 133–153.

The constructed images of racial/ethnic minorities, women and gays/lesbians as damaged and different have given way to processes of self-definition. The mission has been to re-claim and re-(in)state their own subjectivities and to dispel the myths that have been perpetuated by their dominating groups.

The irony is that our differences are also semantic traps. They are institutionalized by an ideology of separatism that set us against each other, reproducing the 'deviations' that depart from the 'norm' (Minh-Ha, 1989).[1] The colossal number of works which focus on deconstructing and demystifying the wrongs that have been perpetuated by dominant groups will leave intact much of the power of the 'norm' to define reality as if somehow natural and predetermined (Foucault, 1978).

The ability of privileged and dominant groups (who are often white, male, heterosexual) to determine our realities of marginalized groups and to pass as 'normal' has severely limited our analyses of race, gender, class and sexuality. Hazel Carby (1992) argues that the theoretical paradigm of differences has been consumed with identity politics rather than the forms of domination and power. In psychology, the obsession with studies on ethnic, racial and gender (trait) differences has consistently ignored the social, political and cultural complexity of racial minorities (Jones, 1991; Fine and Gordon, 1989). Often, studies of 'difference' focused on differences from the white/male norm or, in other cases, have focused on the complexity of the white participant's response to a Black other. These reductionistic measures fail to examine the systems of domination and subjugation that structure the racialization and socialization of *all* peoples. In this article, I will try to address an aspect of this missing discourse: specifically, the unproblematized construction of 'whiteness' as a privileged site in psychology.[2]

The article is divided into two main sections. First, the discussion will revolve around the di(s)-section of 'whiteness' as the privileged site in psychology. The second will center around a discussion of the three manifestations of 'whiteness' and the psychologist's abilities to secure a normative 'absence' in texts. By exposing the 'technologies of obfuscation'[3] that have retained racial hierarchies and distorted the nature of 'whiteness' within psychological texts, I will exorcise the phantom of racial minorities in psychological discourse and methods and observe how their objectification and control have informed the construction of 'whiteness'. The phantom of racial minorities, by virtue of the power of 'whiteness', materializes into a cardboard figure; as a repository of culture, values, attitudes and behaviors to function as the 'symbolic representative' of the group (Marable, 1992). In the section on 'porno-raced methods', I will describe the experimental studies that desecrate the cardboard figures as independent variables, that are used to test the responses of the white subjects. Throughout these discussions, I will also draw on a content analysis of *Psychology of Women Quarterly* (*PWQ*) and *Journal of Personality and Social Psychology* (*JPSP*) from 1990 to 1992 to substantiate and exemplify the three ways in which 'whiteness' as psychological subtext reveals its power and status.

DI(S)-SECTING 'WHITENESS'

In the history of African-American and 'third world' communities, 'whiteness' has been associated with violence/killings (hooks, 1989), servility (Palmer, 1989) and ressentiment (Rollins, 1985). Vron Ware (1992) and David Roediger (1991) recount the collusion of the first wave of white feminism and the white working class with the dominant white, bourgeois male society to expedite their own gains and status. We read about white researchers' forays into 'urban ghettos' to study, research and ameliorate the plight and conditions of the 'colored' poor without reflecting and problematizing their race and class. Recently, Fine (1993) urged a predominantly white audience that they should critically interrogate their privileged manner of race-ing and that they should be responsible for doing their own race,[4] as also argued by Omi and Winant (1986). By 'doing race', 'chains of equivalences'[5] are linked and fused to enact a better vision of social activism, autonomy, rights and justice (Mouffe, 1988).

In recent years, there have been critical self-examinations within feminist psychologies showing that 'differences' and 'norms' (white, heterosexual, middle-class, able-bodied woman) are socially constructed (Kitzinger et al., 1992; Griscom, 1992; McIntosh, 1988; Russo, 1991; Caraway, 1991). Part of this has been a response to the deconstruction of 'Woman' brought about by Black feminist theorists, 'third world feminists'[6] and lesbians (hooks, 1990; Moraga and Anzaldua, 1981; Mohanty, 1991). The homogeneity of 'Woman' has been delegitimized and displaced.

Lesbians/'third world women' have reminded white heterosexual feminists of the manner in which race, class and sexuality shape experiences, identities, choices and communities; and how different multiple positions may privilege, subjugate and (dis)empower all at the same time. They challenge white heterosexual feminists in arguing that if feminism is to empower all Women and indeed to change all Women's lives, it must take up the issues of racism, heterosexism and classism embedded within their theorizing. White feminists are located at the 'peculiar paradox of identity politics' (Cohen, 1991) which defines for them positions that (re)produce the contradictory processes of oppression and privilege.

Increasing numbers of white feminists have begun to raise issues of their own 'whiteness' and their relationships to politics, passion and power. The first dialogues about 'whiteness' and privilege have been written by white lesbians (Frye, 1983; Pratt, 1984). These writers offer insightful analyses of how race has influenced their lives and they offer suggestions for a movement that will allow for the (re)creation of spaces where differences within and between women are negotiated and discussed. Hence, Russo (1991) urges white feminists to face up to their own racism, classism and (hetero)sexism in order to empower themselves and to forge/negotiate alliances and differences across race, class and sexuality.

Works such as here cited earlier are reminders to white feminists of their race and privileges. Their efforts to 'fix' the norm spring from a genuine desire to forge a collective movement that will allow different stories, nations, cultures and communities to (e)merge into a 'multicultural feminist politics of solidarity' (Caraway, 1991).

DIS(S)-CLOSING 'WHITENESS'

When asked to discuss 'whiteness', one of Tatum's (1992) students put it in this way;

> I realized that it was possible to simply go through life totally oblivious to the entire situation or, even if one realizes it, one can totally repress it. It is easy to fade into the woodwork, run with the rest of society, and never have to deal with these problems. So many people I know from home are like this. They have simply accepted what society has taught them with little, if any, question. My father is a prime example of this ... (Carl, a white male, quoted in Tatum, 1992: 14).

'Whiteness' is about a topic within psychology that does not seem to exist but one whose power and presence are continuously felt. It is a subject that asserts its centrality or dominance on social and cultural levels yet remains shrouded within a veil of transparency that ensures its absence, thus evading the subject of discourse. In psychology, we often ask the question: what racial categories (or gender/sexuality/class) are excluded and/or gain admittance and expression at the center. Psychologists do not ask how the magic of displacements, the law of exclusion and the theory of control are used to sketch and shadow the spaces and latitudes of meaning, desires and power of the dominant groups (Fine and Wong, in prep; Fine et al., in prep). In this article, I would like to delineate the contours and outlines of white power within psychology and argue that racial minorites have not been consigned to the margins of psychological texts. On the contrary, we have always been forced to 'sit' at the perimeter but hover over the center of mainstream psychology; neither inside nor outside (Hall, 1988). The perimeter is the circumference and boundary of a figure and most often, its length, texture and durability are defined and determined by the center. The center of the figure is also dependent and decided by the perimeter. Therefore, only by sketching out the silhouettes of 'Blackness' situated at the perimeters will 'whiteness' be dragged out into the foreground. Stallybrass and White (1986: 5) write:

> A recurrent pattern emerges: the 'top' attempts to reject and eliminate the bottom for reasons of prestige and status, only to discover, not only that it is in some way dependent upon that low-Other . . . but also that the top includes that low symbolically, as a primary eroticized constituent of its own fantasy life. The result is a mobile, conflictual fusion of power, fear and desire in the construction of the subjectivity: a psychological dependence upon precisely those Others which are being rigorously opposed and excluded at the social level. It is for this reason that what is socially peripheral is so frequently symbolically central ...

Within the intergroup literature, psychologists have been locked into an oppo-sitional model — pitting center against margins; ingroup versus outgroup — and have not seriously considered a dialogical model (see Billig, 1987, for an excep-tion) whereby, in mapping the topography of the center ('whiteness') and the margins (racial minorities, sexuality, gender), the points of differences, similari-ties and intersections among race/class/gender/sexuality are (re)produced through, constructed by, overlap and intersect with one another. By virtue of exclusion, regulation and control of the presence of 'coloreds' (non-white) at the perimeters of mainstream psychology, psychologists have granted racial minori-ties 'a shadowless [colorless] participation in the dominant cultural body'; specifically, to construct the powerful white body. The shadowless participa-tions of racial minorities — invisible and objectified — emerge only behind the white researcher when s/he deems them important. But only in the space when 'whiteness' has appropriated and used 'Blackness' to construct its own mean-ings and desires. I will illustrate with two examples: e-racing theory and the porno-raced method. These examples will discuss the assumptions and practices that some psychologists have adopted to distance and to 'white-out' their works and to inform the meaning of 'doing differences'.

E-RACING THEORY

> There are many subjects close to my own concerns which I would like to see studied in more depth. I would like to see a qualitative study of female drug users; a comparative study of girls in single-sex schools with those in mixed-sex schools; an interactive study of girls as TV-viewers in relation to family life and more research of this type which concentrated on race and ethnicity (*an element which is unfortunately missing in my own work*) (Angela McRobbie, 1991: xii, my emphasis).

There is a tendency to disregard and ignore 'whiteness' as a racial category in most psychological texts. A content analysis of the last three years of published empirical pieces in *Psychology of Women Quarterly* (*PWQ*) and *Journal of Personality and Social Psychology* (*JPSP*) reveals a similar story. Out of the 76 reports in *PWQ* (1990 to 1992), 43 percent have failed/ignored to report 'white-ness' for their samples. In *JPSP* (1990 to 1992), 79 percent of the 337 reports have not reported the race of their participants. They have simply described the participants as 'subjects', assuming that the reader will know that they are white. A mere 6.5 percent in *PWQ* and only 5.5 percent of *JPSP* addressed the 'white-ness' of their sample.[7] There are only two (2.6 percent)[8] empirical pieces of research that exclusively examine the concerns, processes or interests of racial minority women[9] in *PWQ*. There were *no* articles in *JPSP* that examined only the concerns of racial minorities.

Within social psychology, researchers continue to subscribe to the doctrine of universalism — the belief that the attitudes, behaviors and cognitive processes of the 'generic subject' are generalizable to the populations of racial minorities. Meanwhile, the official journal of Division 35 and the most prestigious journal of social and personality psychologists are still directed by 'standardized guidelines' that promote the erasure of 'whiteness' and the subscription to the 'generic college (wo)man' (Reid, 1992).

In the special edition of 'Theorizing Heterosexuality' in *Feminism & Psychology*, we celebrate, question, dismantle and deconstruct the privileges and legitimacy of heterosexuality. However, even here, the authors' intentions of demystifying heterosexuality have inevitably perpetuated the 'unexamined Whiteness' of psychology, including white feminist psychologists. And in the section on 'Heterosexual Feminist Identities: The Personal and the Political', feminists relate their dis-eased impressions regarding heterosexuality, identities, passions and politics. However, 'white heterosexual feminists' shunned and/or neglected discussions of race. The discourses of white heterosexuality are trans(mute)d and re-positioned as relational discourses about family, children, outrage and guilt. But in an act of defiance and refusing to be 'boxed', Kanneh (1992: 432) comments:

> I do intend to suggest or intimate a possible reading of heterosexuality which would insist on the value and significance of racial and cultural loyalties within a feminist politics . . . I find the imperative within my self-understanding as a feminist is to view the politics of anti-imperialism, black struggles, nationalism, within the perspectives of gender and feminist movement. In contrast, and to my own confusion, I find myself viewing women-identified theories unshakingly from the perspective of my own racial positioning, my own experience of racism, the histories of black people and my own family. These two strategies need not be mutually exclusive, experientially or theoretically, and I will not make the decision to abandon feminism in an either/or dynamic which would unacceptably limit and reduce my life.

The editors by tokenizing race and class from the discussion (see Bhavnani, 1993, for a discussion of this process in Women's Studies), leave unchallenged the differently classed and raced 'versions' of heterosexuality that serve the white man's palate (hooks, 1992). Identities are fluid, shifting and contradictory (Harding, 1986; de Lauretis, 1986; Alcoff, 1988) and the construction of the white heterosexual woman is located at a nexus of relational power where sexuality, race and class intersect (Carby, 1987; Collins, 1990; Crenshaw, 1992; Hull et al., 1982; King, 1988). Any dialogues that attempt to problematize issues of privilege and normality have to take into consideration the intricate webs of privilege, 'whiteness', heterosexuality, able-bodied, middle class and youth.

Another way in which 'whiteness' has been repres(s)-ented and e-raced in psychological texts is through its displacement and substitution by synonyms of 'whiteness'. In the content analysis, I found that 22 percent of the empirical pieces in *PWQ*, the writers substituted 'white' with 'Caucasians', 'whites (non-Hispanics' and 'European-Americans'. 'Whiteness' moves from one set of literature to another, unburdening the discourse of ambivalence and anxiety onto the

'Other'. 'Whiteness' is difficult to examine since it breaks apart and shifts to synonyms as soon as one attempts to bring it into focus. Except in cross-racial studies where racial minorities play a significant role, 'whiteness' remains absent yet present. 'Whiteness' in psychology is almost always defined only in comparative racial studies. In the content analysis, 21 percent of the empirical pieces in *PWQ* and 3.8 percent in *JPSP* reported the 'whiteness' of their participants only in comparative race research. In Black/white comparison, the word 'white' is almost always used, in studies of Latinos and Mexicans (Chicanos), 'Anglo' is preferred and in cross-cultural studies, the word 'American' or 'Caucasians' is preferred. The contradictory positions of 'whiteness' fluctuate and mutate; evading examination. When we focus on 'whiteness', we find its legitimacy is defined by shifting its language to 'Caucasians', 'Americans', 'Anglos', 'Non-colored' and 'Raceless'.

In a recent issue of the *American Psychologist*, Graham (1992) surveyed six APA journals between 1970 and 1989, including *JPSP*. She was interested in the number of studies which controlled for socioeconomic status (SES) of subjects; and whether the race of experimenter or therapist was reported. She reported that only 3.6 percent of all articles published by the six APA journals between 1970 and 1989 represented research on African-American populations. Graham concluded that psychological knowledge fails to represent racial minority populations and is in danger of becoming 'raceless'. But psychological texts are not raceless; the meaning of these texts is constructed through an active process which defines them as, or in relation to, white (Wong, 1992). In deconstruction (Culler, 1982), the concept of 'différance' focuses on meaning that is generated on a series of binary oppositions, one having an identity only in relation to the other. The first gains meaning from what the second is not; male/female; white/black, etc. The identities are built on a series of hierarchical oppositions where the differences in the socially valued and powerful subsumes and devalues the other. So what is present in (whites) is reflected in the text by the absence of the other (non-whites).

When Sandra Graham describes psychological discourse as raceless, she also effaces what Toni Morrison (1992) has referred to as the role of the Africanist presence in the white imagination.[10] In *Playing in the Dark* (1992), she investigates the construction of a non-white African-like, or Africanist, presence or persona in the United States, and how the imaginative uses of this fabricated presence have served in literary discourse.

> These images of impenetrable whiteness need contextualizing to explain their extraordinary power, pattern and consistency. Because they appear almost in conjunction with representations of black or Africanist people who are dead, impotent, or under complete control, these images of blinding whiteness seem to function as both antidote for and mediation on the shadow that is companion to this whiteness — a dark and abiding presence that moves the hearts and texts of American literature with fear and longing (Morrison, 1992: 33).

Like the abiding shadow that is companion to blinding 'whiteness' in literary discourse, a formless, shapeless and disembodied phantom that is under the white gaze can also be found in psychological texts. This phantom is not simply framed, controlled and manipulated in psychological discourse but is also used to articulate the meaning of 'whiteness'.

Signithia Fordham (1988) also made a similar point when she argued that 'race-lessness' is an important factor in Black students' school success. In Signithia Fordham's work, she presents two cases of high achieving 'raceless' (1988) Black students who 'act white' (Fordham and Ogbu, 1986). Basically, she argues that Black students are pulled apart by the contradictory relationships between the indigenous black-fictive kinship systems and the individualistic and competitive ideology of the contemporary mainstream education system. Fordham argues that there are competitive ideologies from both the white mainstream and the general African-American culture community. She finds that Black students are trying to juggle an optimal position where they can minimize the conflicts and anxieties generated by the competing ideologies of their schools and community. The Black students who perform well in the education system express continual dismay regarding their social positions. For many Black adolescents, the fact that they are attending school is either a conscious or unconscious rejection of African-American culture. So in order to be 'authentic' members of their community, they create an environment that will support their cultural beliefs. But in the recreation of an indigenous culture, they inadvertently ensure their own failure. In order to succeed, racial minorities, as in the case of African-American communities, will have to find the means to juggle their contradictory positions. That is, they either have to 'act white' or 'forfeit their race/become raceless'. Fordham reports in her ethnography that Black students who succeed

> ... consciously and unconsciously sense that they have to give up aspects of their identities and of their indigenous cultural system in order to achieve success as defined in dominant group terms; their resulting social selves are embodied in the notion of racelessness (1988: 81).

Fordham reports and sets up a dichotomy between Black/white and argues that the only means by which Black students can succeed in the school environment is to dissociate themselves from their Black communities and to contradict an identification and solidarity with Black culture. My problem is with Fordham calling them raceless.

We could easily recast Fordham's finding to celebrate and embrace the clever strategies that these high achieving African-American students have employed in moving up the educational system.

Fordham's work informs us of the different ways multiple and varied constructions of identity are suppressed and denied. It dismisses differences among us by labeling some folks black and others not. The varied and complex ways of understanding 'being black' or even reclaiming the different ways of understanding subaltern or marginal identities are negated. It reproduces the oppositions of school by negating the complex maneuvers of students and by supporting the hegemonic structures of white, male, Eurocentric cultures to normalize and universalize (Giroux, 1992). bell hooks (1990) argues that postmodernist thought would be helpful in re-formulating outdated notions of identity. She laments that the African-American community has been circumscribed for too long from both the outside and the inside by a narrow construction of 'Blackness'. Only by criticizing essentialism will African-Americans acknowledge how class mobility, gender differences or sexual orientation have altered the collective Black experience (also see Hall, 1988). Such critiques will open up the possibility of affirming multiple Black positions and varied Black experiences through deconstruction of the unidimensional representation of 'Blackness'. This undimensional representation has created,

> ... a discourse of the primitive and promoted the notion of an 'authentic' experience ... Contemporary African-American resistance struggle must be rooted in a process of decolonialization that continually opposes re-inscription notions of 'authentic' black identity (hooks, 1990: 28).

Like Fordham, works by most contemporary 'Orientalists' like Markus and Kitayama (1991), Triandis (1989), and Stevenson and Stigler (1991) have also drawn from the dichotomy of individualism and collectivism to inform their analysis. The works of Markus, Kitayama and Triandis also draw from the dichotomy of individualism (West)/Collectivism (East) to describe the motivational, affective and cognitive processes of Americans and 'Easterners' which inevitably fix rigid differences between people of the 'West' and the 'East'. In their decontextualized valorization of Asian educational practices, Stevenson and Stigler (1991) arguably serve to perpetuate the model minority stereotype of Asian Americans and may have seemingly translated it into virulent anti-Asian American policies and violence (Wong, 1993).

While bell hooks has cautioned us against essentialist conceptions of identity, Renato Rosaldo (1989), Lila Abu-Lughod (1991), and Akhil Gupta and James Ferguson (1992) warn us against static, discrete and bounded conceptions of culture. Rosaldo has claimed that the classic conceptions of culture in anthropology emphasize coherence and stability at the expense of change, inconsistencies and contradictions. By limiting culture within such clean coherent groups, it is difficult to analyse 'the zones of difference within and between cultures' (Rosaldo, 1989: 28).

In 'Culture Diversity and Methodology in Feminist Psychology', Landrine et al. (1992) have committed the same problematic errors. In their article they argue for a revision in the methodology of feminist psychological research because the present methods do not allow for the incorporation of cultural differences. So they suggest a methodology that integrates etic (objective, behavioral) and emic (subjective, phenomenal) approaches. In their results, they found

> ... [w]hite women did not differ from women of color in self-ratings on several gender-role stereotypic items (etic data). However, the two groups differed significantly in how they had defined and interpreted those terms while rating themselves (emic data), and these subjective, culturally constituted interpretations predicted the self-ratings (Landrine et al., 1992: 145).

By analysing the data 'white women versus women of color', they assume that African-American, Latina and Asian-American women belonged together as a monolithic 'colored' group. Hazel Carby (1992: 13) describes her reservation about this phrase:

> This phrase [women of color] carries a series of complex meanings. It has its origin in the need of subordinated, marginalized, and exploited groups of women to find common ground with each other and in the assertion of their desire to establish a system of alliances as 'women of color' ... Do white women and men have no color?

In the second set of analyses, the authors separate 'women of color' into separate categories for analysis. Also, they fail to consider the possible diversity among these women such as generational and class statuses. By providing a checklist which consists of seven gender-stereotypic adjectives, such as 'I am sensitive to the needs of others'; 'I am assertive', the authors are imposing a set of predominantly male Eurocentric and individualistic presumptions on their participants. If we take seriously the view that 'women of color' and 'white women' are predominantly collectivistic and communal (Gilligan, 1982; Collins, 1990; Markus and Oyserman, 1989), what forms of interpretations are the authors enforcing on their participants prior to interpreting the data? Furthermore, asking 'women of color' to simply restrict their definitions to such statements denigrates their historical experiences, collective consciousness and subjectivities.

Landrine et al. (1992) report that they have borrowed emic approaches from cross-cultural psychology (closely akin to anthropology) which will allow for the interpretations of their participants. But just simply 'borrowing' directly from cross-cultural psychology leaves much of the epistemological assumptions unchallenged and unexamined. Furthermore, they fail to consider and contextualize the wider debates surrounding interpretation, methods and writing within feminist and anthropological circles (Behar, 1993; Alcoff, 1991; Scott, 1991; Clifford and Marcus, 1986).

The concept of culture may speak against essentialism but it tends to freeze differences between groups. In Landrine et al.'s case, 'women of color' and 'white women' are separated as if the former is culture-full and the latter is culture-less. Within Fordham's work, the other is not 'whiteness' but other Blacks whose racial identities are delegitimized because they do not adhere to the 'normative' definitions of 'Blackness'. Fordham's failure to theorize against the colonial distinctions of 'Blackness' and 'whiteness' presumes differences as

'either/or' — mutually exclusive, independent and discrete. The binary categorizations overlook differences within the construction such as class and gender
(Young, 1990); and such dividing practices ignore the ways in which 'black'
experiences may have been shaped outside of representation (Hall, 1992); exac-
erbate the 'dilemma of differences' (Minow, 1990) in our society; and denies
how 'Blackness' may have changed over time historically (Abu-Lughod, 1991).
Finally, such categorizations leave much of the connections between those on
the divide untheorized and unexamined, and unable to understand the dialogic
ways that groups function.

One step that could be taken to develop dialogic insights would be to dismantle the concept of the 'essential being' in our assumptions and practices. The
practices of social psychology embrace the notion of an essential racial being
with his/her definite cultural and behavioral code. Social (feminist?) psychology
uses this 'essential being' to represent 'Blackness' and subsequently to inform
and test 'whiteness'. This essential being is also used to represent what
'Blackness' means and to reveal what 'acting white' Blacks have to give up in
order to succeed in the school system. In certain spheres of feminist psychology
and psychology, we use the 'essential being (generic women)' to pervert gender,
race and sexuality into studies of differences (Fine and Gordon, 1989; Jones,
1991). In other words priviliging the concept of the 'essential being' masks the
power inequalities inherent in otherness and difference.

I have shown how 'whiteness' is ignored, e-raced, denied and displaced in
psychological texts but there is another form of its paradoxical manifestation. In
this instance 'whiteness" functions as the dominant epistemological assumption
guiding much of psychological discourse. In psychology, we have predominantly white psychologists using white subjects dictated by a history of
Eurocentric philosophy. By choosing university sophomores (Sears, 1986),
issues of class, gender, sexual orientation, ableness and race are either included
or excluded. Within experimental psychology, the lack of attention to issues of
external validity has resulted in an unacknowledged genderized and racialized
discourse. As whiteness is e-raced, racial minorities (e)merge as cardboard figures — essentialized and prepared to embody the virtues, desires, traits and culture of their groups. A similar account of this essentialized cardboard figure is
found in the porno-raced method. But in this case, the invention, development
and understanding of 'whiteness' is contingent on manipulating and extrapolat-
ing from the expressions and significations of this cardboard figure (Wong,
1991).

THE PORNO-RACED METHOD

In many instances, social psychologists have been cloaked by the doctrine of
objectivity; distancing and denying the hyphen between researcher and participant. They believe that objectivity via the experimental method will generate

'good' and 'accurate' results and will prove the hypothesized causality in speci-
fied relationships.

In their effort to show causality (cause–effect relationship), psychologists
manipulate the independent variables and the outcome is measured by dependent
variables. Independent variables are antecedent causes created and controlled so
that other causative influences will not interfere in the experiment. They are said
to be manipulated so that their effects are measured using dependent variables.
When matters pertaining to non-whites or, in most cases, 'Blackness' are located
and called attention to in social psychology, race conveniently occupies the role
of the 'independent variable' (Pastor and Wong, 1992). 'Blackness' exists
within what I call an 'essentialized pornography of coloreds'[11] in psychological
experiments. Representations of race come in the form of psychological stimuli
— stereotypes, social representations or stigmas. They are inaccurate and false
depictions that stand in for other possible realities. As 'provocative' independent
variables, non-whites are framed and displayed as objects to motivate and arouse
the responses of the white subjects. Here are the allusions to pornography:

> Our race manipulation was introduced by way of the partner's personal folder.
> Specifically, all subjects received identical and rather uninformative preference
> information about their fictitious partner, 'Laura', except that half of the sub-
> jects received a picture of a black woman, whereas the other half found a photo
> of a white woman in the folder (Omoto and Borgida, 1988).

By using representations associated with 'Blackness', it was hoped that the
white subjects would be fooled into thinking that they were interacting with a
Black individual, allowing researchers to test the white participants' responses.

Furthermore, in most studies of prejudice and racism, the typical scenario of
an experimental priming study substitutes with what is considered 'real' to
images and words of Blacks;

> Words that are labels for the social category, Blacks (e.g. Blacks, Negroes, nig-
> gers) or are stereotypic (e.g. poor, lazy, athletic) were the priming stimuli.
> Twenty-four primes were used to generate two stimulus replications. Efforts
> were made to produce roughly equivalent content in the two replications.
> Replication 1 primes included the following: nigger, poor, afro, jazz, slavery,
> musical, Harlem, busing, minority, oppressed, athletic and prejudice.
> Replication 2 primes included the following: Negroes, lazy, Blacks, blues,
> rhythm, Africa, stereotype, ghetto, welfare, basketball, unemployed, and plan-
> tation (Devine, 1989).

Another way in which white subjects are deceived into thinking that they are
interacting with a Black partner is to introduce voices and information that are
stereotypically 'Black':

> Subjects were nested within one of four cells representing a factorial combina-
> tion of two speech styles (SE or BEV)[12] and two racial labels (black or white)
> within a matched guise format. The speech styles were incorporated in a 90 sec

stimulus tape, ostensibly containing the self-description of a university student. The actual speaker for all four experimental cells were a bidialectal black graduate student. For the first speech sample, the actor read a typical student self-description in Standard English. For the second Black English Vernacular (i.e., many of the more striking grammatical features of BEV, such as the 'invariant be,' were either not used or used infrequently. An example of a BEV passage is the following: I don't get off into the political thang much, 'cause it's always the old same old. Sports would be my thang but the teams in Chicago ain't 'bout nothing. The corresponding English SE version is: I'm not interested in politics — none of it seems to have much to do with me personally, and it's always just the same old stuff. I like to follow sports, except Chicago teams are always so bad (McKirnan et al., 1983: 438).

Aronson et al. (1985) in the *Handbook of Social Psychology*, liken the set up of an experiment to a theater production, 'Blackness' as an independent variable in psychological experiments is analogous to the props in the play. Props are used to establish the character and reinforce the style and environment of the play. The roles of 'Blackness' as props serve the vital function of informing, testing and constructing the meaning of 'whiteness'. Here is an example:

In addition to the white, naive subject other participants included two accomplices, a Negro who played the role of the victim and a Negro or white accomplice who served as an aggressive model. Upon arriving at the experimental room, subjects were told that they were participating in a study to evaluate the effect of shock upon learning. Thus, one participant would play the role of a learner, whereas the other two would serve as experimenters. In order to determine who would play the victim or learner's role, the participants were asked to select a number from 1 to 10. Insofar as this procedure was rigged, the same Negro accomplice was selected as the learner for all subjects. The remaining participants, the subject and the accomplice, were told that they would play the role of experimenters in a study on the effects of shock upon learning. This role would be played by shocking the learner for incorrectly anticipating the stimulus words presented serially on a memory drum. It was emphasized that the experimenter could press any one of the five buttons clearly marked from very low to very high. At this point, the remaining accomplice (Negro or white) 'spontaneously' requested to play the role of the experimenter first since his time was limited. In this manner, the accomplice always served as the aggressive model. The naive subject was requested to observe and record the accomplice's selection of shock so that level of shock could be related to the rate of learning. In this manner, the subject was given the opportunity to observe the level of shock employed by the second accomplice, now serving as an aggressive model. Depending on the appropriate condition, the model was either Negro or white, low or high status. In the low status condition, the model wore old, dishevelled clothes and responded to an orally administered questionnaire so as to reveal the following information about himself within the hearing distance of the naive subject: family income, less than $3000; parental occupation, unemployed. In the high status condition, the model appeared well-dressed and responded in the following manner: family income $15000 per annum; parental occupation, executive in an advertising firm. The Negro victim made a programmed series of responses such that 32 shocks were administered by the naive subject in a seven-trial learning series. Unknown to the subject, however, a locked switch precluded the actual administration of shock to the victim. Furthermore, after an initial warm-up period in which the model delivered the highest level of shocks to the victim for errors during the first serial presentation, he delivered the highest level of shock namely 'very high shock' for subsequent errors. After the victim had learned the correct order of serially presented words, the subject was given the opportunity to play the role of the experimenter. This time the victim was asked to learn a new set of words (Epstein, 1966: 575).

It is worth quoting this experiment at length since this study is an excellent example of the way the black body is controlled and fetishized to inform 'whiteness' as a privileged site of power where racial divisions and otherness are reinforced.

The psychological experiment has become a 'political anatomy'. Foucault (1979) describes political anatomy as a device which has; the 'mechanics of power' to define, dominate and dissect over others' bodies, not only that they may do what one wishes, but also to determine how they operate. After the bodies have been subjected, disciplined and punished, they are known as 'docile' bodies. In this case, the black 'docile' bodies, depicted as victims and confederates, are punished by electrocution to test the reactions of whites. The production of 'docile bodies' requires uninterrupted intimidation on the bodily activities of 'Blackness'. In this respect, the construction of the powerful 'whiteness' screams at the reader's face: the power of the white researcher to control and manipulate the bodies of the black confederates and the power of the white participants to deliver the voltage to the black confederate. The construction of 'whiteness' as benevolent or sadistic can be seen from the amount of voltage delivered to the black confederate. But in most cases, we read about the obedient and benevolent 'white' participant who struggles with his/her moral conscience (Milgram, 1974). The power of the white researcher to control 'Blackness' remains. This is not only symptomatic of psychological research but is evident in wider society; racial minorities continue to face segregation and domination by whites. Within psychological texts, racial minorities are often reported as independent variables and not as subjects.

In this cautionary tale, I have raised the need to be aware of the practices that may serve to perpetuate white dominance and the reification of racialized minorities into an 'essentialized pornography of coloreds'. When I read cross-racial experiments or any studies which frame Asians/Blacks/Latinos as objects for response, I wonder about how my fellow psychologists of 'color' feel about reading their own objectifications and how we are *all* implicated by these practices.

However, what concerns me with respect to the use of 'Blackness' as objects and independent variables (especially when these are stereotypes) are the possible 'racist' effects on the 'generic participants'. The constant reification of 'Blackness' in the white imagination needs to be examined especially in the context of a 'scientific lab'.

What do the practices of using only 'Blackness' as confederates and priming stimulus signify? One response could be: these practices will help us to explain much of the intergroup conflict and to find ways to alleviate and deal with white prejudice against non-whites. However, the recognition that white prejudice lies with their irrational processes leaves much of the institutional and cultural racism unexplained and unchanged (Henriques, 1984). By theorizing a middle class 'whiteness' as the predominant site of intervention against racism, the white researcher leaves the class divisions within and between racial groups untouched.

In psychology, the prevailing approach is to rely on statistical and empirical methodologies. Such reductionistic approaches always take racism to be due to socialization factors, authoritarian personality or irrational cognitive processes. Despite all this work, racisms have changed and persisted. Explanations and rationalizations have also changed and persisted. A large body of work has been consumed with seeking the origins of white prejudice and the impact of racism and discrimination on its victims. It is also important to examine the 'victims' who have resisted and challenged racism. Equally important is to examine how the notions of racial hierarchy and exclusion have also affected whites (Bowser and Hunt, 1981). The methodological practices that we cling to dearly in psychology need to be further examined, especially in circumstances where whites hold considerably more power than racial minorities but are nonetheless highly dependent on racial minorities to inform their own constructions and processes (Morrison, 1992; Palmer, 1989).

CONCLUSION

The 'metaphor of travel' has become popular in recent years to allow us to traverse and cross borders within and across groups and disciplines (Giroux, 1992; Rosaldo, 1989; Lugones, 1987; Caraway, 1991). These theories emphasize the celebratory notions of occupying multiple contradictory positions of spaces and the need for commuting across/within spaces. Gloria Anzaldua (1987) has argued that the traversal of boundaries and borders will help to develop better understanding of ethnicities, cultures, genders, sexualities, etc. For most of us, traveling across ethnic/racial/national boundaries is mandatory. This article is an invitation to white psychologists to imagine, contest and enforce spaces, places, peoples and texts that will permit issues of 'whiteness', difference, sameness, privilege and oppression to travel within and across diverse groups. White psychologists have always been mobile but they have been cloaked by a veil of transparency that continues to hide their tracks. But the torch has been lit by some white psychologists who have refused to 'stay put' in their little safe space of 'whiteness' and privilege. 'They' have continued to promote and enrich the 'multicultural feminist politics of solidarity' that have built across some groups.

On a final note, I would like to suggest that *all* psychologists take the 'essentialized body' and observe a Buddhist funeral rite — cremate the body, scatter the ashes in the sea and let them float to Amitabha Buddha's Western paradise.

NOTES

A shorter version of this article was presented at the 14th Ethnography in Education Conference in Philadelphia. Much of the thinking that went into this article resulted from many discussions with Michelle Fine. I want to thank her for her support, guidance and encouragements, and the '(in)justice gang'. I am indebted to Judith Addelston, Kum-Kum Bhavnani, Candice Clarke, Meg Coulson, Liz Dalton, Calliope Haritos, Louise Kidder, Halina Maslanka, Vita Rabinowitz, Pamela Reid and one anonymous reviewer for their multiple and partial perspectives, constructive suggestions and editorial support.

1. Audre Lorde (1984) refers to the mythical norm as 'white, thin, male, young, heterosexual, Christian and financially secure'. These characteristics define the standards that most of us, the subjugated and oppressed, deviate from. In this article, I am specifically examining 'whiteness' as multiple, heterogenous and incoherent forms of representation, identities and/or racial group and do not begin to even tackle the complexities of gender, race, class and sexuality. An unfortunate aspect of this article is the lack of theorizing about class. Often within psychology, we leave class out of our analyses, perpetuating a white middle-class analysis.

2. Some efforts have been made to examine 'whiteness' as a racial norm as evident with the proliferation of papers on 'whiteness' within women's studies (hooks, 1989; Ware, 1992; McIntosh, 1988; Caraway, 1992; Russo, 1991), education (Weis, 1990; Tatum, 1992), literary criticism (Morrison, 1992), film studies (Dyer, 1988), history (Roediger, 1991; Ware, 1992) and counseling psychology (Helms, 1990).

3. To borrow a term from de Lauretis (1987).

4. By 'doing race', I mean that white peoples should seriously interrogate their 'whiteness' and question their own privileges that are afforded by their race. I do not want to prescribe a cookbook of 'doing race' and will leave this to the individual reader to decipher for themselves the means of 'proper' contextualized race-ing.

5. The phrase 'chain of equivalences' is borrowed from Chantal Mouffe's point about democratic struggles. She frames her discussion of democratic rights in the context of coalition building to form what Gramsci called 'expansive hegemony'. She uses the metaphor of 'chain of equivalences' to help us to think about democratic demands fused together to forge a collective will to struggle against subjugation and subordination and to demand for political and individual autonomy, and collective and individual rights.

6. I am borrowing this term from Chandra Mohanty. She defines 'third world women' as a designation of 'political constituency, not a biological or even sociological one. It is a sociopolitical designation for people of African, Caribbean, Asian and Latin American descent, and native peoples of the US' (p. 7). The basis of struggle is an oppositional alliance of a common context of struggle. I realize the implications of the term 'third world women' implying hierarchical and native, for an assessment of the term, refer to Minh-Ha (1989).

7. In this group, only studies that examine white participants are included.
8. Both of these empirical papers appeared in 1990. There were no articles on race or ethnicity in 1991 and 1992.
9. Pastor and Wong (1992) found similar results in their content analysis of six mainstream social psychological journals. Within the last decade (1981 to 1991), only 2.2 percent of the articles exclusively examine American racial/ethnic (excluding cross-cultural samples) groups in their studies.
10. Africanist is a term that describes a 'denotative and connotative "Blackness" that African peoples have come to signify; as well as the entire range of views, assumptions, readings and misreadings that accompany Eurocentric learning about these people' (Morrison, 1992: 6).
11. Thanks to Michelle Fine for coining this phrase.
12. SE stands for Standard English and BEV stands for Black Vernacular English.

REFERENCES

Abu-Lughod, L. (1991) 'Writing Against Culture', in R. Fox (ed.) *Recapturing Anthropology*, pp. 137–62. Santa Fe, NM: School of American Press.

Alcoff, L. (1988) 'Cultural Feminism Versus Post-structuralism: The Identity Crises in Feminist Theory', *Signs* 13(3): 405–36.

Alcoff, L. (1991, Winter) 'The Problem of Speaking for Others', *Cultural Critique* 5–32.

Anzaldua, G. (1987) *Borderlands: The New Mestiza = La Frontera*. San Francisco, CA: Spinsters/Aunt Lute.

Aronson, E., Carlsmith, M. and Brewer, M. (1985) 'Experimentation in Social Psychology', in Lindsey and Gardner (eds) *Handbook of Social Psychology*, Vol. 1. New York, NY: Random House.

Behar, R. (1993) *Translated Woman: Crossing the Border with Esperanza's Story*. Boston, MA: Beacon Press.

Bhavnani, K.-K. (1993) 'Talking Racism and the Editing of Women's Studies', in D. Richardson and V. Robinson (eds) *Thinking Feminist: Key Concepts in Women's Studies*, pp. 27–48. New York, NY: Guilford Press.

Billig, M. (1987) *Arguing and Thinking: A Rhetorical Approach to Social Psychology*. New York, NY: Cambridge University Press.

Bowser, B. P. and Hunt, R. G. (1981) *Impacts of Racism on White Americans*. Newbury Park, CA: Sage.

Caraway, N. (1991) *Segregated Sisterhood: Racism and the Politics of Feminism*. Knoxville, TN: University of Tennessee Press.

Carby, H. V. (1987) *Reconstructing Womanhood: The Emergence of the Afro-American Woman Novelist*. New York, NY: Oxford University Press.

Carby, H. V. (1992) 'The Multicultural Wars', *Radical History Review* 54: 7–18.

Clifford, J. and Marcus, G. E. (1986) *Writing Culture: The Politics and Poetics of Ethnography*. Berkeley, CA: University of California Press.

Cohen, E. (1991) 'Who are "We"? Gay "Identity" as Political (E)Motion (A Thousand Rumination)', in D. Fuss (ed.) *Inside/Out*, pp. 71–92. New York, NY: Routledge.

Collins, P. (1990) *Black Feminist Thought: Knowledge, Consciousness and the Politics of Empowerment*. London: Harper Collins.

Crenshaw, K. (1992) 'Whose Story Is It Anyway? Feminist and Antiracist Appropriations of Anita Hill', in T. Morrison (ed.) *Race-ing Justice, En-gendering Power*, pp. 402–40. New York, NY: Pantheon Books.

Culler, J. (1983) *On Deconstruction*. Ithaca, NY: Cornell University Press.

de Lauretis, T. (1986) *Feminist Studies/Critical Studies*. Bloomington, IN: Indiana University Press.

de Lauretis, T. (1987) *Technologies of Gender*. Bloomington, IN: Indiana University Press.

Devine, P. (1989) 'Stereotypes and Prejudice: Their Automatic and Controlled Components', *Journal of Personality and Social Psychology* 56: 5–18.

Dyer, R. (1988) 'White', *Screen* 29(4): 44–65.

Epstein, R. (1966) 'Aggression Toward Outgroups as a Function of Authoritarianism and Imitation of Aggression Models', *Journal of Personality and Social Psychology* 3(5): 574–9.

Fine, M. (1993) 'Working the Hyphen: Reinventing "Self" and "Other" in Qualitative Research', paper presented at the 14th Ethnography in Education at the University of Pennsylvania in Philadelphia.

Fine, M. and Gordon, S. M. (1989) 'Feminist Transformations of/Despite Psychology', in M. Crawford and M. Gentry (eds) *Gender and Thought*, pp. 146–74. New York, NY: Springer.

Fine, M. and Wong, L. M. (in prep) 'Desperately Seeking (In)Justice'.

Fine M., Genovese, T., Ingersall, S., McPherson, P. and Roberts, R. (in prep) 'White Li(v)es'.

Fordham, S. (1988) 'Racelessness as a Factor in Black Students' School Success: Pragmatic Strategy or Pyrrhic Victory?', *Harvard Educational Review* 58(1): 54–84.

Fordham, S. and Ogbu, J. U. (1986) 'Black Students' School Success: Coping with the Burden of "Acting White" ', *The Urban Review* 18(3): 176–205.

Foucault, M. (1978) *The History of Sexuality*, Vol. 1. New York: Vintage.

Foucault, M. (1979) *Discipline and Punish*. New York, NY: Vintage.

Frye, M. (1983) *The Politics of Reality*. Trumansburg, NY: Crossing Press.

Gilligan, C. (1982) *In a Different Voice*. Cambridge, MA: Harvard University Press.

Giroux, H. (1992) *Border Crossings*. New York, NY: Routledge.

Graham, S. (1992) 'Most of the Subjects were White and Middle Class', *American Psychologist*, 47(5): 629–39.

Griscom, J. (1992) 'Women and Power: Definition, Dualism and Difference', *Psychology of Women Quarterly* 16(4): 389–414.

Gupta, A. and Ferguson, J. (1992) 'Beyond "Culture": Space, Identity, and the Politics of Difference', *Cultural Anthropology* 17(1): 6–23.

Hall, S. (1988) 'New Ethnicities', in K. Mercer (ed.) *Black Film, British Cinema. ICA Documents* 7, 26–31.

Hall, S. (1992) 'What is This "Black" in Black Popular Culture?', in G. Dent (ed.) *Black Popular Culture*, pp. 21–33. Seattle, WA: Bay Press.

Harding, S. (1986) *The Science Question in Feminism*. Ithaca, NY: Cornell University Press.

Hare-Mustin, R. T. and Marecek, J. (1990) *Making a Difference: Psychology and the Construction of Gender*. New Haven, CT: Yale University Press.

Helms, J. (1990) *Black and White Racial Identity Attitudes' Theory*. Westport, CT: Greenwood Press.

Henriques, J. (1984) 'Social Psychology and the Politics of Racism', in J. Henriques,

W. Holloway, C. Urwin, C. Venn and V. Walkerdine (eds) *Changing the Subject*, pp. 60–89. New York: Methuen.

hooks, b. (1989) 'Representing Whiteness in the Black Imagination', in L. Grossberg, C. Nelson and P. Treichler (eds) *Cultural Studies*, pp. 338–46. New York, NY: Routledge.

hooks, b. (1990) *Yearning: Race, Gender and Cultural Politics*. Boston, MA: South End Press.

hooks, b. (1992) *Black Looks: Race and Representation*. Boston, MA: South End Press.

Hull, G. T., Scott, P. B. and Smith, B. (1982) *All the Women are White, All the Men are Black, But Some of Us are Brave*. Old Westbury, NY: Feminist Press.

Jones, J. M. (1991) 'Psychological Models of Race: What Have They Been and What Should They Be?', in J. D. Goodchilds (ed.) *Psychological Perspectives on Human Diversity in America*, pp. 7–46. Washington, DC: American Psychological Association.

Kanneh, K. G. (1992) 'Sisters Under the Skin: A Politics of Heterosexuality', *Feminism & Psychology* 2(3): 432–3.

King, D. K. (1988) 'Multiple Jeopardy, Multiple Consciousness: The Context of a Black Feminist Ideology', *Signs* 14(1): 42–72.

Kitzinger, C., Wilkinson, S. and Perkins, R. (1992) 'Theorizing Heterosexuality', *Feminism & Psychology* 2(3): 293–324.

Landrine, H., Klonoff, E. A. and Brown-Collins, A. (1992) 'Cultural Diversity and Methodology in Feminist Psychology', *Psychology of Women Quarterly* 16(2): 145–63.

Lorde, A. (1984) *Sister Outsider*. Trumansburg, NY: Crossing Press.

Lugones, M. (1987, summer) 'Playfulness, "World"-Travelling, and Loving Perception', *Hypatia* 2(2): 3–19.

Marable, M. (1992) 'Race, Identity and Political Culture', in G. Dent (ed.) *Black Popular Culture*, pp. 292–302. Seattle, WA: Bay Press.

Markus, H. and Kitayama, S. (1991) 'Culture and Self: Implications for Cognition, Emotion and Motivation', *Psychological Review* 98(2): 224–53.

Markus, H. and Oyserman, D. (1989) 'Gender and Thought: The Role of the Self Concept', in M. Crawford and M. Gentry (eds) *Gender and Thought*, pp. 100–27. New York, NY: Springer.

McIntosh, P. (1988) 'White Privilege and Male Privilege: A Personal Account of Coming to See Correspondences Through Work in Women's Studies', working paper, p. 189. Wellesley, MA: Center for Research on Women, Wellesley College.

McKirnan, D. J., Smith, C. E. and Hamayan, E. V. (1983) 'A Sociolinguistic Approach to the Belief-Similarity Model of Racial Attitudes', *Journal of Experimental Social Psychology* 19: 434–47.

McRobbie, A. (1991) *Feminism and Youth Culture*. Boston, MA: Unwin Hyman.

Milgram, S. (1974) *Obedience to Authority*. New York, NY: Harper Row.

Minh-Ha, T. T. (1989) *Woman, Native, Other*. Bloomington, IN: Indiana University Press.

Minow, M. (1990) *Making All the Difference: Inclusion, Exclusion and American Law*. Ithaca, NY: Cornell University Press.

Mohanty, C. (1991) 'Under Western Eyes: Feminist Scholarship and Colonial Discourse', in C. T. Mohanty, A. Russo and L. Torres (eds) *Third World Women and the Politics of Feminism*, pp. 51–80. Bloomington, IN: Indiana University Press.

Moraga, C. and Anzaldua, G. (1981) *This Bridge Called My Back*. New York, NY: Kitchen Table.

Morawski, J. (1988) *The Rise of Experimentation in American Psychology*. New Haven, CT: Yale University Press.

Morrison, T. (1992) *Playing in the Dark: Whiteness in the Literary Imagination*. Cambridge, MA: Harvard University Press.

Mouffe, C. (1988) 'Hegemony and New Political Subjects: Towards a New Concept of Democracy', in C. Nelson and L. Grossberg (eds) *Marxism and the Interpretation of Culture*, pp. 89–101. Urbana, IL: University of Illinois Press.

Omi, M. (1989) 'In Living Color: Race and American Culture' in I. Angus and S. Jhally (eds) *Cultural Politics in Contemporary America*, pp. 111–22. New York, NY: Routledge.

Omi, M. and Winant, H. (1986) *Racial Formation in the United States*. New York, NY: Routledge.

Omoto, A. and Borgida, E. (1988) 'Guess Who Might Be Coming to Dinner?: Personal Involvement and Racial Stereotyping', *Journal of Experimental Social Psychology* 24: 571–93.

Palmer, P. (1989) *Domesticity and Dirt: Housewives and Domestic Servants in the United States 1920–1940s*. Philadelphia, PA: Temple University Press.

Pastor, J. and Wong, L. M. (1992) 'The Concept of Race in Social Psychology — The Sequel', paper presented at the 100th American Psychological Association Meeting in Washington, DC.

Pratt, M. B. (1984) 'Identity: Skin Blood Heart', in E. Bulkin, M. B. Pratt and B. Smith (eds) *Yours in Struggle: Three Feminist Perspectives on Anti-semitism and Racism*. Brooklyn, NY: Long Haul Press.

Reid, P. T. (1992) 'Poor Women in Psychological Research: Shut Up and Shut Out', paper presented at the 100th American Psychological Association Meeting in Washington, DC.

Roediger, D. R. (1991) *The Wages of Whiteness*. New York, NY: Verso.

Rollins, J. (1985) *Between Women: Domestics and Their Employers*. Philadelphia, PA: Temple University Press.

Rosaldo, R. (1989) *Culture and Truth: The Remaking of Social Analysis*. Boston, MA: Beacon Press.

Russo, A. (1991) '"We Cannot Live Without Our Lives": White Women, Anti-racism and Feminism', in C. T. Mohanty, A. Russo and L. Torres (eds) *Third World Women and the Politics of Feminism*, pp. 297–313. Bloomington, IN: Indiana University Press.

Scott, J. W. (1991, Summer) 'The Evidence of Experience', *Critical Inquiry* 17: 773–97.

Sears, D. O. (1986) 'College Sophomores in the Laboratory: Influences of a Narrow Data Base on Social Psychology's View of Human Nature', *Journal of Personality and Social Psychology* 51(3): 515–30.

Stallybrass, P. and White, A. (1986) *The Politics and Poetics of Transgression*. Ithaca, NY: Cornell University Press.

Stevenson, H. W. and Stigler, J. W. (1991) 'How Asian Teachers Polish Each Lesson to Perfection', *American Educator* (Spring): 12–47.

Tatum, B. D. (1992) 'Talking About Race, Learning About Racism: The Applications of Racial Identity Development Theory in the Classroom', *Harvard Educational Review*, 62(1): 1–24.

Triandis, H. C. (1989) 'Cross-cultural Studies of Individualism and Collectivism', in J. J. Berman (ed.) *Cross-cultural Perspectives*, pp. 41–133. Lincoln, NE: University of Nebraska Press.

Ware, V. (1992) *Beyond the Pale: White Women, Racism and History*. New York, NY: Verso.

Weis, L. (1990) *Working Class Without Work: High School Students in De-industrializing Economy*. New York, NY: Routledge.

West, C. (1990) 'The New Cultural Politics of Difference', in R. Ferguson, M. Gever, T. T. Minh-Ha and C. West (eds) *Out There: Marginalization and Contemporary Culture*, pp. 19–38. Cambridge, MA: Massachusetts Institute of Technology Press.

Williams, J. E. (1966) 'Racial Concepts and Color Names', *Journal of Personality and Social Psychology* 3(5): 531–40.

Wong, L. M. (1991) 'From the Next Generation of Psychologists: The Discourse of Ethnicity', paper presented at the 100th American Psychological Association in Washington DC.

Wong, L. M. (1992) 'Reflecting and Refracting Whiteness: Using Model Minority as Blackbox and Prism', paper presented at the American Educational Studies Association Meeting in Chicago.

Young, I. M. (1990) *Justice and the Politics of Difference*. Princeton, NJ: Princeton University Press.

L. Mun WONG is a doctoral student in Social-Personality Psychology at the City University of New York, where he is completing his dissertation about the welfare state. His interests are critical psychological feminist, race and queer theories, the politics and passions of methods and issues of injustice and moral exclusion. He is a member of Division 35 and an executive member of American Psychological Association Graduate Students. ADDRESS: Social-Personality Psychology, CUNY: Graduate Center, 33 W 42nd Street, New York, NY 10036-8099, USA; email WON@CUNYVMS1

Erica BURMAN

Experience, Identities and Alliances: Jewish Feminism and Feminist Psychology

This article develops a theoretical perspective on identities as relational and produced through histories of oppression and resistance. The arguments are applied to their expression in issues for feminists teaching psychology and feminists organizing around psychology. As an illustration of key questions around the construction of counter-histories and self-representations, I focus on the changing forms and expressions of Jewish feminism in Britain. The analysis of Jewish identifications draws on recent calls to interrogate the notion of whiteness, and fracture the hegemony of racialization by attending to 'different degrees of othering'. This is developed in relation to the possibilities of, and obstacles to, alliances between Jewish and black feminists. In order to document a counter-history, I present an analysis of the presences and absences of Jewish feminist representations, particularly in relation to factors contributing to the non-publication of a British Jewish Feminist Anthology. The article finishes with a reminder of the wider political arenas in which discussions of identity, agency and collective action become increasingly urgent.

In this article I am going to address a set of issues about the political role of experience and identifications in relation to alliances between black and white people in combating racism. From an initial focus on exclusions and absences in relation to questions of identity, representation and self-representation in theoretical and pedagogical frameworks in feminist psychology, I move on to analyse the state and status of Jewish feminism in Britain. Attending to the specificities of this particular issue illustrates key questions of the representation and conceptualization of 'race' in ways that also address feminist and psychological practices. Despite the difficulties, I will be arguing for the importance of retaining a notion of identity as a political category, taking this as describing a partial, transitory and temporary position to promote change and alliance rather than enclosure and division.

Feminism & Psychology © 1994 SAGE (London, Thousand Oaks and New Delhi), Vol. 4(1): 155–178.

SPEAKING POSITIONS

Questions of commonality, unity and difference are now central themes of feminist discussions. Since the 1980s black[1] (Amos and Parmar, 1984; Carby, 1987) and lesbian (e.g. Rich, 1983) critiques have highlighted the racist and heterosexist exclusionary practices that have structured much of what used to pass as feminism in the UK and North America. While the term 'difference' carries a multiple theoretical burden (Barrett, 1987), the category 'woman' is itself in question (e.g. Riley, 1988): as Stevi Jackson (1992) has aptly noted, 'she' is in danger of disappearing altogether. In terms of feminist groups and campaigns the attention to 'difference' took the form, often in separate groups, of 'identity politics' addressing the multiple and diverse identities women held. The corollary of this in terms of political activity has been the move away from broad-based to single-issue campaigns. While 'identity politics' has been treated as symptomatic of the drift from action to self-contemplation (sometimes in the form of therapy), this should be seen within the general context of the crisis of confidence of the Left generally in response to the break-up of the Soviet Union and the entrenchment of the New World Order. However, the more recent convergence of postmodernist and feminist analyses has produced a move away from categories of oppression to a focus on difference. In the more bizarre and divisive manifestations of this convergence (such as in racism awareness training, see Sivanandan, 1985, 1989) oppressions were arranged hierarchically as if they were additive. If attending to one's multiple identities threatened to usher in a new form of solipsism (since by definition no one can precisely share your particular configuration of positions), the casting of inequalities between women, and between men and women as 'difference' can function as a disavowal of relationships of oppression (e.g. Burman, 1990a).

Within some current feminist analyses the essentialism–constructivism debate is now replaced by notions of strategic essentialism which allow some forms of mobilization and collective action on the basis of coalitions or affinities (Haraway, 1989; Spivak, 1990a). Now the tensions between foundational and deconstructive tendencies within feminism can be complementary rather than mutually exclusive (Ferguson, 1991). In line with this, and as my starting point for this account, I want to draw on the notion of *positionality* rather than identity, that is attending to the process of constructing identifications, with identities thereby rendered as textual productions rather than as some personal attributes or references to events. Hence insofar as I assume an autobiographical voice for this account, I do so more to inscribe than to authorize a particular set of positionings. That is, writing in this journal, and in this issue, produces a particular address. The positions from which I speak, or rather write, are not composed of some prior essential and individual qualities that are simply *arranged* for purposes of exposition (cf. Marcus, 1987). They are clearly also structured by a material history. This site of enunciation in some senses constitutes, rather than provides an outlet for, the positions adopted: I assume particular positions in order to speak in particular places. This narration of experiences and events here, therefore, not only allows me to articulate particular sets of preoccupations, but is also rhetorically constructed as an intervention. That is, in this account I am assuming the speaking positions of feminist, feminist teacher of psychology (and women's studies), and Jewish feminist, in order to interrogate the concept of identity in relation to antiracist practice.

IDENTIFICATIONS AND DIS-PLACEMENTS

Kobena Mercer (1992) argues that in addition to analysing the 'burden of representation' carried by (what he calls) 'minoritized subjects', the challenge for contemporary cultural and political analysis is to make whiteness visible 'as a culturally constructed ethnic identity historically contingent upon the disavowal and violent denial of difference' (p. 20). In this vein, Vron Ware (1992) documents how colonialism produced contradictory but nevertheless profoundly racialized conceptions of femininity. The antislavery campaign of the 19th century mobilized white women by drawing upon, in the main, women's traditional forms of work and organization. British imperialist authorities countered resistance to colonial occupation and consolidated and escalated the brutality of their rule by claiming to maintain the purity and safety of white women from the clutches of black men. It is not, or not only, that dominant notions of femininity fail to represent black, minority and poor women's experiences but also that the circulation of these ideas was central to a strategy of control, effected through the threat and reality of racist murders, such as lynching.

There are two important points here that Ware's account illustrates. First, that racism profoundly structures forms of femininity. This makes a nonsense of treating categories of oppression as separate and additive. Similarly, it is not only a question of models of femininity (including the psychology of women) having omitted black and minority women's experience; but that they are repressing how they are moulded to reflect and inform racial and colonial domination. Second, just as the paradoxes of patriarchal and colonial oppressions meant that becoming a missionary or teacher in India could be promoted as a *feminist* enterprise, as a means for British unmarried women to be independent and self-supporting at a time when there were few such opportunities at 'home', so also did white women build alliances with black women and men to join in the struggle to abolish slavery. That is, alliances were made, which were successful enough to be effective. This has its corollaries in terms of psychological models of subjectivity. Hence social learning theory is manifestly inadequate because (among other reasons) it cannot theorize how we fail to conform, and cognitive developmental models are inadequate for failing to account for how we do conform (Sayers, 1986). Ignoring the multiple and fragmentary positions wrought by racialization (the oppressive structuring of identities according to the racist notion of 'race') shores up ambivalence, conflict and doubt and renders alliance and action difficult.

We need then to attend to the disjunctions and contradictions of the different positions we occupy, as both materially structured and subjectively experienced, to disrupt the hegemony of single factor dimensions of difference. The failure to attend to class and other power relationships within white groups functioned to psychologize and essentialize racism as a quality to position all white people as equally racist. By this model, racism is portrayed as inevitable, paralysing well-intentioned white people with guilt and disenfranchising other experiences of oppression. The fact that, for example, in the late 1980s Manchester City Council, like other local authorities, dropped class from its equal opportunity policy was rightly identified by the McDonald Inquiry (1989) into the murder of an Asian boy, Ahmed Iqbal Ullah, in his school playground as symptomatic of the way the particular variety of antiracism implemented (and resisted) in the school polarized black and white children and parents.[2] Similarly, efforts of local authorities to consult with black and minority groups have often been tokenistic, treating the communities as homogeneous and, in the process of identifying 'representatives', simply confirming existing power structures (that is reproducing the marginalization of women and young people as well as radical political tendencies) within communities and the structures set up often functioning more to inform than to consult (Gibson, 1987).[3]

EXPERIENCE: USES AND LIMITS IN FEMINIST PSYCHOLOGY

I want to take up these ideas by exploring how questions of identity, authenticity and experience enter into the practice of feminist psychology. Psychology has assumed that identities are single, static and uniform. Once acquired (in the form of 'self-concept', for example) the 'self' is portrayed as an enclosed, completed entity, integrated and safely sealed off from disturbances from the 'outside' world (except when registered in quantitative terms through levels of 'self-esteem'). As post-structuralist critiques suggest (Henriques et al., 1984; Parker and Shotter, 1990; Rose, 1990; Walkerdine and Lucey, 1989) this bourgeois, masculinist representation of subjectivity is predicated on a liberal notion of the self-governing citizen. Psychology plays a critical part in the production and regulation of subjects by providing technologies of normalization and naturalization. As Phoenix and Woollett (1991) discuss in relation to the representation of mothers, difference is either effaced or it is noted only as a pathological deviation from the norm.

The drive towards homogenization is a tendency that feminist psychological interventions struggle to ward off. This can be seen first in relation to the elaboration of the arena of the 'psychology of women'. It has been a struggle to create intellectual and organizational space for women in psychology. But the danger of intervening in a structure is that the oppositional forms inadvertently reproduce aspects of the structures they seek to change. All too often, in the name of providing critique to mainstream/malestream psychology, we threaten to fall into a homogenization of our own in identifying an alternative to its exclusions. Just as postmodernism fragments feminism, femininity and even the category 'woman' itself into a set of transient configurations, so these debates that are so central to feminism also hammer home the *impossibility* of psychology, and thus necessarily the impossibility of a psychology of women. The culture-free, western, middle class heterosexist assumptions that inscribe gender norms and sex roles threaten to find new life in models of women's development (Squire, 1989). Unless conceived of as the strategic elaboration of an arena of critique *between* psychology and feminism (rather than simply as an area of psychology), the psychology of women will turn into another normative apparatus that essentializes its own activity and treats the outcome (both its existence as a topic, and the representation of women's experience it provides) in abstraction from the conditions that gave rise to it.

Equivalent issues are reflected in the organization of feminist psychologists. Although the issue is more complex than this, a similar development can be seen in the effort to contain the 'Psychology of Lesbianism Section' within the Psychology of Women Section of the British Psychological Society — although the very language, and apparatus, of 'sections' and 'divisions', speaks volumes of the supposed unity and splits of institutionalized psychology (Parker, forthcoming). An indication of how the 'divide and rule' tactic operates in psychology is the asymmetrical and entirely separate treatment of 'Living in a Multiethnic Society' and 'Psychology and Gender Issues' within the important British Psychological Society document *The Future of the Psychological Sciences* (BPS, 1988). While 'Psychology of Women' courses were, at least in rhetoric, hailed as an important area to be fostered within psychology, the 'multi-cultural issues' received much less favourable and detailed treatment — perhaps intimating that this is a much more threatening arena in which to address issues of difference. This indicates how the psychology of women can be incorporated, literally taken into the body of psychology, leaving its boundaries and functions intact.

Similarly the content of the British Women and Psychology annual conference tends to focus on issues presumed (see, for example, Carby, 1987) to be of common feminist concern to women — such as reproductive issues and motherhood. Up to now the conference has been pretty silent on discussions of racism. The lesson here for feminist psychologists is that a Section within the British Psychological Society cannot act on their feminist aspirations. Rather we need to produce/organize around another set of positions — such as that provided by the Alliance of Women in Psychology (formerly Women In Psychology, a feminist organization for mainly British women in and interested in psychological practice which is independent of the British Psychological Society, see Wilkinson and Burns, 1990. It was relaunched as WAPS in early 1993) — to express feminist psychologists' political identifications.

SPEAKING FROM EXPERIENCE

Second, problems about the role of identity and experience arise in the feminist teaching of psychology. Stemming from the political and pedagogical practice of the feminist tenet that 'the personal is political', a major strategy in feminist psychology, as in women's studies, has been to focus on personal experience, and to privilege autobiography as an instrument for teaching and for analysis. However, the aim to 'give voice' to devalued perspectives, whether within curricula or research practice, poses some dilemmas for the positions that are set out for students. Psychology of women courses typically engage students as perhaps the first (and often only) parts of their psychology degree where, owing to the denial of subjectivity within positivist rhetoric of psychology, they can own and express their personal experience and opinions (e.g. Hollway, 1989). But self-expression can turn into an injunction to self-disclose, this through structural power relationships both with tutors and within the group expressed through real or perceived relationships between classroom performance and contexts of assessment (McNeil, 1992). While some students are happy to speak of areas which had formerly been silenced, in this context the dangers of both exposure and disenfranchisement for black and lesbian students are particularly acute, where the mainly white, middle class and heterosexual lecturers themselves overdetermine the absences they/we try to acknowledge. Here, as in research contexts (as Bhavnani, 1990, notes), silence may be more empowering than speech.

On the other hand, the alternative to the sometimes patronizing magnanimity, of 'giving voice' or inviting students to 'paint her/himself thick with authenticity' (Minh-ha, 1987: 14) is to focus on how the general model has been structured according to its absences (this is the way I teach both Developmental Psychology and the Psychology of Women, e.g. Burman, 1990b, in press). Yet this focus on structural exclusions can still maintain the marginalization of black perspectives. It is therefore necessary both to problematize the essentialism of identity politics, and to recognize that assuming the voice of authenticity can function tactically as a position of critique.

My third concern with appeals to 'authenticity' in the teaching arena, as in the cultural–political sphere, is that claims to specificity and authenticity can isolate and paralyse rather than promote recognition and alliance. There are general questions here about the incipient individualization and incontestability structured within the commitment of some varieties of feminist research to prioritizing experience (see Currie and Kazi, 1987). Liz Bondi (1993) argues that what she calls the 'hyphenated feminisms' of identity politics assume that knowledge flows only from experience and hence that what one knows is indistinguishable from what one is. The important issue is that we locate experience within a *politics* of subjectivity, and that we recognize the location of that politics. Otherwise the move within current discussions (including this one) away from notions of 'identity' to that of 'subject positionings' can allow essences to creep back in the form of locations. If, as Bondi argues, notions of 'where I am' have replaced 'who I am' , then the move from abstracted integrated (male) consciousness (so rampant in psychology) to 'positions' or 'locations' demands that we attend to the creation and production of those positions rather than implicitly treat them as immanent. It is the constructed and provisional character of positions and identifications that should help us to configure and reconfigure relationships between different kinds of identities, and politics based on coalitions and alliances.

Moreover, identification may be important but it is not always necessary within a political framework. As discussions in cultural studies (Walkerdine, 1990) and feminist teaching (Moss, 1989) suggest, the mappings of identifications may be multiple and complex in ways that do not necessarily relate to simple conceptions of class, 'race' or gender positions (for example). Solidarity is more than knowing it could happen or has happened to you. While for some it may be a start, a politics cannot be driven only by spontaneous feeling. Dismantling the apparatus of difference need not produce a collapse into sameness, or a fragmentation into equal, and equally different differences. As Trinh T. Minh-ha (1987: 20) puts it: 'speaking near-by or together-with certainly differs from speaking for or about'. Further, Gayatri Chakravorty Spivak (1990b) discusses how deferring to special categories of experience can function as a reverse 'othering', as an excuse not to engage in discussion. She talks about the need to do 'homework', taking the example of the 'young white male student, politically correct who will say "I'm only a bourgeois white male, I can't speak"' to argue that this is a safe, lazy and pernicious escapism.

It is in the spirit of doing this homework that I now move away from considerations of feminist psychology, psychology of women and the exclusionary practices it is both subject to, and culpable of, to consider a particular category of political identification relevant to feminist and antiracist work, i.e. Jewish feminism.

REPRESENTATION AND RESISTANCE

Taking up both the call to interrogate the notion of whiteness (e.g. Charles, 1992) and Mercer's (1992) notion of 'different degrees of othering', I want to explore the shifting and relational identifications available for British Jewish feminists, most of whom are white.[4] My uneasy position, as a white Jew, an unease mobilized anew in the act of writing here (for a very 'mixed' — in multiple ways — audience), highlights how the category of whiteness is not monolithic. Just as the category of 'whiteness' is therefore the absent presence in relation to which blackness functions, so the Jewish question that has preoccupied political theorists of Left as well as Right persuasions is (also) a non-Jewish question (Cohen, 1984). This is not to deny my racial privilege within a white supremacist society nor to lay claim to some intermediate position within a hierarchy of oppressions but rather to indicate how positionings are fractured and multiple. Attending to such fractures and overlaps can form the *basis* for alliance. From the resistances brought about through discontinuities and fractures (or counter-discourses) within the dominant culture there may arise some hope for the 'split' subject of (late) modernity, and some basis for collective organization (Venn, 1992).

A strategy for resisting the subordinate position set up by racialization in politics as in pedagogy is to highlight what is left out, left over, what cannot be contained within that structuring. As a longstanding minority, the production of Jewish identities provides a clear example (although a similar analysis could be developed for Irish and gypsy experiences, with whom the Jewish experience of oppression is probably closest). In a long parenthesis Elizabeth Grosz (1990) points to the paradox of producing an autonomous Jewish history: it cannot be separate for it is a history of oppression, persecution and suffering effected because of the actions of others. But it also cannot be seen as *only* the catalogue of oppression since this would be to deny or omit any agency. Jewish history is therefore a counter-history, produced, but yet subversive of, what she calls Hellenic/Christian history, the narrative of western progress. She draws a parallel with the dilemma of the Third World intellectual who must both resist and assume the language of the colonizer since there is no other language in the struggle to represent the interests and positions of the colonized. She argues that 'the Judaic' provides a counter-tendency, a 'repressed but subversive tradition ... that is uneven, scattered, a series of interruptions, irruptions, outbreaks and containments — an intellectual history of skirmishes in an undeclared war' (Grosz, 1990: 78).

Grosz (1990) analyses the historical and textual construction of the Jew as a radical alterity that evades categorization. Jews are a landless people (the creation of a state of Israel has inflected but not resolved this issue in complex ways, as the discussion later in this article highlights), with a hermeneutic tradition of interpretation and revision that deconstruction explicitly draws upon in privileging textuality over identity, and unsettling the idealism, abstraction or, in deconstructive terms, 'logocentrism' of the Hellenic/Christian tradition (see also Handelman, 1983). The identification therefore is both produced by and against the dominant tradition, with the corresponding tensions of being both part of, and other from, this. There is no choice between the two positions. Rather, straddling the tensions is a resource, a position of critique 'uniquely privileged in terms of social transgression and renewal' (Grosz, 1990: 87).

The possibilities offered by the multi-perspectivity of the 'exile' are clearly fruitful for the analysis of feminists in relation to academic practices, and for the radical uncertainties of the positions of feminists in relation to psychology. The complexities of the question of self-representation for feminist psychologists are at play in our investments in newsletters, journals, conferences, etc., and in the tensions between: keeping up the pressure on orthodox psychological structures (such as BPS committees) versus becoming dependent or participating actors within them, and contributing to them (by, for example, having conferences and producing journals); versus maintaining an active presence within feminism (both academic and activist forms). The point is that, like any oppositional tendency, there is no feminist psychology tradition or history separate from that of the struggle for representation: feminist psychology therefore necessarily both must be part of, and must refuse to be part of, psychology.

In the next part of this article I take up the issue of self-chosen representations in relation to their presence and absence within Jewish feminism. I want to refer to this particular case in the spirit of producing a counter-discourse, recovering from a history of suppression some general intimations of political strategies and a specific vantage point from which to view recent debates and developments in feminist and other progressive social movements. As with feminist psychology, the contents of such positioning have been structured by, produced in relation to, particular debates and events. These events highlight the impossibility of abstracting debates in the women's movement from those within the left, and from the broader cultural-political arena. At this point I want to emphasize that I can/will not assume some representative voice for Jewish feminists nor demarcate some specific qualities of Jewish experience. I regard the discourse of 'specialness' (within Jewish experience in the form of 'the chosen') as the combined resignation and arrogance of the victim who has no choice; simply adopting and celebrating the projections of the oppressor. So while I hesitate to lay claim either to a commonality or to a specificity of Jewish experience, since this has so often been used to preclude alliances, I think there are important lessons to be learnt from the histories, struggles and questions posed by long-standing and recent discussions of Jewish, and Jewish feminist, identifications.

BETWEEN A HARD PLACE AND A ROCK

From the US context, Barbara Smith in her influential paper 'Between a Rock and a Hard Place' (1988) discusses the relationships between Jewish and black feminists as historically tense and divided but as a potential site of coalition based on mutual recognition of common oppression by virtue of racism and anti-semitism, as well as the specificity of their different and contradictory enactments. In the British context, where until recently policies of overt assimilation prevailed over the cultural pluralism of the 'melting pot', the investments in denying difference, facilitated by the ambiguities for Jews of 'passing' as white gentiles, have been particularly great. It is worth tracing the historical continuities in migration and immigration.

There has been a long-standing Sephardic (of Spanish and Portuguese origin) Jewish presence in Britain. Jews were expelled from Britain in the 13th century but, expelled from Spain along with Muslims in 1492, were allowed to settle in Britain under Cromwell. From the late 19th century, Jews succeeded Irish people both chronologically and in terms of areas of settlement and occupation (typically in the garment-making industry). These Jews were mainly Ashkenazi

Jews from Eastern Europe, seeking refuge from pogroms (massacres) and systematic racialized impoverishment. There were therefore major cultural and class differences between the groups of established Jewish communities and the new immigrants (Williams, 1985). Now, black people live in areas that were formerly primarily Jewish, and in particular Asian people are now associated with the clothing industry. It is important to emphasize that there is overlap as well as succession between these patterns of settlement and occupation.

As well as the different expressions of antisemitism and racism, with correspondingly different stereotypes, part of what divides Jewish and black people is the desire of the dominant Jewish middle class to forget their working class origins, ignoring the past and present existence of a Jewish working class. Since Jews do not get counted in the census, the only available measure is synagogue membership which not only grossly underestimates those who identify as Jewish but also provides a religious, and religiously practising, definition. This also selects on the basis of class through synagogue membership fees and, also, gender, since, as current debates within British orthodox Jewish communities indicate, women who are not members as part of a male-headed household are marginalized and are accorded little decision-making role within synagogues. In the study of Redbridge (Kosmin and Levy, 1983), a large proportion of Jews are shown to be lower middle class or working class, which suggests that Jews conform neither to antisemitic stereotypes (of all being rich) nor do they reflect the middle class establishment that claims to represent them.

As well as the enormous diversity within both Jewish and specific black experiences, there are both some continuities and asymmetries between them. While concepts of exile and migration figure prominently within contemporary cultural theory, as Jenny Bourne (1992) has argued, this still retains a sense of place, of originality, even though constituted through the act of leaving. But the place is a position in counter-discourse rather than a geographical space to recover. Its elaboration is part of the project of producing a politically progressive, transgressive cultural imaginary, not a territorial appropriation of space (cultural or otherwise). (The attempt to realize this imaginary within an actual geographical space by means of the zionist state of Israel has been a disaster for Palestinians and Jews.)

JEWISH IDENTITY: CONTRADICTIONS AND COLLUSIONS

The question of when and why it is appropriate to organize around a Jewish feminist identity is a particular variant of the more general issue of organizing as Jews or as feminists or feminist psychologists for that matter. Three historical and conceptual points are important here. First, a general critique of identity politics was first directed specifically at 'Jewish Feminism' (see Bourne, 1987). Second, debates have played a part in constituting the very forms of Jewish feminist organization they critique (in the forms of response and resistance) and therefore are part of the material structure of their topic. And third, Jewish feminists have a specific positioning in relation to the broader communities of Jews, of feminists (black and white) and of black people. As a case study in the changing forms and meanings of identities in relation to challenging racisms, I want to explore what Grosz's (1990) notion of self-chosen representations has meant in the context of Jewish feminist activity in Britain over the last decade, that is to consider the question of when and why it is, and is not, important to assume such a specific positioning.

The trajectory of Jewish feminism in Britain has been a disparate and fluctuating affair, emerging in the early 1980s with the first Jewish feminist and Jewish lesbian conferences in Britain but now (like feminist activity in general) it is more fragmented. That the conferences have not become regular events is indicative of the ways debates on the complexities and difficulties in defining identities and reformulating what we mean by political activity have entered Jewish feminism. In British Jewish feminist and socialist circles, one of the key current debates concerns what a secular Jewish identity looks like. Since 1945 at least, the mainstream expressions of Jewishness have tended to be structured either around religion or, as its substitute, zionist identifications (particularly after the Nazi genocide of Jews and immigration controls imposed by other countries). The perspective of Jewish socialist or feminist identification as arising primarily from a history of oppression is largely understood as a 'negative identity', with efforts made to assert some 'positive' aspects. There is some dismay if the cultural–political features being celebrated by Jewish feminists/socialists turn out as derivative in some respects from religion.[5] Here Grosz's (1990) analysis highlights how the 'positive' and 'negative' features cannot be absolutely separable and how they function in relation to each other.

In spite of the dangers of reification, homogenization of Jewish feminist identifications and correlative polarization from other groups (cf. Attar, 1985), I want to argue that in some contexts it both has been, and may yet be, important to assume this positioning as a political identification. Far from celebrating a history of victimization and oppression (including the oppression of Jewish women both by Jewish men and a patriarchal culture — though no more so than any other), asserting a Jewish feminist identification can be part of the wider feminist and antiracist struggles in at least two ways.

First, there is a need to create public representations to counter the effacing of secular Jewish (feminist) existence and traditions. Recently when some British Jewish feminist friends gathered in Manchester to watch a television programme about Jewish feminism, we were disappointed to find that this was defined as the attempt to reconcile Jewish religious practices with feminism (and that it was North American). Asserting the specificity and diversity of Jewish feminist cultures is part of the project of warding off the elision of religion and culture. This conflation abstracts cultural practices from their material context. It both renders multiculturalism incapable of challenging the functioning of misogynist practices within minority communities for fear of being dubbed racist, and affords the appropriation of the language of cultural difference by fundamentalists (Bard, 1991). In this context it is vital to document the existence and practice of secular cultural traditions, particularly for minority groups that historically have been identified through religion or who, as a product of racism and then as an expression of anti-imperialism, have increasingly come to merge national and religious identifications.

Second, it is necessary to highlight the historical continuities between Jewish and black experience in Britain in ways that develop solidarity between minority communities, and elaborate a basis for collective organization. The first immigration controls passed in Britain in 1905 were directed to the regulation and exclusion of Jews coming from Eastern Europe. Steve Cohen (1984, 1987, 1988) argues that the structural antisemitism that brought about Britain's first immigration legislation has contributed to the seeming naturalness, reasonableness and hence inevitability of immigration control that laid the basis for restrictions on the immigration of black peoples today. The history of immigration control in Britain thus both reflects and weaves together antisemitism and racism. Recalling this is to demonstrate the total fiction of any claims Britain has to honourable treatment of refugees (Cohen, 1988) and to highlight, with some exceptions, a long history of the reformist Left and working class movements' collaboration with the political Right in calling for and enacting immigration controls. To identify the common threads of Jewish, black and Asian experiences in relation to structural racism and antisemitism is also to document a tradition of struggle and resistance against immigration control, in the early 20th century in the form of Jewish working class struggle, and currently in the form of black and Asian self-organization.

The response of the Anglo-Jewish establishment to the introduction of immigration controls provides a case history of negotiation and collusion that other minorities can learn from. The story of immigration is also one of class divisions within communities as well as racialized and class divisions between them (Cohen, 1984), although of course for some Jews and black people social class is more important than their Jewishness or blackness. The obstacles to joint Jewish and black organization are heir to the history of Jewish communal leadership disowning and disenfranchising the Jewish working class and allying with the British state to pressurize Jews into anglicization and assimilation. One factor was the suppression of Yiddish as a 'foreign' language because of its association with political mobilization of the Jewish proletariat in Jewish-owned factories (and Jewish workers were very active in the early strikes against sweatshop conditions). Another was the mistaken assumption exhibited by the Anglo-Jewish establishment from the 1880s onwards that assimilation would protect against antisemitism. This perhaps reached its most overt form in the 'Helpful Information and Guidance for Every Refugee' issued in 1938 by the 'German Jewish Aid Committee in conjunction with the Jewish Board of Deputies', which (although Britain was imposing stringent immigration controls against them and) while lauding Britain's hospitality to Jews insisted on prescriptions for behaviour considered to guarantee tolerance. These included: only talking English, not talking loudly, not being conspicuous in dress or custom, not being critical of government or British customs and not joining any political organization or participating in any political activity (see Cohen, 1984: 74).

This approach does much to explain (but not excuse) the reluctance of Jews to make explicit alliances with other oppressed groups, since Jews were taught that asserting difference or being politically active is tantamount to inciting anti-semitism. As a sad reflection of this, in Manchester where I live the supposedly representative body of the Jewish community refused to participate in the City Council 'race subcommittee' because it claimed that Jews were not an 'ethnic minority'. It is this history that feeds into the silencing of public expressions of criticism of the actions of the Israeli state towards Palestinians, and (combined with anti-Muslim racism) makes it difficult to persuade Jews to adopt the voice of the refugee/survivor to argue for British interventions in support of Bosnia. An important project for Jewish feminists and socialists has been, therefore, to document the radical Jewish traditions (often typified by Yiddish and the Jewish Workers Bund) and thereby to present analyses of why and how these have been suppressed (e.g. Gilbert, 1982). Reclaiming this history is a vital tool to mobilize the Jewish community to organize with other oppressed groups. In terms of specifically feminist work, this has, for example, demonstrated how norms of British femininity (and masculinity for that matter) in relation to work as well as family commitments came far from naturally to Jewish immigrants from Eastern Europe (e.g. Burman, 1982; Jewish Women In London Group, 1989). Notwithstanding moral panics over intermarriage rates and falling synagogue attendance, the assimilationist tendencies within British Jewish community leadership have contributed to the dismay and bewilderment of the mainstream at being outstripped by Jewish fundamentalist movements who have found a particular constituency in young people. In this context then the assertion of Jewish feminist and socialist identifications functions both as a critical movement in relation to mainstream Jewish communities and as a counter to the homogenization of feminism (treating all varieties of women's experiences as if they were diverse tokens of an essentially unitary female experience).

PRESENT ABSENCES: JEWISH FEMINISM IN BRITAIN

So far I have been talking in general terms about Jewish history in Britain rather than specifically about Jewish feminists. But, indicating another parallel between Jewish and black feminists, this lack of gender specificity highlights the common struggle of Jewish women with Jewish men against antisemitism, as well as that of Jewish women in relation to patriarchal structures within Jewish culture and practices.[6]

If it seems rather strange to be going into this level of detail in this forum, then I should point out that it is a matter of some irony that these discussions have not achieved their circulation within a specifically Jewish feminist forum, an irony that I am going to treat with some 'serious play' in Haraway's (1989) sense, by focusing on the non-appearance of a key self-chosen representation of Jewish feminist presence in Britain, a British Jewish Feminist Anthology with which I was involved. It should be noted that there is still no British Jewish Feminist Anthology. (My argument that the non-appearance of the British Jewish Feminist Anthology is significant is lent weight by the fact there is also a British Jewish Lesbian Anthology that has never appeared.) As an enterprise conceived and commissioned as early as 1981 to document Jewish feminist presence in Britain and to analyse the differences between British and US Jewish feminists, this has clearly failed: it does not exist. There was no shortage of material: there are man-uscripts which date back to the early 1980s. As the very *absence* of this sign of Jewish feminist presence suggests, the picture of Jewish feminism that emerges is far from a coherent and linear elaboration of a fully formed, integrated identity but rather the interruptions, the disruptions and the diversions from this project of self-representation reveal the constitutive forces structuring British Jewish femi-nist identifications over the last decade. It is important to stress that this analysis is very much concerned with the British context in which Jewish feminist identifica-tion takes place. In the US the philosophy (if not the practice) of the melting pot has permitted Jewish experience much more public and confident exhibition, with a corresponding proliferation of Jewish feminist publications such as *Nice Jewish Girls* (Torton Beck, 1982), *The Tribe of Dina* (Kaye/Kantrowitz, 1984), *Speaking for Ourselves* (Zahava, 1990), *On Being a Jewish Feminist* (Heschel, 1989), *Dreams of an Insomniac* (Klepfisz, 1990) and *The Issue is Power* (Kaye/ Kantrowitz, 1992), as well as a Jewish feminist magazine *Lilith*.

The first disruption was associated with the Israeli invasion of Lebanon in response to which Jewish feminists and socialists organized to break the overt Jewish consensus on Israel, both by their actions within the left and by opening up debate within the Jewish community. But the emergence of antisemitism in the form of antizionism focused around the suppression of debate over an article in the then high-circulation British feminist magazine *Spare Rib*. Ruth Wallsgrove, a former member of the *Spare Rib* collective, recently reflected on how the oppression of Palestinians and the massacres of Sabra and Shatilla (with which the Israeli army colluded) became symptomatic of a whole range of anti-imperialist struggles:

> Somehow, women who were angry about Ireland and Latin America, Black women, an Iranian woman who hated America for what it had done in Iran, and a hard-Labour Left Jewish woman came together on the collective to agree, or at least feel unable to disagree, that Israel was intrinsically evil, and that no women could have a voice as Jewish without first denouncing Zionism (Wallsgrove, 1993: 6).

This meant that Jewish feminist identifications were increasingly being premised on a kind of antizionist credentialism that only recognized Jewish feminists on the condition that they also claimed to be antizionist. Whatever the (very) diverse views of Jewish feminists on this matter, the denial of the legitimacy of Jewish feminism outside of a position on Israel paradoxically colluded in the antisemitic equation of Jews and the Israeli state. I say 'paradoxically', for it is in the context of double-bind demands on Jewish feminists that we/they should continually speak about Israel when we/they were trying to speak of other things that have angered and silenced us. Making Jewish feminist identity conditional upon claims to antizionism conflated Jewish and zionist identifications and thereby presupposed precisely those features that Jewish feminists were trying to tease apart in developing secular non/antizionist positions.

Denied a voice within the women's movement through the suppression of over 40 letters of protest to *Spare Rib*, Jewish feminists set up their own magazine, *Shifra* (it ran for four issues). In its short life the response to *Shifra* was both rapturous and hypercritical (of the latter readers complained of too much — literature, politics, poetry, history, etc.) — perhaps indicating the overwhelming and impossible burden of representation the magazine carried for British Jewish feminists and Jewish women at that time. Similar investments no doubt attended the enterprise of a British Jewish Feminist Anthology.

When in 1987 Jenny Bourne's general critique of identity politics was cast specifically in terms of an attack on the notion of Jewish feminist identity, Jewish feminist energies then went into developing a set of critical responses in *A Word in Edgeways* (JF publications, 1988). The resurgence of this discussion in *Spare Rib* before the magazine's demise in 1993 suggests that the tensions in this area were far from resolved (Bard, 1992). My point is that the need to react and respond to political developments (whether within the women's movement(s) or in relation to the international scene) has absorbed the energies of the women who would otherwise have produced the Jewish Feminist Anthology or at least this is at least part of the story — there were of course political differences within and between the various cohorts of women involved in editing the anthology. Whether or not this would have enriched or hampered the production process is now only a matter of speculation. All this highlights the relational basis of identifications, in this case Jewish feminist identifications.

My contribution to the missing anthology (on a topic that the then editors specifically asked me to address) was precisely on the problems of 'identity politics', taking seriously the critique provided by Bourne (1987) (having elsewhere countered the way it singled out Jewish feminism, e.g. Burman, 1988a). I regarded (and still regard) Jewish feminism as a political identification rather than some absolute or stable personal attribute. I argued that the dangers of identity politics are that they threaten to decouple introspection from action; to level out oppressions (including those between women); that they fragment women into a potentially infinite regress of 'different' positions, making it difficult to elaborate a basis for common organization, and ushering in the solipsism of dissipated but nevertheless still highly individualized (what some would perhaps call 'postmodern') subjectivity. The difficulties of basing an identity on negative solidarity with a history of oppression, as opposed to some positive affirmation of intrinsic worth, turns out to be something of a false opposition when considered as linked by a history of struggle and resistance. Thus Jewish feminist identity, insofar as it exists, may be a necessary fiction in the maintenance of a collectivity that unites not only Jewish women but provides a basis for broader organization.[7] In this it is therefore shifting and strategic: its fluctuations are therefore indicative of temporary alliances between what are diverse and otherwise divided groups (Burman, 1988b).

Applying this analysis to the more contemporary scene, the silence of Jewish feminists as a collectivity testifies to a number of important strands and developments affecting forms of feminist activity, and politics generally. First, the absorption within specific struggles has meant that there was no time to write our history; second, there has been both a movement away from identity politics as defining monolithic identities for minorities, and the increasing polarization between lesbian and heterosexual feminists has been reflected in Jewish feminism too. Third, like other political strands, Jewish feminism has been subject to the privatization of politics — into lifestyle, and for some women motherhood, taken up by second wave feminists in their late thirties and early forties, has brought further political issues to the fore. Fourth, the reflection of the demise of the grand (feminist, marxist) narratives within the sphere of Jewish cultural–political activity can be seen in the development of specific projects with a variety of forms of organization and activity which include exhibitions and oral history projects (e.g. Jewish Women in London Group, 1989) and a move towards organization on the basis of single-issue campaigns, such as Jews Against the Clause (organizing against anti-gay and lesbian legislation). Along with this is the emergence of more alliance-oriented forms of organization, such as Women in Black, which draws together black, Asian, Jewish, Palestinian and other Arab as well as white women worldwide in opposing the Israeli oppression of Palestinians, and is now also organizing against the oppression of Muslims in former Yugoslavia. The emergence of Women Against Fundamentalism in 1990 is a similar expression of this general trend.

What is 'Jewish feminism' then? Does it exist? Does this matter? The short answer appears to be, sometimes it has existed, sometimes it does exist and right now maybe it does not and perhaps this does not matter. This is not to say that there are not British Jewish feminist or lesbian groups, which there are. The key difference from the 1980s appears to be that currently there are no sustained attempts at national organizations or presumption of public forms of expression, except in relation to particular arenas of intervention. (The last Jewish feminist conference was in 1987, and the Jewish Feminist Newsletter — which was London-based — is no longer being produced.) Currently, it feels as though reviving the project of a British Jewish Feminist Anthology would be to attempt to heave together too many disparate tendencies. Unless presented as a historical retrospective its content would now need to be dramatically revised. But its absence still testifies to the history that precluded its appearance. Now it seems that the homogenization that follows from ascribing to, or being categorized as, a particular cultural identification may be tenable for limited goals (such as countering racism or antisemitism or mobilizing with others) but is otherwise unworkable. Treating identities as essences naturalizes and thereby exoticises difference and draws attention away from the structural relationships that give rise to those positions (see also Sivanandan, 1989). Attending to those relationships, and their changing forms, may empty identification of its content but this may, at base, be unimportant compared with the psychic and physical violence committed in the name of affirming 'specialness' (Minh-ha, 1987).

HAVENS AND HOMELANDS

Questions of identity have an urgent political character outside the academy. Alongside postmodernist celebrations of the fragmentation of subjectivity, are laments of the dissipation of political agency that must presume some (albeit partial) integration, and some basis for collective organization. It is a bitter irony — but no coincidence — that just as academics hail the end of the grand narratives and, in psychology, the demise of the rational unitary subject, we are witnessing a resurgence of national and religious identities. In Britain the multiculturalist discourse of respect for cultural difference has elided religion with culture, and abstracted both from the lived experience of black and minority groups in such a way that it could be appropriated by the new Right to mean that cultural difference and cultural autonomy necessarily involve cultural conflict. This analysis is used to fuel the call for repatriation of minorities, thereby also constructing all black and minority-identified groups as 'non-indigenous migrants' (Seidel, 1986a).

The emergence of fundamentalism as a vital political tendency may testify to the effort to construct a sense of certainty and security in an uncertain and insecure world (Sahgal and Yuval-Davis, 1992) but 'ethnic cleansing' in Bosnia and communal violence in India, for example, originate in the deliberate manufacture of religious and national identities as the central organizers and divisors of individual subjectivity and collective alliance by expansionist and self-seeking politicians and parties. Just as the wearing of the yellow star worked as a sign not only to demarcate difference but also to terrorize many non-Jews into abandoning Jews to the Nazi genocide, so in India non-Muslim protesters and protectors against attacks on Muslims were subject to the same violence (Vanaik, 1992). The very notion of unity or alliance is also what is under attack. In former Yugoslavia the (literal as well as psychological) territory at the core of the struggle is precisely in Bosnia where integration between Muslims, Croats and Serbs was greatest (while the asymmetry between the religious and cultural–national categories employed in this conflict is by a self-fulfilling prophesy fast collapsing) (Borden, 1993; Magaš, 1992). That this is a feminist issue as well as an issue for all concerned with progressive politics is clear in that the battles over national and cultural identities are waged with and through women's bodies, both symbolically and literally in the raping of women to inscribe racial identifications (e.g. Grech, 1993; Patel, 1993; Women's Aid to Former Yugoslavia, 1992, 1993).

At the same time as a new European identity is being forged, with movements towards common currency and trade, Europe is tightening up its immigration controls. The production of European identity is explicitly based on practices of exclusion: the workings of the 'free market' of goods and labour within the EC presupposes its global regulation (Friedman, 1993), such that asylum seekers as 'political' let alone 'economic' refugees (a false opposition if ever there was one — considering the economic crippling of the South by the North) will be stonewalled by Fortress Europe instead of negotiating the multiple and variable policies of individual European countries.

Recently, on a single day (31 May 1993), the newspapers carried reports of three related events that highlight the intersections between the politics and identities of 'race', ethnicity and gender. Three days after the German parliament voted to tighten Germany's asylum laws, neo-Nazis burnt the home of a Turkish family in a German village, Solingen, killing two women and three girls, and leaving three other children seriously ill. This event coincided in Britain with reports of the Tory MP Winston Churchill's — grandson of the wartime leader — speech to the Bolton (a small town in the North of England in an area where there is an organized fascist presence) Conservative Club calling for a 'halt' to the 'relentless flow of immigrants ... and urgently — if the British way of life is to be preserved':

> Mr Major promises us that 50 years from now, spinsters will still be cycling to Communion on Sunday mornings — more like the muezzin will be calling Allah's faithful to the High Street mosque (Churchill, quoted in the *Guardian*, 31 April 1993).

The response of the British liberal left newspapers was to juxtapose Churchill's claims with the 'facts' about immigration and black presence in Britain. But the implication that correcting the numbers will undo the damage ignores the effects of the reproduction of anti-black and anti-Muslim sentiments. In some ways it is a concession to the racists to attempt to counter their outpourings with facts and numbers but it is a sad reflection of the currency of racist ideas that this is deemed necessary (as is also the case with holocaust denial myths, see Seidel, 1986b). It is not insignificant that the image of threat to 'the British way of life' is cast within the familiar guise of the need to protect English (Christian) femininity, now from a Muslim threat. The same newspaper carried the front page story of EC ministers deciding on a new European-wide immigration policy, employing an ethnocentric definition of 'family' to rationalize racist, immigration policy — a narrow definition including only 'husband' and 'wife' with their children up to 18 years. This resurgence of racist attacks, immigration controls and definitions of femininity indicates how the patriarchal and xenophobic themes of imperialism live on in Europe, and specifically the UK, beyond Enoch Powell's racist rantings of the late 1960s and Margaret Thatcher's 'swamping' speech of the late 1970s.

I grew up surrounded by elderly relatives and their friends who regularly reiterated — it was almost a liturgical chant — how grateful they were to be here, how Britain was a wonderful place, qualifying it in the very next breath with 'and here you would know, you'd have some warning before anything happened'.

I am not grateful. And now I know that even they had nothing to be grateful for. And that the injunction to be grateful is an inadequate and silencing response to the increasingly urgent need to be very vocal. The question of shifting identities in challenging racisms is not about discovering who we are but about what we do (cf. Spivak, 1990a, 1990b). Agonizing over identifications does not necessarily help us to become or do something else. The issue is one of the necessity for a vision of the future, 'historicising the imaginary identifications that enable democratic agency' (Mercer, 1992: 22).

In this article I have thrown some of the presuppositions of identity politics into question by highlighting the relational basis of identifications. Nevertheless, it is sometimes tactically important, and quite consistent with this analysis to support mobilization around identities. I have considered in some detail the example of Jewish feminist identifications and (self) representations as not only an issue of personal significance for me but as a particular expression of a general set of problems about political categories, experience and activity. As the discussion in the early part of this article indicates, there are continuities between the global political context and more parochial questions of how and what we teach and do in psychology. If collectively constructed cultural imaginaries and illusory identifications help us to mobilize collectively, to acknowledge rather than suppress differences, to forge alliances between, as well as within, categories of identification, then they are part of a dynamic that makes psychology a vital part of politics.

NOTES

Thanks to Julia Bard, Janet Batsleer, Liz Bondi, Leah Burman, Rickie Burman, Ian Parker and Heather Walton for their comments, to the reviewers of this article for their close reading and suggestions, and to Ann Phoenix and Kum-Kum Bhavnani for their encouragement in writing this piece, and their patience with my delays.

This piece is dedicated to Catherine and Amanda, and, for different and similar reasons, to Kathleen.

1. I am using the term 'black' within a British context to refer to groups subject to racism on the basis of skin colour (unlike the position of most British Jews and Irish

people who suffer oppression on a different basis). I use this term therefore to refer only to a political (not a national, cultural or religious) collectivity. I therefore do not mean to imply that black (or any other) communities are internally homogeneous. Where it is relevant for my argument to distinguish aspects of the different histories of different black groups in Britain as they connect in different ways with Jewish experiences, I move to use the formulation 'black and Asian', where the former then refers to people of Afro-Caribbean background. The difficulties of terminology themselves betray shifting histories and debates about 'race' and identity that it is beyond the scope of this article to elaborate further.

2. Contrary to the media reports at the time, the antiracist policy was primarily the displaced forum in which management problems within the school were played out. The issue here is *why* it could be played out through this.

3. The very process of 'ethnic monitoring' produces a catalogue of supposed identifications, with 'white' generally portrayed as either homogeneous or fractured by the category of 'other' — a nice example within foucauldian terms of how administrative technologies construct the categories they then proceed to regulate.

4. That this is so reflects both a common and separate history of exclusion and persecution of Arabic and black Jews with that of non-Jewish black people.

5. Although two issues should be noted. First, there is a revival of interest in egalitarian and pro-gay and lesbian forms of Jewish religious practice, particularly in London and Birmingham where new communities have been set up. Second and, on the other hand, there is also increasing recognition from the mainstream Jewish communities of secular, humanistic Jewish traditions (such as the ideas of Martin Buber and Isaac Deutscher), although these are also thinly disguised attempts to tempt the secularists back into the religion.

6. An indication of this was that it was Jewish women who called for and organized the publication of an analysis of antisemitism on the left written by a man, Cohen (1984) to counter the permeation of antisemitism from the left into the women's movement.

7. Of course within a lacanian psychoanalytic framework all moments of identification, including and especially self-identification, are *mis*recognitions.

REFERENCES

Amos, V. and Parmar, P. (1984) 'Challenging Imperial Feminism', *Feminist Review* 17: 3–19.

Attar, D. (1985) 'Why I Am Not a Jewish Feminist', *Shifra* 2: 8–10.

Bard, J. (1991) 'Backwards to Basics', *Women Against Fundamentalism Journal* 2: 10–11.

Bard, J. (1992) '*Spare Rib*: Magazine Defends Exclusion Policy', *Jewish Socialist* 27: 3–4.

Barrett, M. (1987) 'The Concept of Difference', *Feminist Review* 26: 29–41.

Bhavnani, K.-K. (1990) 'What's Power Got To Do With It? Empowerment and Social Research', in I. Parker and J. Shotter (eds) *Deconstructing Social Psychology*. London: Routledge.

Bondi, L. (1993) 'Locating Identity Politics', in M. Kett and S. Pile (eds) *Place and the Politics of Identity*. London: Routledge.

Borden, A. (1993) 'The Bosnians: A War on Identity', *Balkan War Report, Bulletin of the Institute for War and Peace Reporting, April/May*, 19, special briefing paper supplement, 1–8.

Bourne, J. (1987) 'Homelands of the Mind: Jewish Feminism and Identity Politics', *Race and Class* 29 (2): 1–23.

Bourne, J. (1992) 'Re-locations –– from Bradford to Brighton', *New Formations* 17: 86–94.

British Psychological Society (1988) 'The Future of the Psychological Sciences', report of the Scientific Affairs Board from the Harrogate Conference. Leicester: British Psychological Society.

Burman, E. (1988a) 'Identity: Paradoxes and Dilemmas', contribution to *Jewish Feminist Anthology*, unpublished.

Burman, E. (1988b) 'The Politics of Identity Politics', in JF Publications (ed.) *A Word In Edgeways: Jewish Feminists Respond*. London: JF Publications.

Burman, E. (1990a) 'Differing with Deconstruction: A Feminist Critique', in I. Parker and J. Shotter (eds) *Deconstructing Social Psychology*. London: Routledge.

Burman, E. ed. (1990b) *Feminists and Psychological Practice*. London: Sage.

Burman, E. (in press) *Deconstructing Developmental Psychology*. London: Routledge.

Burman, R. (1982) 'The Jewish Woman as Breadwinner', *Oral History* 10 (2): 27–39.

Carby, H. (1987) 'Black Feminism and the Boundaries of Sisterhood', in M. Arnot and G. Weiner (eds) *Gender and the Politics of Schooling*. London: Hutchinson.

charles, H. (1992) 'Whiteness — the Relevance of Politically Colouring the "Non"', in H. Hinds, A. Phoenix and J. Stacey (eds) *Working Out: New Directions for Women's Studies*. Basingstoke: Falmer Press.

Cohen, S. (1984) *That's Funny You Don't Look Antisemitic: An Antiracist Analysis of Left Antisemitism.* Leeds: Beyond the Pale.

Cohen, S. (1987) *It's the Same Old Story.* Manchester: Manchester City Council.

Cohen, S. (1988) *From the Jews to the Tamils: Britain's Mistreatment of Refugees.* Manchester: Manchester Law Centre.

Currie, D. and Kazi, H. (1987) 'Academic Feminism and the Process of De-radicalization', *Feminist Review* 25: 77–98.

Ferguson, K. (1991) 'Interpretation and Genealogy in Feminism', *Signs: Journal of Women in Culture and Society* 16 (2): 322–39.

Friedman, H. (1993) 'The Political Economy of Food: A Global Crisis', *New Left Review* 197: 29–57.

Gibson, D. (1987) 'Hearing and Listening: A Case Study of the "Consultation" Processes Undertaken by a Local Education Department and Black Groups', in B. Troyna (ed.) *Racial Inequality in Education*. London: Tavistock.

Gilbert, C. (1982) *The Jewish Workers' Bund*. London: Jewish Socialist Publications.

Grech, J. (1993) 'Resisting War Rape in Bangladesh', *Trouble and Strife* 26: 17–21.

Grosz, E. (1990) 'Judaism and Exile: the Ethnics of Otherness', *New Formations* 12: 77–88.

Handelman, S. (1983) 'Jacques Derrida and the Heretical Hermeneutic', in M. Krupnick (ed.) *Displacement, Derrida and After*. Madison: University of Wisconsin Press.

Haraway, D. (1989) 'A Manifesto for Cyborgs: Science, Technology and Socialist Feminism in the 1980s', in *Simians, Cyborgs and Women*. London: Verso.

Henriques, J., Hollway, W., Venn, C., Urwin, C. and Walkerdine, V. (1984) *Changing the Subject: Psychology, Social Regulation and Subjectivity*. London: Methuen.

Heschel, S. (1989) *On Being a Jewish Feminist*. New York: Shocken Press.

Hollway, W. (1989) *Subjectivity and Method in Psychology*. London: Sage.

Jackson, S. (1992) 'The Amazing Deconstructing Woman', *Trouble and Strife* 25: 25–31.

Jewish Women in London Group (1989) *Generations of Memories: Voices of Jewish Women*. London: Women's Press.

JF Publications ed. (1988) *A Word in Edgeways*. London: JF Publications.

Kaye/Kantrowitz, M. (1984) *The Tribe of Dina: a Jewish Women's Anthology*. Beacon Press: Boston.

Kaye/Kantrowitz, M. (1992) *The Issue is Power: Essays on Women, Jews and Violence*. San Francisco: Aunt Lut.

Klepfisz, I. (1990) *A Few Words In the Mothertongue*. Portland, OR: Eighth Mountain Press.

Klepfisz, I. (1990) *Dreams of an Insomniac: Jewish Feminist Essays, Speeches and Diatribes*. Portland, OR: Eighth Mountain Press.

Kosmin, B. and Levy, C. (1983) *Jewish Identity in an Anglo-Jewish Community*. London: Board of Deputies of British Jews.

Magaš, B. (1992) 'The Destruction of Bosnia-Herzegovina', *New Left Review* 196: 102–13.

Marcus, L. (1987) '"Enough About You, Let's Talk About Me", Recent Autobiographical Writing', *New Formations* 11 (1): 77–94.

McDonald, I. (1989) *Murder in the Playground: the Report of the McDonald Inquiry into Racism and Racial Violence in Schools*. Manchester: Longsight Press.

McNeil, M. (1992) 'Pedagogical Praxis and Problems: Reflections of Teaching About Gender Relations', in H. Hinds, A. Phoenix and J. Stacey (eds) *Working Out: New Directions for Women's Studies*. Basingstoke: Falmer Press.

Mercer, K. (1992) 'Skin Head Sex Thing: Racial Difference and the Homoerotic Imaginary', *New Formations* 16: 1–25.

Minh-ha, T. T. (1987) 'Difference: "a Special Third World Women Issue"', *Feminist Review* 25: 5–22.

Mitchell, J. (1984) 'Femininity, Narrative and Psychoanalysis', in *Women: The Longest Revolution: Essays in Feminism, Literature and Psychoanalysis*. London: Virago.

Moss, G. (1989) *Un/Popular Fictions*. London: Virago.

Parker, I. (forthcoming) 'The Unconscious State of Social Psychology', in T. Ibañez and L. Iniguez (eds) *Critical Social Psychology*. London: Sage.

Parker, I. and Shotter, J. eds (1990) *Deconstructing Social Psychology*. London: Routledge.

Patel, V. (1993) 'Gender Implications of Communalisation of Socio-political Life in India', presented at the Round-table on Communalism and Women organized by the Association of Asian Studies, 25–28 March, Los Angeles.

Phoenix, A. and Woollett, A. (1991) 'Motherhood: Social Construction, Politics and Psychology', in A. Phoenix, A. Woollett and E. Lloyd (eds) *Motherhood: Meanings, Practices and Ideologies*. London: Sage.

Rich, A. (1983) 'Compulsory Heterosexuality and Lesbian Existence', in A. Snitow, C. Stansell and S. Thompson (eds) *Desire: the Politics of Sexuality*. London: Virago.

Riley, D. (1988) *Am I that Name? Feminism and the Category of Woman in History*. London: Macmillan.

Rose, N. (1990) *Governing the Soul*. London: Routledge.

Sahgal, G. and Yuval-Davis, N. (1992) 'Introduction: Fundamentalism, Multiculturalism and Women in Britain', in G. Sahgal and N. Yuval-Davis (eds) *Refusing Holy Orders: Women and Fundamentalism in Britain*. London: Virago.

Sayers, J. (1986) *Sexual Contradictions: Psychology, Psychoanalysis and Feminism*. London: Tavistock.

Seidel, G. (1986a) 'Race, Culture and Nation in the New Right', in R. Levitas (ed.) *The Ideology of the New Right*. Oxford: Blackwell.

Seidel, G. (1986b) 'The Holocaust: the Facts', in *Holocaust Denial: Antisemitism, Racism and the New Right*, Ch. 2. Leeds: Beyond the Pale.

Sivanandan, A. (1985) 'RAT and the Degradation of Black Struggle', *Race and Class* 26: 1–33.

Sivanandan, A. (1989) 'All That Melts into Aid is Solid: the Hokum of New Times', *Race and Class* 31 (3): 1–30.

Smith, B. (1988) 'Between a Rock and a Hard Place: Relationships between Black and Jewish Women', in E. Bulkin, M. Bruce Pratt and B. Smith (eds) *Yours in Struggle: Three Feminist Perspectives on Antisemitism and Racism*. Ithaca, NY: Firebrand Books.

Spivak, G. C. (1990a) 'Questions of Multi-culturalism', in S. Harasym (ed.) *The Post-colonial Critic*. London: Routledge.

Spivak, G. C. (1990b) 'Practical Politics at the Open End', in S. Harasym (ed.) *The Post-colonial Critic*. London: Routledge.

Squire, C. (1989) *Significant Differences: Feminism in Psychology*. London: Routledge.

Torton Beck, E. (ed.) (1982) *Nice Jewish Girls: A Lesbian Anthology*. Massachussetts: Persephone Press.

Vanaik, A. (1992) 'Reflections on Communalism and Nationalism in India', *New Left Review* 196: 43–65.

Venn, C. (1992) 'Subjectivity, Ideology and Difference', *New Formations* 16: 40–61.

Walkerdine, V. (1990) 'Video Replay', in *Schoolgirl Fictions*. London: Verso.

Walkerdine, V. and Lucey, H. (1989) *Democracy in the Kitchen: Regulating Mothers and Socialising Daughters*. London: Virago.

Wallsgrove, R. (1993) 'Sweet and Sour: the Demise of *Spare Rib*', *Trouble and Strife* 26: 4–6.

Ware, V. (1992) *Beyond the Pale: White Women, Racism and History*. London: Verso.

Wilkinson, S. and Burns, J. (1990) 'Women Organising Within Psychology: Two Accounts', in E. Burman (ed.) *Feminists and Psychological Practice*. London: Sage.

Williams, B. (1985) *The Making of Manchester Jewry, 1740–1875*. Manchester: Manchester University Press.

Women's Aid to Former Yugoslavia (1992) Press release, Manchester, December.

Women's Aid to Former Yugoslavia (1993) 'Behind the Lines', *Trouble and Strife* 26: 31–3.

Zahava, I. (1990) *Speaking for Ourselves*. California: Crossing Press.

Erica BURMAN is a Senior Lecturer in Developmental and Educational Psychology at the Discourse Unit, Centre for Qualitative and Theoretical Research on the Reproduction and Transformation of Language and Subjectivity, the Manchester Metropolitan University. Her publications include *Feminists and Psychological Practice* (edited, 1990, Sage), *Discourse Analytic*

Research (co-edited with Ian Parker, 1993, Routledge) and *Deconstructing Developmental Psychology* (1994, Routledge). She is politically active in feminist and Jewish antiracist organizations in Britain. ADDRESS: Discourse Unit, Department of Psychology and Speech Pathology, the Manchester Metropolitan University, Hathersage Rd, Manchester, M13 0JA, UK. Tel: 061 247 2557. Fax: 061 224 0893.

Nira YUVAL-DAVIS

Women, Ethnicity and Empowerment

This article critically examines the ideology of empowerment and its links to debates about solidarity and difference among women, especially those from oppressed and minority collectivities. The notions of community, identity, culture and ethnicity are examined together with issues of women's citizenship and coalition politics. The article argues against simplistic notions of empowerment based on identity politics which homogenize and naturalize social categories and groupings and which deny shifting boundaries as well as internal power differences and conflicts of interest. As an alternative, the article suggests the idea of 'transversal politics' based on situational dialogues.

'Empowerment' has been a central item, at least since the late 1960s, on the political agenda of all grass roots resistance movements, whether they have called for black power, raising women's consciousness or for a more general 'return' to 'the community' (see e.g. Gorz, 1982; Wainwright, 1985; Cain and Yuval-Davis, 1990). One of the major issues the anti-racist and feminist movements have been struggling with has been the effects of that self-negation which powerlessness carries with it. These effects and, hence, the solutions called for, often have psychological implications. For example, Franz Fanon (1952) called on the 'Black man' to 'regain his manhood'; and the feminist movement has called on women to reclaim their 'womanhood' (or 'humanhood' — depending on their specific ideology). These calls are a result of the view that the internalization by the powerless of the hegemonic value system according to which they are invisible, valueless and/or 'dangerous' is a major obstacle to their ability to resist their discrimination and disadvantage. Of particular influence in this trend of thought has been the work of Paulo Freire (1972) which intimately links knowledge and power.

Jill M. Bystydzienski (1992: 3) claims:

> Empowerment is taken to mean a process by which oppressed persons gain some control over their lives by taking part with others in development of activities and structures that allow people increased involvement in matters

Feminism & Psychology © 1994 SAGE (London, Thousand Oaks and New Delhi), Vol. 4(1): 179–197.

which affect them directly. In its course people become enabled to govern themselves effectively. This process involves the use of power, but not 'power over' others or power as dominance as is traditionally the case; rather, power is seen as 'power to' or power as competence which is generated and shared by the disenfranchised as they begin to shape the content and structure of their daily existence and so participate in a movement for social change.

Bystydzienski and other feminists who have written about empowerment (e.g. Bookman and Morgen, 1988; Macy, 1983; Hartsock, 1981; Kitzinger, 1991) see empowerment as a process which breaks the boundaries between the public and the private domain, that comes out of the personal into the social and which connects the sense of the personal and the communal. Empowerment can be felt momentarily or can be transformative when it is linked to a permanent shift in the distribution of social power. Great emphasis is put on autonomous grass roots activity:

> Offering subordinate groups new knowledge about their own experiences can be empowering. But revealing new ways of knowing that allow subordinate groups to define their own reality has far greater implications (Hill Collins, 1990: 222).

The ideology of empowerment, however, is not without its pitfalls, as has become clearer the more successful collective empowerment resistance movements have become. The aim of this article is to evaluate critically the ideology of empowerment and its links to debates about solidarity and difference among women, especially those from oppressed and minority collectivities. In doing so it explores themes which have relevance for feminism and psychology as well as for politics and sociology. The notions of community, identity, culture and ethnicity are examined as well as questions about women's citizenship and coalition politics.

'EMPOWERMENT' AND THE IDEOLOGY OF 'THE COMMUNITY'

The work of Freire and those who followed him links the notion of empowerment closely to the notion of 'the community'. Its progressive political connotations of 'power of' rather than 'power over' firmly situates the individual inside a more or less egalitarian and homogeneous grouping which is 'the community', the members of which share in the process of empowerment and collectively manage to fight their oppression and become the controllers of their own destiny.

The ideology of 'the community' has become popular in wide circles of the Left since, in recent years, in the western world in general, and in Britain in particular, representations based on political parties and trade union memberships have come to be seen as less and less satisfactory, reflecting imbalances of power and access which exist within the civil society itself as well as in the

state. Women and ethnic minorities have been the primal foci of attempts to create new selection mechanisms which will be more 'just' in their representative
and distributive power. The notion of autonomous 'community organizations' as
the basis of an alternative mechanism of representation to the more traditional
ones has been promoted for that purpose (Gorz, 1982).

As has been elaborated elsewhere (Young, 1990; Yuval-Davis, 1991; Anthias
and Yuval-Davis, 1992: Ch. 6), certain analytical (as well as political) problems
arise with these formulations. The notion of 'the community' assumes an
organic wholeness. The community is perceived as a 'natural' social unit. It is
'out there' and one can either belong to it or not. Any notion of internal difference within the 'community', therefore, is subsumed to this organic construction. It can be either a functional difference which contributes to the smooth and
efficient working of 'the community' or it is an anomaly, a pathological deviation. Moreover, the 'naturalness' of the 'community' assumes a given collectivity with given boundaries — it allows for internal growth and probably differentiation but not for ideological and material reconstructions of the boundaries
themselves (Bhabha, 1990). It does not allow for collectivities to be seen as
social constructs whose boundaries, structures and norms are the result of constant processes of struggles and negotiations or more general social developments. Indeed, as Homi Bhabha (in GLC, 1984) and Paul Gilroy (1987) have
shown, the fascination of left-wing intellectuals with the 'working class community' has resulted in their adoption of a model of 'Englishness' which is unques-
tionably racist, culturally discriminatory and invariably sexist. The perspective
of the community as fixed can create exclusionary boundaries of 'the community' which would keep as 'the other' all those perceived as different — in other
words, they can become extremely conservative, racist and chauvinist (e.g. ten-
ants associations on some housing estates which mobilize the neighbourhood to
exclude Afro-Caribbeans and Asians in Britain; and on a much more horrific
scale some of the fights in Lebanon, Bosnia and other 'ethnic cleansings').

These inherent problems within the notion of 'community' are shared, in
somewhat different ways, with the notion of 'empowerment'. The automatic
assumption of a progressive connotation of the 'empowerment of the people',
assumes a non-problematic transition from individual to collective power, as
well as a pre-given, non-problematic definition of the boundaries of 'the people'. Moreover, it also assumes a non-problematic, mutually exclusive boundary
between the notion of 'power of' and the notion of 'power over', as if it is
always possible for some people to take more control over their lives without it
sometimes having negative consequences on the lives of other powerless people.
Two very different examples can demonstrate the naivety of such an assumption
— first, the price children often pay when their mothers break out of oppressive
family situations (which is not to deny that they also often make real gains out
of this); and second, the destabilization and often persecution of internal minorities as a result of successful struggles of liberation and independence of
oppressed and colonized people.

The automatic assumption that no inherent conflicts of interest can arise during the process of people gaining empowerment has been, as has been shown (Cain and Yuval-Davis, 1990; Phillips, 1991), a cornerstone of the 'equal opportunity' policies. The promoters of those policies, both in formal institutions and in the voluntary sector have assumed that the interests of all the oppressed and disadvantaged — be it women, ethnic and racial minorities, the disabled, the working class, etc. — are not only always 'progressive' but also automatically shared and reconciled (see Walkerdine and Lucey (1989) for a discussion of this in relation to the white, working class). The ideological construction of these policies did not allow for possible conflict of interests among them. 'White backlash' and 'working class racism' were, therefore, never taken seriously, except as 'false consciousness' or a personal pathology of despair. Nor was 'infighting' and the growing clashes between 'women's units' and 'race units', between 'Afro-Caribbeans' and 'Asians' etc. taken seriously.

I am far from believing, and especially far from hoping, that solidarity among different people, as individuals and as groupings, in struggles against racism, sexism and other forms of discrimination and disadvantage, are impossible. I shall expand on this later. However, I do not believe that such struggles can be taken forward successfully by simplistic notions of empowerment of the oppressed.

ETHNICITY, CULTURE AND IDENTITY

Some of the underlying assumptions of the ideologies of both 'the community' and of 'empowerment', relate to their analytical collapse of ethnicity into culture, on the one hand, and into identity on the other. Within psychology, social identity theory has also tended to reflect and perpetuate the reduction of ethnic differences to social identity. Such collapses, evident in various forms of 'identity politics' movements and 'equal opportunities' policies based on both 'multiculturalist' and 'anti-racist' schools of thought, need examining and unpacking.

There is no space here to enter into a full elaboration of a theoretical framework on ethnicity and the ways it is linked with race and racism (see Anthias and Yuval-Davis, 1992). Ethnicity relates to the politics of collectivity boundaries, dividing the world into 'us' and 'them' around, usually, myths of common origin and/or destiny and engaging in constant processes of struggle and negotiation. These are aimed, from specific positionings within the collectivities, at promoting the collectivity or perpetuating its advantages, via access to state and civil society powers. Ethnicity, according to this definition, is, therefore, primarily a political process which constructs the collectivity and 'its interest', not only as a result of the general positioning of the collectivity in relation to others in the society but also as a result of the specific relationships of those engaged in 'ethnic politics' with others within that collectivity. Gender, class, political and other differences play central roles in the construction of specific ethnic politics and different ethnic projects of the same collectivity can be engaged in intense competitive struggles for hegemonic positions. Some of these projects can involve different constructions of the actual boundaries of the collectivity. Ethnicity is not specific to oppressed and minority groupings. On the contrary, one of the measures of the success of hegemonic ethnicities is the extent to which they succeed in 'naturalizing' their social constructions.

Ethnic projects mobilize all available relevant resources for their promotion. Some of these resources are political, others are economic and yet others are cultural — relating to customs, language, religion, etc. Class, gender, political and personal differences mean that people positioned differently within the collectivity could, while pursuing specific ethnic projects, sometimes use the same cultural resources for promoting opposite political goals (e.g. using various Koran surras to justify pro- and anti-legal abortion politics, as was the case in Egypt or using rock music pro- and anti- the Extreme Right in Britain). In other times, different cultural resources are used to legitimize competing ethnic projects of the collectivity — e.g. when Bundists used Yiddish as 'the' Jewish language — in an ethnic-national project whose boundaries were East European Jewry, and Zionists (re)-invented modern Hebrew (till then used basically for religious purposes) in order to include in their project Jews all over the world. Similarly, the same people can be constructed in different ethnic-racial political projects in Britain to be 'Paki', 'Black Asians' and 'Muslim fundamentalists'.

Given this, it is clear why ethnicity cannot be reduced to culture, and why 'culture' cannot be seen as a fixed, essentialist category. As Gill Bottomley (1991: 305) claims when discussing relationships between ethnicity and culture:

> Categories and ways of knowing ... are constructed within relations of power and maintained, reproduced and resisted in specific and sometimes contradictory ways.

Different ethnic projects can also play different roles in the construction of individual identities. I recently heard a presentation by a Bosnian woman refugee who described how Islam, from a virtually non-significant 'if quaint' element in her background has become, through the recent war, her primary identity. Different historical situations can enforce individual as well as collective identities and thus promote certain ethnic projects more than others (Chhachhi, 1992). Moreover, in certain historical circumstances, certain ethnic projects can result in the construction of new collectivity boundaries which would include people who previously would not have defined themselves as being part of the same collectivities, and sometimes would have even been hostile (e.g. 'Asians' in Britain as including people from Sikh, Hindu and Muslim origins, from both Pakistan and Bangladesh, who were fighting each other on the Indian subcontinent). As Avtar Brah points out (1991: 58): 'Difference is constructed differently within various discourses. These different meanings signal differing political strategies and outcomes.'

Moreover, because specific ethnic projects tend to suit certain members of the collectivity more than others who are positioned differently in terms of class, gender, stage in the life-cycle etc., there can be no automatic assumption, as has been so prevalent within 'identity politics' (Bourne, 1987) that specific individuals, just because they are members in certain collectivities, can automatically be considered as 'representing their community'. Only those elected in democratic ways can even partially be considered so. Otherwise, the best and most committed 'community activists' should be considered only as advocates, not as representatives of their 'community' (Cain and Yuval-Davis, 1990). In terms of equal-opportunities policies, the fact that certain individuals of the groupings become employed in a category of work that previously excluded members of their grouping, although positive in itself, can by no means automatically guarantee the overall improvement in the situation of those who belong to it as a whole. The widening gap of class positions among African Americans is a case in point.

The collapse of ethnicity to culture, on the one hand, and identity, on the other hand, can also create what Kobena Mercer (1988) calls ' the burden of representation' which can handicap members of groupings subject to positive actions and equal-opportunities policies. In the collection Mercer edited on this subject, Judith William remarked:

> The more power any group has to create and wield representations, the less it is required to be representative ... the visible demand to 'speak for the black community' is always there behind the multi-culturalism of public funding (Mercer, 1988: 12).

Moreover, specific individuals are usually, especially in contemporary urban settings, members in more than one collectivity. The boundaries of these collectivities sometimes partially overlap and often cross-cut each other. 'Identity politics' which called people to organize (and empower themselves) according to their particular identities, came up against this reality. In the 'equal-opportunities' policies of the GLC and other local authorities' 'popular planning' groups, for instance, fights broke out concerning the question of whether a certain black woman worker should become part of the 'Race unit' or the 'Women's unit'. On the other hand, once budgets were tight, the same black woman would probably be asked to represent all the interests of all minority 'communities' in the area, notwithstanding conflicts and differences of interests among them.

As Kobena Mercer points out, these assumptions are part and parcel of the ideology of multi-culturalism which, with some changes, 'anti-racists' and 'popular planners' have adopted as well (Rattansi, 1992; Anthias and Yuval-Davis, 1992; Sahgal and Yuval-Davis, 1992).

'MULTI-CULTURALISM'

'Multi-culturalism' (and later on 'anti-racism') has been a major ideological response in the West to the obvious failure of previous liberal approaches which assumed that racism is caused by the 'strangeness' of the immigrants, and that with the 'acculturation' and eventual 'assimilation' of the immigrants — or their children — the issue would disappear. The 'melting-pot', however, did not melt, and ethnic and racial divisions were reproduced from generation to generation (Glazer and Moynihan, 1965, 1975; Wallman, 1979; Watson, 1977).

Multi-culturalism constructs society as composed from basically internally homogeneous units — an hegemonic majority, and small unmeltable minorities with their own essentially different communities and cultures which have to be understood, accepted and basically left alone (since their differences are compatible with the hegemonic culture), in order for the society to have harmonious relations.

Multi-culturalist policies construct cultures as static, ahistoric and in their 'essence' mutually exclusive from other cultures, especially that of the 'host society'. Moreover, 'culture' in the multi-culturalist discourse is often collapsed to 'religion', with religious holidays becoming the signifiers of cultural difference within 'multi-cultural' school curricula.

Fundamentalist leaderships, who use religion in their ethnic political projects, have benefited from the adoption of multi-culturalist norms (Sahgal and Yuval-Davis, 1992). Within the multi-culturalist logic, their presumptions about being the keepers of the 'true' religious way of life are unanswerable. External dissent is labelled as racist and internal dissent as deviance (if not sheer pathology, as in the case of 'self-hating Jews'). In the politics of identity and representation they are perceived as the most 'authentic' 'others' to be included in the multi-culturalist project (see Wetherell and Potter [1992] for a discussion of Maon elders as the most 'authentic' Maons). At the same time, they are also perceived as a threat, and their 'difference' as a basis for racist discourse and exclusion. Unlike previous proponents of multi-culturalism, fundamentalist activists refuse to respect the 'limits of multi-culturalism' which would confine 'ethnic cultures' to the private domain or to some limited cultural community spheres. Fundamentalists aim to use modern state and media powers in order to impose their version of reality on all those whom they perceive as their constituents.

This has proved to be very confusing for the Left, and impossible to grapple with within the paradigm of multi-culturalism based on identity politics. An ILEA document in 1977 promoted multi-culturalism as a policy 'which will ensure that, within a society which is cohesive though not uniform, cultures are respected, differences recognized and individual identities are ensured'. While the contents of the ideology promoted by religious fundamentalist activists are often anathema to all that people on the Left generally believe in, in terms of women's equality, individual freedom, etc., they are committed to 'respect different culture and ensure different identities'. The ideology of autonomous self-determination and empowerment, which is at the base of identity politics and multi-culturalism, for-bids 'intervention in the internal affairs of the community' as Eurocentric and racist, part of a tradition of cultural imperialism which must be rejected.

Women have been primary victims of fundamentalist politics (Sahgal and Yuval-Davis, 1992). Nevertheless, many women have also joined fundamental-ist movements and gained a certain sense of empowerment from them in spite of this (Afshar, 1989; Yuval-Davis, 1992). Subjective feelings of empowerment and autonomy, however, cannot be the full criterion for evaluating the politics of a certain action. In a conference in Ireland on Gender and Colonialism (Dublin, Spring 1992) Gayatri Chakravorty Spivak defined 'effective gendering' as 'con-structing constriction as choice' which is an accurate description of the situation of these women. Feelings and knowledge are constructed as a result of specific power relations and are not outside them (Haraway, 1988). As Richard Johnson, (1991: 17) points out:

> Frameworks are embodied in practical strategies, tacit beliefs, detailed stories ... I may feel empowered or disempowered, heroic, a victim, or stoical, depending on the framework.

'Choosing the framework' is, therefore, not just a question of applying 'posi-tive thinking' — as some of the more simplistic feminist and 'human growth' workshops on 'women and empowerment' would tend to imply. As Foucault (1988: 119) has shown us: 'Power doesn't only weigh on us as a force that says no ... it induces pleasure, forms of knowledge, produces discourse'. This is why it is so important to examine questions of women and empowerment, therefore, in relation to the ways women affect and are affected by ethnic and national processes.

WOMEN, CITIZENSHIP AND 'THE COMMUNITY'

The specific ways women affect and are affected by ethnic and national processes have been elaborated elsewhere (Yuval-Davis, 1980; Yuval-Davis and Anthias, 1989; Walby, 1992; Yuval-Davis, 1993). They include the roles of women: as biological and cultural national reproducers; as cultural embodiments of collectivities and their boundaries; as carriers of collective 'honour' and as participants in national and ethnic struggles. All these ways are vitally important to any analysis not only of the specific position of women but also for any ade-quate perspective about the ways state and society operate in general.

The construction by the state of relationships in the private domain, i.e. mar-riage and the family, is what has determined women's status as citizens within the public domain (Pateman, 1989; Vogel, 1989). In some non-European coun-tries, the right of women even to work and travel in the public domain is depen-dent on formal permission of her 'responsible' male relative (Kandiyotti, 1991), and until 1948 women marrying 'aliens' would have lost their British citizenship altogether.

There have been attempts to explain some of the recent changes in Eastern and Central Europe, in terms of the reconstruction of civil society. This is defined as a presence of a social sphere which is independent of the state. Many western feminist analyses of the relationships between women and the state have shown this 'independence' to be largely illusory, as it is the state which constructs, and often keeps surveillance of, the private domain (especially of the lower classes, e.g. Wilson, 1977; Showstack Sassoon, 1987). However, in third world societies there is sometimes only partial penetration of the state into civil society, especially in its rural and other peripheral sections. In these cases, gender and other social relationships are determined by cultural and religious customs of the national collectivity. This may also happen in 'private domains' of ethnic and national minorities in other states.

However, it is not only in the 'private domain' that gender relationships differ within different groupings. Often the citizenship rights and duties of women from different ethnic and racial groupings are different as well. They would have different legal positions and entitlements; sometimes they might be under the jurisdiction of different religious courts; they would be under different residential regulations, including rights of re-entry when leaving the country; might or might not be allowed to confer citizenship rights on their children, or — in the case of women migrant workers who had to leave their children behind — may or may not receive child and other welfare benefits as part of their social rights.

With all these differences, there is one characteristic which specifies women's citizenship. That is its dualistic nature — on the one hand women are always included, at least to some extent, in the constructions of the general body of members of national and ethnic collectivities and/or citizens of the state; on the other hand — there is always, at least to a certain extent, a separate body of regulations (legal and/or customary) which relate to them specifically as women.

Marshall (1950, 1965, 1981) defines citizenship as 'full membership in the community' which includes civil, political and social dimensions of citizenship. The problematic notion of 'the community' discussed above notwithstanding, the ambivalent nature of women's citizenship creates an inherent ambivalence within women's politics vis-a-vis their collectivities, on the one hand, and vis-a-vis women from other collectivities, on the other hand. The famous quotation by Virginia Woolf that 'As a woman I have no country' emphasizes the realization of many women that they are positioned in a different place from men vis-a-vis their collectivity and that the hegemonic cultural and political projects pursued in the name of their collectivities can be against their interests. On the other hand, especially among subordinated and minority women, there is a realization that to fight for their liberation as women is senseless as long as their collectivity as a whole is subordinated and oppressed.

Feminist politics are affected by this ambivalence. Many Black and minority women have pointed out the racist, Eurocentric and middle class biases which have been at the heart of most feminist agendas, at least until the last few years. As bell hooks claimed (1990: 29):

> The vision of sisterhood evoked by women liberationists was based on the idea of common oppression — a false and corrupt platform disguising and mystifying the true nature of women's varied and complex social reality.

There are many examples of this varied and complex social reality of women, which, as a result, problematize any simplistic assumptions about what is 'the feminist agenda'. Debates relating to these issues can be found in all areas of feminist politics — whether it is the debate on reproductive rights and prioritizing forbidden abortions versus forced sterilizations; the attitudes feminists should have towards 'the family' as an oppressive or protective social institution or the extent to which women should come out against all forms of violence or should campaign for participation in the military (Kimble and Unterhalter, 1982; Anthias and Yuval-Davis, 1984; Spelman, 1988; Hill Collins, 1990; Yuval-Davis, forthcoming).

If we add to membership in particular ethnic, national and racial collectivities as well as dimensions of identity and difference among women, such as class, sexuality, stage in the life course, etc., it would be very easy to reach a postmodernist deconstructionist view and a realization that 'everyone is different'. The question, then, is whether any collective political action in general, and feminist collective action in particular, is possible once such a deconstructionist analytical point of view is conceded as valid (see the critique of Barrett and McIntosh (1985) of Anthias and Yuval-Davis (1984)). Are effective politics and adequate theoretical analysis inherently contradictory to each other? My basic answer to this question is the same as that of Gayatri Chakravorty Spivak (1991: 65) when she claimed:

> Deconstruction does not say anything against the usefulness of mobilizing unities. All it says is that because it is useful it ought not to be monumentalized as the way things really are.

Or, to put it in Stuart Hall's succinct way: 'all identity is constructed across difference' (1987: 44).

WOMEN AND 'COALITION POLITICS' — LINKING THEORY AND PRACTICE

Adopting such a political perspective of boundary construction of 'units' or 'unities' can keep us aware of continuous historical changes and keep our perceptions of the boundaries between collectivities sufficiently flexible and open so that exclusionary politics are not permitted. At the same time it still enables us not to be paralysed politically. Concretely this means that all feminist (and other forms of democratic) politics should be viewed as a form of coalition politics in which the differences among women are recognized and given a voice, without fixating the boundaries of this coalition in terms of 'who' we are but in terms of what we want to achieve. As Caryn McTighe Musil says:

> The challenge of the nineties is to hold on simultaneously to these two contra-dictory truths: as women, we are the same and we are different. The bridges, power, alliances and social change possible will be determined by how well we define ourselves through a matrix that encompasses our gendered particularities while not losing sight of our unity (Albrecht and Brewer, 1990: vi).

The question is, of course, how to go about this task concretely. I shall now look critically at several approaches which have attempted to tackle that task — two which, although creative and thoughtful in many ways, have, I believe, some major flaws relating to some of the issues discussed earlier in the article, and two which, although very different from each other, might point the way forward in effectively tackling the problem.

The first approach has been described in the article by Gail Pheterson in the *Bridges of Power* collection (1990). It describes an experiment in Holland in which three mixed women's groups (more or less in half and half proportions) were constructed — one of Black and White women, one of Jews and Gentiles and one of Lesbian and Heterosexual women. The groups operated very much within the usual pattern of feminist consciousness-raising tradition. Pheterson (1990: 3) found that:

> ... in every group, past experiences with oppression and domination distorted the participants' perceptions of the present and blocked their identification with people in common political situations who did not share their history.

She talks about the need to recognize and interpret how we internalize both oppression and domination in order to create successful alliances. Her position constructs ethnicity as including a power dimension — of oppression and domi-nation and not just as made of 'cultural stuff'. She also shows that women can experience internalized oppression and domination simultaneously as a result of different experiences — people and identities are not just unidimensional. On the other hand her approach implies that there is such a thing as an 'objective truth' that can be discovered rather than a constructed one. I would say that rather than using a discourse of 'distortion', one should use a discourse of ideo-logical positioning. I will come back to this point later.

The discourse of 'distortion' creates its own distortions. Pheterson discusses, for instance, the reluctance of some women (Black women born in the colonies rather than in Holland; Jewish women who have only one Jewish parent) to identify with their groups and sees it as a distortion and 'blocked identifica-tions'. Such a perspective assumes essentialist homogeneity within each cate-gory (such as 'Blacks', 'Jews', etc.) and refuses to accept that these women are genuinely located in different positionings from other members of their groups.

Moreover, it assumes that the centrality and significance of these categories would be the same to different women members and disregards differences of class, age and other social dimensions among the participants as inherently irrelevant for the group.

Such an approach is typical of the 'identity politics' which were discussed above and which have been very central to western feminism. The whole idea of consciousness-raising techniques assume, as a basis for political action, a reality that has to be discovered and then changed, rather than a reality which is being created and re-created when practised and discussed (Yuval-Davis, 1984). Moreover, this reality is assumed to be shared by all members of the social category within which the consciousness-raising movement operates who are perceived to constitute a basically homogenous social grouping sharing the same interests. Individual identity has become equated with collective identity whereas differences, rather than being acknowledged, have been interpreted by those holding the hegemonic power within the movement as mainly reflections of different stages of raised consciousness. Although to a large extent this has been acknowledged by the women's movement(s) in recent years, the solution has often been to develop essentialist notions of difference, such as, for example, between Black and White women, or middle class and working class women. Within each of these idealized groups, the assumptions about 'discovered' homogenous reality, and the other problems of 'identity politics' and the politics of 'the community' discussed above, usually continue to operate. Moreover, as Linda Gordon (1991: 103) points out, such essentialist notions of difference are necessarily exclusive:

> We are in danger of losing any ability to offer any interpretation that reaches beyond the particular groups ... it does not capture the experience of all ... women.

Even more importantly, as Bonnie Thornton Dill (1988: 106) points out:

> As an organizing principle, difference obliterates relation ... Difference often implies separation, but these relationships frequently involve proximity, involvement.

An attempt at a more sophisticated type of identity politics was theorized by Rosalind Brunt who writes in the influential collection *New Times* (Brunt, 1989: 150). Brunt argues that:

> ... unless the question of identity is at the heart of any transformatory project, then not only will the political agenda be inadequately 'rethought' but more to the point, our politics aren't going to make much headway beyond the Left's own circles.

Reflecting upon one's own identity, the return to the 'subjective', does not imply for Brunt withdrawal from politics, but rather the opposite — locating grids of power and resistance — in the Foucauldian way, which are horizontal and not just vertical, while keeping political frameworks of action heterogenous and floating. She rejects the logic of 'broad democratic alliances' and 'rainbow coalitions' because, she argues, political action should be based on 'unity in diversity' which should be founded not on common denominators but on

> ... a whole variety of heterogeneous, possibly antagonistic, maybe magnificently diverse, identities and circumstances ... the politics of identity recognizes that there will be many struggles, and perhaps a few celebrations, and writes into all of them a welcome to contradiction and complexity (Brunt, 1989: 158).

As a positive example of this type of political struggle Brunt points to the support activities which surrounded the British miners' strike of 1984–5, which was against pit closures and redundancies. This is, however, an unfortunate example, because, with all its positive features, the strike ended up in a crushing defeat, not only of the miners and trade-union movement, but of the anti-Thatcherite movement as a whole.

Defeats and real politics aside, Brunt's model of politics can be seen as very seductive — it incorporates theoretical insights of highly sophisticated social analysis, is flexible, dynamic and is totally inclusive. However, it is in this last point that the danger lies. What ultimately lies behind Brunt's approach is a naive populist assumption that, in spite of contradictions and conflicts, in the last instance all popular struggles are inherently progressive. She shares with other multi-culturalists a belief in the inherent reconcilability and limited boundaries of interest and political difference among those who are disadvantaged and discriminated against. Such a belief, as discussed above, has created a space for fundamentalist leaderships to rise.

The next example which I want to discuss is of feminist politics which has progressed beyond such assumptions. It is that of Women Against Fundamentalism (WAF), which was organized in London at the wake of the Rushdie Affair (when, in 1989, the Ayatolla Khomeni issued a *fatwah* against Rushdie following publication of his Satanic Verses and Rushdie was forced to go into hiding for his own protection) to struggle exactly against such fundamentalist leaderships of all religions as well as against expressions of racism which masqueraded themselves as anti fundamentalism.

WAF includes women from a variety of religious and ethnic origins (Christians, Jews, Muslims, Sikhs, Hindus, etc.). Many of the members also belong to other campaigning organizations, often with a more specific ethnic affiliation — such as the Southall Black Sisters (SBS), the Jewish Socialist Group, and the Irish Abortion Support Group. However, except for SBS which has had an organizational and ideological initiatory role in establishing WAF, women come there as individuals rather than as representatives of any group or ethnic category. On the other hand, there is no attempt to 'assimilate' the women who come from the different backgrounds. Differences in ethnicity and points of view — and the resulting different agendas — are recognized and respected. But what is celebrated is the common political stance of WAF members, as advocating 'the Third Way' against fundamentalism and against racism.

Patricia Hill Collins in her book *Black Feminist Thought* (1990) discusses the importance of recognizing the different positioning from which different groupings view reality. Her analysis (which follows to a great extent the feminist epistemological perspective elaborated by Donna Haraway (1988)), echoes exactly the agenda which has been guiding the members of WAF:

> Each group speaks from its own standpoint and shares its own partial, situated knowledge. But because each group perceives its own truth as partial, its knowledge is *unfinished* [to differentiate from invalid (NY-D)] ... Partiality and not universality is the condition of being heard; individuals and groups forwarding knowledge claims without owning their position are deemed less credible than those who do ... Dialogue is critical to the success of this epistemological approach (Hill Collins, 1990: 236).

In this Hill Collins side steps the trap in which Marxists and many sociologists of knowledge have been caught of relativism, on the one hand, and locating specific social groupings as the epistemological 'bearers of the Truth', on the other hand. Dialogue, rather than fixity of location, becomes the basis of empowered knowledge. The campaigns of WAF on, for instance, state religious education or on women's reproductive rights has been informed by the differential experiences of the women of different positionings and backgrounds in the group.

The last example I want to discuss is also based on dialogue. A dialogue which has been developed by Italian feminists (from the movement Women In Black — especially the women from the Bologna and Torino Women's Centres) working with feminists who are members of conflicting national groups, like the Serbs and the Croats but especially Palestinian and Israeli Jewish women. On the face of it, such a dialogue does not seem very different from the more common 'identity politics' type of dialogue such as was described by Gail Pheterson. However, several important differences exist.

The boundaries of the groupings are not determined by an essentialist notion of difference but by a concrete and material political reality. Also, the women involved in the different groups are not perceived simplistically as representatives of their groupings. While their different positioning and background is recognized and respected — including the differential power relationships inherent in their corresponding affiliations as members of the Occupier and the Occupied collectivities — all the women who were sought and invited to participate in the dialogue are committed to 'refuse to participate unconsciously in the reproduction of the existing power relations' and are 'committed to finding a fair solution to the conflict' (Italian letter of invitation, December, 1990).

The basic perspective of the dialogue is very similar to that of Patricia Hill Collins. The terminology is somewhat different. The Italian women use as key words 'rooting' and 'shifting'. The idea is that each participant brings with her the rooting in her own membership and identity but at the same time tries to shift in order to put herself in a situation of exchange with women who have different membership and identity. They call it 'transversalism' — to differentiate from 'universalism' which by assuming a homogeneous point of departure ends up being exclusive instead of inclusive.

Two things are vital in developing the transversal perspective. First, that the process of shifting would not involve self de-centring, i.e. losing one's own rooting and set of values. There is no need for it, as Elsa Barkley Brown (1989: 922) claims:

> All people can learn to center in another experience, validate it and judge it by its own standards without need of comparison or need to adopt that framework as their own ... one has no need to 'decenter' anyone in order to center someone else; one has only to constantly pivot the center.

It is vital in any form of coalition and solidarity politics to keep one's own perspective on things while empathizing and respecting others. In multi-culturalist types of solidarity politics there can be a risk of uncritical solidarity. This was very prevalent, for instance, in the politics of some sections of the Left around the Iranian revolution or the Rushdie Affair. They saw it as 'imperialist' and 'racist' to intervene in 'internal community matters'. Women are often the victims of such a perspective which allows the so-called representatives and leaders of 'the community' to determine policies concerning women.

Second, and following from the first point, the process of shifting should not homogenize the 'other'. As there are diverse positions and points of view among people who are similarly rooted, so there are among the members of the other group. The transversal coming together should not be with the members of the other group 'en bloc' but with those who, in their different rooting, share compatible values and goals to one's own.

A word of caution, however, is required here. Transversal politics are not always possible, as conflicting interests of people who are situated in specific positionings are *not* always reconcilable. However, when solidarity is possible, it is important that it is based on transversalist principles so as not to fall into the pitfalls of 'identity politics' of the feminist, nationalist or the anti-racist kinds.

CONCLUSION

Empowerment of the oppressed, whether one fights for it for one's own — individual or group — sake, or that of others, cannot by itself be the goal for feminist and other anti-oppression politics. Recently, for instance, memoirs by former members, especially Elaine Brown, have brought to light the 'disciplinary' practices of brutality and violence which became part of the daily reality of the American Black Panthers (Walker, 1993), and the murder of the teenager to which Winnie Mandela has allegedly been party has been just one dreadful demonstration of the old truism that 'power corrupts'. This can also apply to the power of previously disempowered people, and to power which is only relative and confined to specific contingencies.

The ideology of 'empowerment' has sought to escape this dilemma by confining 'positive' power to 'power of' rather than 'power over'. However, in doing that, empowerment has been constructed as a process which breaks the boundaries between the individual and the communal. As Bookman and Morgen (1988: 4) point out, the notion of empowerment connotes:

> ... a spectrum of political activity ranging from acts of individual resistance to mass political mobilizations that challenge the basic power relations in our society.

This article pointed out that such constructions assume a specific 'identity politics' which homogenizes and naturalizes social categories and groupings, denying shifting boundaries and internal power differences and conflicts of interest. Also in such an approach cultures and traditions are transformed from heterogenous, sometimes conflicting reservoirs of resources into unified, a-historical and unchanging essence.

As an alternative to this kind of 'identity politics' the article suggests that the idea of 'transversal politics' provides the way forward. In 'transversal politics', perceived unity and homogeneity is replaced by dialogues which give recognition to the specific positionings of those who participate in them as well as to the 'unfinished knowledge' that each such situated positioning can offer. Transversal politics, nevertheless, does not assume that the dialogue is boundariless, and that each conflict of interest is reconcilable. However, the boundaries of such a dialogue are determined by the message, rather than the messenger. The struggle against oppression and discrimination might (and mostly does) have a specific categorical focus but is never confined just to that category.

If empowerment of women is to transcend some of the pitfalls discussed in this article, it is perhaps wise to adhere to Gill Bottomley's (1991: 309) warning:

> The dualistic approach of a unitary Us vs a unitary Them continues to mystify the interpenetration and intermeshing of the powerful constructs such as race, class and gender and to weaken attempts at reflexivity ... both the subjective and the objective dimensions of experience need to be addressed as well as the thorny issue of the extent to which observers remain within the discourses they seek to criticise.

The transversal pathway might be full of thorns but at least it leads in the right direction.

NOTE

The last part of the article is based on a paper presented at the Women's Studies Conference, July 1992, in Preston.

REFERENCES

Ackelsberg, Martha (1991) *Free Women of Spain*. Bloomington, IN: Indiana University Press.

Afshar, Haleh (1989) 'Three Generations of Muslim Women in Bradford', paper presented at the CSE conference, London.

Albrecht, Lisa and Brewer, Rose M., eds (1990) *Bridges of Power, Women's Multicultural Alliances*. Philadelphia: New Society.

Anthias, Floya and Yuval-Davis, Nira (1984) 'Contextualizing Feminism: Gender, Ethnic and Class Divisions', *Feminist Review* 15: 62–75.

Anthias, Floya and Yuval-Davis, Nira, in association with Cain, Harriet (1992) *Racialized Boundaries: Race, Nation, Gender, Colour and Class and the Anti-Racist Struggle*. London: Routledge.

Antrobus, Peggy (1989) 'The Empowerment of Women', in R. S. Gallin, M. Aronoff and A. Feguson (eds) *The Women and International Development Annual,* Vol. 1, pp. 189–207. Boulder, CO: Westview Press.

Barkley Brown, Elsa (1989) 'African-American Women's Quilting: A Framework for Conceptualizing and Teaching African-American Women's History', *Signs* 14 (4): 921–9.

Barrett, Michelle and McIntosh, Mary (1985) 'Ethnocentrism in Socialist Feminism', *Feminist Review* 20.

Bhabha, Homi K. ed. (1990) *Nation and Narration*. London: Routledge.

Bookman, Ann and Morgen, Sandra eds (1988) *Women and the Politics of Empowerment*. Philadelphia: Temple University Press.

Bottomley, Gill (1991) 'Culture, Ethnicity and the Politics/Poetics of Representation', *Diaspora* (3): 303–20.

Bourne, J. (1987) *Homelands of the Mind: Jewish Feminism and Identity Politics*. Race and Class pamphlet no. 11.

Brah, Avtar (1991) 'Difference, Diversity, Differentiation', in S. Allen, F. Anthias and N. Yuval-Davis (eds) *Gender, Race and Class* special issue of *International Review of Sociology* 2: 53–72.

Brunt, Rosalind (1989) 'The Politics of Identity', in S. Hall and M. Jacques (eds) *New Times*. London: Lawrence & Wishart.

Bystydzienski, Jill M. ed. (1992) *Women Transforming Politics: Worldwide Strategies for Empowerment*. Bloomington, IN: Indiana University Press.

Cain, Harriet and Yuval-Davis, Nira (1990) '"The Equal Opportunities Community" and the Anti-racist Struggle', *Critical Social Policy* (Autumn): 5–26.

Chhachhi, Amrita (1992) 'Forced Identities, the State, Communalism, Fundamentalism and Women in India', in Deniz Kandiyotti (ed.) *Women, the State and Islam*, pp. 144–75. London: Macmillan.

Fanon, Franz (1986(1952)) *Black Skin, White Masks*. London: Pluto Press.

Foucault, Michel (1980) 'Truth and Power', in Colin Gordon (ed.) *Power/Knowledge: Selected Interviews and Other Writings 1972–1977*. Brighton: Harvester Press.

Freire, Paulo (1972) *The Pedagogy of the Oppressed*. Harmondsworth: Penguin.

Gilroy, Paul (1987) *There Ain't no Black in the Union Jack*. London: Hutchinson.

Glazer, Nathan and Moynihan, Patrick (1965) *Beyond the Melting Pot*. Cambridge, MA: MIT Press.

Glazer, Nathan and Moynihan, Patrick (1975) *Ethnicity, Theory and Experience*. Cambridge, MA: Harvard University Press.

GLC (Greater London Council) (1984) *Challenging Racism in London,* report of the conference held on 12 March 1983, London.

Gordon, Linda (1991) 'On Difference', *Genders* (10, Spring): 91–111.

Gortz, A. (1982) *Farewell to the Working Class*. London: Pluto Press.

Hall, Stuart, (1987) 'Minimal Selves', in *Identity, the Real Me*, ICA Document 6, pp. 44–6. London: ICA.

Haraway, Donna (1988) 'Situated Knowledge: The Science Question in Feminism and the Privilege of Partial Perspective', *Feminist Studies* 14(3): 575–99.

Hartsock, N. (1981) 'Political Change: Two Perspectives on Power', in Charlotte Bunch et al. (eds) *Building Feminist Theory: Essays from the Quest*. New York: Longman.

Hill Collins, Patricia (1990) *Black Feminist Thought: Knowledge, Consciousness and the Politics of Empowerment*. Boston: Unwin Hyman.

hooks, bell, (1990) 'Sisterhood, Political Solidarity Between Women', in Sneja Gunew (ed.) *Feminist Knowledge: Critique and Construct*, pp. 27–41. London: Routledge.

Johnson, Richard (1991) 'Frameworks of Culture and Power: Complexity and Politics in Cultural Studies', *Critical Studies* 3(1) *Cultural Studies: Crossing Borders*.

Kandiyotti, Deniz ed. (1991) *Women, the State and Islam*. London: Macmillan.

Kimble, Judith and Unterhalter, Elaine (1982) '"We Opened the Road for You, You Must Go Forward": ANC Women's Struggles 1912–1982', *Feminist Review* 12.

Kitzinger, Celia (1991) 'Feminism, Psychology and the Paradox of Power', *Feminism & Psychology* 1(1): 111–30.

Macy, J. R. (1983) *Despair and Personal Power in the Nuclear Age*. Philadelphia: New Society.

Marshall, T. H. (1950) *Citizenship and Social Class*. Cambridge: Cambridge University Press.

Marshall, T. H. (1975[1965]) *Social Policy in the Twentieth Century*. London: Hutchinson.

Marshall, T. H. (1981) *The Right to Welfare and Other Essays*. London: Heinemann.

Mercer, Kobena, ed. (1988) *Black Film/British Cinema,* ICA documents, British Film Institute.

Pateman, Carol (1989) *The Sexual Contract*. Cambridge: Polity Press.

Pheterson, Gail (1990) 'Alliances Between Women — Overcoming Internalized Oppression and Internalized Domination', in L. Albrecht and R. M. Brewer (eds) *Bridges of Power, Women's Multicultural Alliances,* pp. 34–48. Philadelphia: New Society.

Phillips, Anne (1991) *Engendering Democracy*. Cambridge: Polity Press.

Rattansi, Ali (1992) 'Changing the Subject? Racism, Culture and Education', in James Donald and Ali Rattansi (eds) *'Race', Culture and Difference*. London: Sage.

Sahgal, Gita and Yuval-Davis, Nira eds (1992) *Refusing Holy Orders: Women and Fundamentalism in Britain*. London: Virago.

Showstack Sassoon, Anne ed. (1987) *Women and the State*. London: Hutchinson.

Spelman, Elizabeth (1988) *The Inessential Woman*. London: The Women's Press.

Spivak, Gayatri Chakravorty (1991) 'Reflections on Cultural Studies in the Post-colonial Conjuncture', in *Critical Studies* 3 (1): 63–78. Special Issue on *Cultural Studies Crossing Borders*.

Thornton Dill, Bonnie (1988) 'The Dialectics of Black Womanhood', in Sandra Harding (ed.) *Feminism and Methodology*. Bloomington, IN: Indiana University Press.

Vogel, Ursula (1989) 'Is Citizenship Gender Specific?', paper presented at the Political Science Association Annual Conference, April.

Wainright, Hilary (1985) *Labour, A Tale of Two Parties*. London: Hogarth Press.

Walby, Sylvia (1992) 'Woman and Nation', *International Journal of Comparative Sociology* XXXII (1–2, Jan. – Apr.)

Walker, Martin (1993) 'Sisters Take the Wraps Off the Brothers', *The Guardian* 6 May.

Walkerdine, Valerie and Lucey, Helen (1989) *Democracy in the Kitchen*. London: Virago.

Wallman, Sandra (1979) *Ethnicity at Work*. London: Macmillan.

Watson, J. (1977) *Between Two Cultures*. Oxford: Blackwell.

Wetherell, M. and Potter, J. (1992) *Mapping the Language of Racisim*. Basingstoke: Harvester Wheatsheaf.

Wilson, Elizabeth (1977) *Women and the Welfare State*. London: Tavistock.

Young, Iris Marion (1990) *Justice and the Politics of Difference*. Princeton, NJ: Princeton University Press.

Yuval-Davis, Nira (1980) 'The Bearers of the Collective: Women and Religious Legislation in Israel', *Feminist Review* 3.

Yuval-Davis, Nira (1984) 'Zionism, Anti-semitism, and the Struggle against Racism', *Spare Rib* (Sept.): 18–22.

Yuval-Davis, Nira (1991) 'The Citizenship Debate: Women, the State and Ethnic Processes', *Feminist Review* (Autumn).

Yuval-Davis, Nira (1992) 'Jewish Fundamentalism and Women's Empowerment', in Gita Sahgal and Nira Yuval-Davis (eds) *Refusing Holy Orders: Women and Fundamentalism in Britain*. London: Virago.

Yuval-Davis, Nira (1993) 'Gender and Nation', *Ethnic & Racial Studies* (Autumn).

Yuval-Davis, Nira (forthcoming) *Gender and Nation*. London: Sage.

Yuval-Davis, Nira and Anthias, Floya eds (1989) *Woman–Nation–State*. London: Macmillan.

Nira YUVAL-DAVIS is a Reader in Gender and Ethnic Studies at the University of Greenwich in London. Among her recent books are *Woman–Nation–State; Refusing Holy Orders: Women and Fundamentalism in Britain* and *Racialized Boundaries*. Forthcoming: *Beyond Dichotomies: Gender, Race, Ethnicity & Class in Settler Societies & Gender & Nation*. ADDRESS: School of Social Sciences, The University of Greenwich, Southwood Site, London SE9 2HB.

I

The Politics of White and Black Bodies

Barbara TREPAGNIER

I had only one desire: to find the beauty ... that had escaped me, but apparently, only me ... the world agreed a blue-eyed, yellow-haired pink-skinned doll was what every girl-child treasured (Toni Morrison, 1970).

A primary function of feminist theories has been to describe the oppression of women, to explain the cause/s of that oppression, and to propose strategies for liberation (Tong, 1989). An area of concern for many, the control of women through their bodies, has been addressed primarily by radical feminists in terms of issues such as reproduction and motherhood (Firestone, 1970; de Beauvoir, 1953; Trebilcot, 1984); femininity/masculinity (Millett, 1970; Daly, 1973; French, 1985); and sexuality (Rubin, 1975; Barry, 1979), including lesbian/female sexuality (Frye, 1977; Rich, 1980), male violence (Dworkin, 1974; Brownmiller, 1975), and pornography (Dworkin, 1974; MacKinnon, 1977; Califia, 1981; Samois, 1981). In addition to radical feminists, theorists from other camps, such as socialist feminists (Jagger, 1983; Young, 1990), black feminists (King, 1988; Hill Collins, 1990) and poststructuralist feminists (Bordo, 1988; Bartky, 1990) have also addressed concerns relevant to the female body.

The phrase 'body-identified identity' was coined by German researcher Frigga Haug and her colleagues (1987) to describe the phenomenon of women's identities being defined primarily through their relationships with their bodies. Very few women can satisfy the requirements of 'beauty' perpetrated in western societies; however, since the standard of beauty portrayed in the mass media designates whiteness, black women are presumably at a disadvantage. For that reason, black women are likely to play a role in the construction of white women's 'body-identified identities'.

Feminism & Psychology © 1994 SAGE (London, Thousand Oaks and New Delhi), Vol. 4(1): 199–205.

The idea that black women are utilized in the construction of white women's 'body-identified identities' follows Simone de Beauvoir's (1953) concept of Self/Other: females are defined in relation to males. Woman is Other, according to de Beauvoir, because 'she is *not*-man' (Tong, 1989: 6, emphasis in the original). Is it not possible that black people, in this case black women, are defined similarly, in terms of being *not*-white? The compelling 'caughtness' of being simultaneously Other and Self — male defined yet *other female* definer — led to this attempt to scrutinize the discourse on women's bodies, keeping in mind those differences among women regarding 'race' differences which, in the area of female bodies, often go untheorized by white authors. De Beauvoir's concept of Self/Other, although somewhat reductionist, provides a foundation upon which other, more complex notions of definition, can be positioned.

Following Foucault, Haug and her colleagues portray women as 'active agents' in the formation of their identities:

> [Women] are not simply stamped with the imprint of their given social relations, but ... acquiesce in them and unconsciously participate in their formation (Haug, 1987: 25).

I do not believe that the suggestion of complicity is intended by the author as an indictment of women. Instead, Haug seems to suggest that since women take part in the construction of their own identities, they must be seen, not as victims, but as active participants. Although not mentioned by Haug, the complicity of white women in terms of their body-identified identities, unconscious or otherwise, results in real effects, both material and psychological, upon the lives of black women. These effects, I believe, should not only be considered by white women as they 'acquiesce' in the formation of their identities but evaluated by theorists writing about female bodies.

WHITE AND BLACK WOMEN'S BODIES

Many white authors dealing with the image of female bodies rightly point out the negative consequences on women's definitions of themselves due to constraints placed upon them by society, in particular the fashion/beauty complex and the media (Coward, 1985; Haug, 1987; Bordo, 1988; Bartky, 1990; Wolf, 1991). The authors, however, seemingly confine their discussion to 'white bodies'. As a result, their theories, while significant, are limited in scope — a point of contention raised by black feminists regarding (white) feminist theory in general. Susan Bordo cautions feminists in their attempts to avoid ethnocentrism, to 'guard against the "view from nowhere"' and from the 'dream of being everywhere' (1988: 140 and 141). Her point is that we all must see from *somewhere*, and in so doing, will inevitably exclude someone or something. Nevertheless, theories of the female body as stated by white feminists, because they so often do exclude black feminists, present an important point of departure for a discussion of the politics of white and black women's bodies.

The sexual stereotyping of females which is accomplished largely through body image is thought by Sandra Bartky (1990) to alienate women from their psyches. Bartky borrows Frantz Fanon's concept of 'psychic alienation' in attempting to demonstrate that women are psychologically oppressed in a way that is parallel to the psychological alienation of black people. Bartky (1990: 22) describes it as being 'weighed down in your mind; … hav[ing] a harsh dominion exercised over your self-esteem'. According to the concept of psychic alienation, the primary purpose of psychological oppression is to ensure that those who 'benefit from the established order of things' will not *appear* to be oppressors (Bartky, 1990: 23). Bartky, however, stops short in her analysis since white women, while admittedly psychologically oppressed, also *benefit* from the established order. This is not to deny or ignore the alienation of white women from themselves. Rather, it is to complicate the issue by focusing upon white women's participation in a process which is, on some grounds, disproportionately alienating to black women.

'The beauty myth' is the phrase Naomi Wolf uses to describe 'a violent backlash against feminism that uses images of female beauty as a political weapon against women's advancement' (Wolf, 1991: 10). The campaign assails women's most private world, that of their bodies, with a pervasive conception of how they should look. Wolf points out that one advantage that compliance with the beauty myth offers is success in the labour force. All women suffer inequities due to sex discrimination in the work force. However, those women who fare least well in procuring positions and advancing are those who score farthest from the ideal standard of beauty, particularly in fields where women are seen as being 'on display', as is often the case for women (Wolf, 1991). Some black women are seen as more 'beautiful' than white women. This occurs when 'exotic' beauty, an impossibility for white women, is achieved or when disability, size or other 'deviance' in white women in relation to the beauty standard overrides skin colour. These occurrences, however, are exceptions rather than the norm.

Whiteness and beauty are tightly intertwined in western cultures. A black woman quoted by Wendy Chapkis (1986) comments that the phrase 'beautiful woman' invokes an image of a white woman, in spite of the fact that she thinks black women are truly more beautiful. In her work on female identity formation in black and white women, white historian Phyllis Palmer (1983) shows how white women have used black women like Sojourner Truth instead of white women as models of strength, directness and integrity. Black women are seen as '"womanly", without affectation or false reticence, and so [are] ideally admirable in the eyes of (white) women today' (Palmer, 1983: 153). Since beauty accounts in large measure for white women's 'affectation' and associated lack of strength, why (and how) does the exclusion of black women from the standard of beauty in this country affect black women negatively?

Relative to the nexus of beauty and whiteness, black author Patricia Hill Collins explains that, influenced by white images and standards,

> African American women experience the pain of never being able to live up to externally defined standards of beauty — standards applied to us by white men, white women, Black men and, most painfully, one another (Hill Collins, 1990: 80).

Beauty, propagated in the US culture by the media, with its assumption of whiteness, implies that black is not beautiful. Like others, black men internalize the white ideal image of 'beautiful', often abusing black women because of their inability to live up to this externally imposed, impossible standard (Hill Collins, 1990). The emotional and physical suffering of black women engendered by the white beauty myth can be seen as one of the many ways black women sustain the 'multiple jeopardy' of gender and race (King, 1988: 42).

Differences in the oppression/s of white and black women are discussed by Gloria Joseph and Jill Lewis (1981) in their study of white and black beauty magazines. The authors found that the message in white advertisements is that, if a white woman buys the product, she will become a real woman. By comparison, the message in black advertisements is that, if a black woman buys the product, she will become like the white woman (Joseph and Lewis, 1981). I do not mean to imply that all black women aspire to the white beauty standard. Black women are noted for their resistance, not only to white beauty standards, but to many other forms of oppression (Omolade, 1980; Davis, 1983). The beauty myth, nonetheless, permeates almost every facet of western culture, most certainly the hegemonic discourse on all women which says that white is (more) beautiful.

The issue I am raising concerns how the unspoken whiteness of the beauty myth excludes, and therefore disadvantages, black women in general. If this is the case, the question is: how do/can white feminists, committed to equality for all women, deal with their own privilege?

PRIVILEGE AND RACISM

According to Haug's hypothesis, women who find themselves constrained in their social relationships use whatever means they can to improve their situations. Buying into the beauty myth is one of those means, and heightened attainment in the labour force one of the rewards. However, just as men's rewards are often achieved at the expense of women, so too white women's rewards sometimes penalize black women.

Hill Collins asserts that access to privilege keeps white women from acknowledging their own racism. She quotes scholar Peggy McIntosh:

> I think whites are carefully taught not to recognize white privilege, just as males are taught not to recognize male privilege. I have come to see white privilege as an invisible package of unearned assets which I can count on

cashing in each day, but about which I was 'meant' to be oblivious (Hill Collins, 1990: 190).

McIntosh's statement is particularly salient when considered in relation to the beauty standard in the US. For the 'invisible package of unearned assets' to which she refers could clearly be the whiteness of the beauty standard.

Many white women, including white feminists, do not see racism as their issue any more than men see sexism as theirs. Yet, most feminists view sexism partly as men's problem, just as many black people see racism partly as white people's problem. I do not believe that white women's complicity in the beauty myth is an intentional move to disadvantage black women, neither do I think that the acknowledgement of racism by white feminists will end the oppression of black women. Nevertheless, black women are excluded and thus disadvantaged by perpetuation of the beauty myth, while white women, also punished by the myth, are simultaneously privileged by it. White women's acquiescence, as Haug suggests, is active, not passive. Therefore, responsibility, though not blame, can and should be attributed to white women. When responsibility is taken by white women for their own part in the perpetuation of racism, we will be able to commit ourselves to ending racism, a prerequisite for securing equality for all women.

The acknowledgement by white women of their part in the perpetuation of racism would also complicate the arguments of some feminists which cast males, or at least patriarchy, as the enemy (Firestone, 1970; Daly, 1973; Brownmiller, 1975). Poststructuralist feminists have debunked 'the long-standing male conspiracy against women, or the fixing of blame on *any* particular participants in the play of social forces' (Bordo, 1988: 91 emphasis in original; Hawkesworth, 1989). Foucault's (1978) conception of power as a force field, comprised of a complex network of impulses reacting in concert, is useful here. Power relationships depend upon multiple and transitory sites of resistance. All points in a force field can simultaneously obtain and produce the effects of power. In terms of the beauty myth, the notion of white women as simultaneously disadvantaged and privileged is illustrative of Foucault's analogy, foregrounding questions of resistance, collusion, oppression and accountability.

While the feminist appropriation of poststructuralism is seen by some feminists as a 'natural ally to feminism' (Nicholson, 1990: 5; Haraway, 1985), others see postmodern thought as dangerous to feminist politics (Hartsock, 1987; DiStefano, 1990). Iris Young (1990) offers a flexible conception of oppression which allows for inclusion of Foucault's insight regarding power relationships without discarding the concept of social categories altogether. Young's definition of oppression includes the processes and rules of everyday life. The consequence of white women 'following the rules' (Young, 1990: 41) of the beauty myth has an impact on the lives of others, in this case, black women.

Acknowledgement by white women of privilege in terms of the beauty standard in western cultures will not end racism. However, it may be a step toward building coalitions with other women by broadening the self-interest of white women to include black women, an event which should enhance the likelihood of further liberation of all women.

REFERENCES

Barry, K. (1979) *Female Sexual Slavery.* Englewood Cliffs, NJ: Prentice-Hall.

Bartky, S. L. (1990) *Femininity and Domination.* New York: Routledge.

Bordo, S. (1988) 'Anorexia Nervosa: Psychopathology as the Crystallization of Culture', in I. Diamond and L. Quinby (eds) *Feminism and Foucault.* Boston: Northeastern University Press.

Brownmiller, S. (1975) *Against Our Will: Men, Women and Rape.* New York: Simon & Schuster.

Califia, P. (1981) 'Feminism and Sadomasochism', *Co-evolution Quarterly* 33 (Spring).

Chapkis, W. (1986) *Beauty Secrets.* Boston: South End Press.

Coward, R. (1985) *Female Desires.* New York: Grove Weidenfeld.

Daly, M. (1973) *Beyond God the Father: Toward a Philosophy of Women's Liberation.* Boston: Beacon Press.

Davis, A. (1983) *Women, Race and Class.* New York: Vintage Press.

de Beauvoir, S. (1953) *The Second Sex*, trans. H. Parshley (1949). New York: Vintage Books.

DiStefano, C. (1990) 'Dilemmas of Difference: Feminism, Modernity and Post-modernism', in L. Nicholson (ed.) *Feminism/Postmodernism.* New York: Routledge.

Dworkin, A. (1974) *Woman Hating: A Radical Look at Sexuality.* New York: E. P. Dutton.

Firestone, S. (1970) *The Dialectic of Sex.* New York: Bantam Books.

Foucault, M. (1978) *The History of Sexuality.* New York: Vintage Books.

French, M. (1985) *Beyond Power: On Women, Men and Morals.* New York: Summit Books.

Frye, M. (1977) 'Some Reflections on Separatism and Power', *Beginnings of our Consciousness.*

Haraway, D. (1985) 'A Manifesto for Cyborgs', *Socialist Review* 80.

Hartsock, N. (1987) 'Rethinking Modernism: Minority vs. Majority Theories', *Cultural Critique* 7: 187–206.

Haug,. F. ed. (1987) *Female Sexualization*, trans. E. Carter. London: Verso.

Hawkesworth, M. (1989) 'Knowers, Knowing, Known: Feminist Theory and Claims of Truth', *Signs* 14 (3): 533–57.

Hill Collins, P. (1990) *Black Feminist Thought.* New York: Routledge.

Jagger, A. (1983) *Feminist Politics and Human Nature.* Totowa, NJ: Rowman & Allenheld.

Joseph, G. and Lewis, J. (1981) *Common Differences: Conflicts in Black and White Feminist Perspectives.* Boston: South End Press.

King, D. (1988) 'Multiple Jeopardy, Multiple Consciousness: The Context of a Black Feminist Ideology', *Signs* 14 (11): 42–72.

MacKinnon, C. (1977) *Feminism Unmodified: Discourses on Life and the Law.* Cambridge, MA: Harvard University Press.

Millett, K. (1970) *Sexual Politics*. Garden City, NY: Doubleday.

Morrison, T. (1970) *The Bluest Eye*. New York: Rinehart & Winston.

Nicholson, L. (1990) *Feminism/Postmodernism*. New York: Routledge.

Omolade, B. (1980) 'Black Women and Feminism', in H. Eisenstein and A. Jardine (eds) *The Future of Difference*. Boston: G. K. Hall.

Palmer, P. (1983) 'White Women/Black Women: The Dualism of Female Identity and Experience in the United States', *Feminist Studies* 9 (1): 151–70.

Rich, A. (1980) 'Compulsory Heterosexuality and Lesbian Existence', *Signs* 5 (4): 631–90.

Rubin, G. (1975) 'The Traffic in Women: Notes on the "Political Economy" of Sex' in R. Reiter (ed.) *Toward an Anthropology of Women*. New York: Monthly Review Press.

Samois (1981) *Coming to Power: Writings and Graphics on Lesbian S/M*. Palo Alto, CA: Up Press.

Tong, R. (1989) *Feminist Thought: A Comprehensive Introduction*. Boulder, CO: Westview Press.

Trebilcot, J. (1984) *Mothering: Essays in Feminist Theory*. Totowa, NJ: Rowman & Allenheld.

Wolf, N. (1991) *The Beauty Myth*. New York: William Morrow.

Young, I. (1990) *Justice and the Politics of Difference*. Princeton, NJ: Princeton University Press.

Barbara TREPAGNIER is a doctoral candidate at the University of California at Santa Barbara. Her current research is focused on white feminists exploring their own unintended racism. She has also used a feminist perspective in writing about the cultural norms which underpin the use of physical force in controlling children. ADDRESS: Department of Sociology, University of California at Santa Barbara, Santa Barbara, CA 93106, USA.

II

White Women's Identity and Diversity: Awareness from the Inside Out

Shari TARVER-BEHRING

It is often argued that many women share a common bond of misunderstood and devalued identity development as a result of gender-based prejudice (Heriot, 1983). Affiliative, nurturing and emotionally expressive characteristics are expected in women but not valued as distinctive and worthy ways of defining oneself in a competitive, patriarchal environment. While women have begun to uncover the truth about the specificity of their identities through theory, research and personal journey (Gilligan, 1982), most of this work pertains to white women. Much less is written about the development of identity formation in minority women, that is those who are members of oppressed and less empowered groups apart from gender-related discrimination. By focusing primarily on the universal struggle for identity in women, the impact of minority group membership is often overlooked. How can white women gain knowledge of the multiplicity of challenges in identity development for minority women? Through self-awareness of one's own distinctive and diverse identity, especially as it is situated in political and cultural parameters, white women can begin to understand the complexities of identity formation and identity achievement among minority women. Awareness from inside out brings an empathy and openness to the implications of diversity and devaluation, first for oneself and, ultimately, for others.

Contrary to early theory and research which stressed independent and achievement-oriented characteristics as the most salient aspects of identity formation (Erikson, 1950), the recent work of Gilligan (1982) and Josselson (1990), among others, reveals that women construct their identity in a distinctive manner through intimacy, nurturance and other relatedness. Previous theory and research based on Erikson's model of identity formation contains a societal bias in that, for example, women have been found to be inferior to men in their identity achievement as defined by male characteristics (Gallatin, 1975). Ironically,

Feminism & Psychology © 1994 SAGE (London, Thousand Oaks and New Delhi), Vol. 4(1): 206–208.

when women attempt to embrace independent, goal-oriented values more acceptable in men and more associated with optimal identity development as defined by Erikson, women often experience mixed support at best (Heriot, 1983).

The work of feminist researchers (e.g. Gilligan, 1982; Josselson, 1990) has given life to the unique way in which women defined themselves and has illuminated the unfairness of forcing solely male-identified values onto women. Unfortunately, in an effort to focus on a common thread of gender-based prejudice, these authors often have overlooked minority status as this affects women's identity development. White women, in general, have frequently overgeneralized aspects of their own identity development to other minority groups of women.

Rarely has women's identity formation been examined in relation to non-white groups. Helms (1990) is one of the few who has examined identity among minorities but has focused on similarities in the process of self-definition across race rather than on the increasingly complex challenges to self-definition which occur with minority status. While it is important to recognize a universal process in identity formation for women, the differences in this process in relation to culture also need to be considered in theory, research and practice.

White women can draw from their experiences as members of devalued subgroups. Women, of course, is one such subgroup. Hacker (1951, 1975) has argued that women constitute a minority group because they are not allowed a separate but equal self-definition from the group which holds the most power, white males. Other devalued groups include those ethnic, sexual or religious affiliations which are deemed less worthy than the majority. Sensitivity to oppression associated with poverty can also develop through awareness of economic diversity.

Awareness of multiple group membership in all people emerges from finding one's own membership in cultural subgroups. Oftentimes white women are not aware of the fact that it is not only minorities that have cultures and ethnicity. Comments such as 'I really don't have a cultural background, I'm white' are typical. When these women begin to trace their roots, they are surprised to discover that they have diverse associations with distinctive social groups. These might include socioeconomic status, geographical region, ethnicity and religion, each of which have their own specific characteristics and identities. Thus, the very descriptor, white, is a misnomer which masks a multitude of hidden subgroups. As a white woman sees herself as multiplistic in identity associations, she can see minority women with a new understanding of the complex influences on identity development. Through broader self-definition, white women can also gain better insight into those groups to which they belong which hold unfair privilege over minorities and use this knowledge to work towards more inclusive and equitable conditions.

As white women obtain an awareness of their own diversity and the related devaluation or privilege, they can begin to shed the blindness of ethnocentricity and hear the voices of their minority sisters. A white women summed it up in these words: 'Having a sense of my own diversity has impacted me deeply and reminded me that although I have a connection to a greater group of women, my experience is also different and not always as difficult.' Self-awareness from the inside out may be the key to unlocking a deeper sensitivity of diversity in all women.

REFERENCES

Claremont de Castillejo, Irene (1973) *Knowing Women.* New York: Harper & Row.
Erikson, E. G. (1950) *Childhood and Society.* New York: Norton.
Gallatin, J. (1975) 'The Recurring Problem of Feminine Identity', in *Adolescence and Individuality.* New York: Harper & Row.
Gilligan, Carol C. (1982) *In a Different Voice: Psychological Theory and Woman's Development.* Massachusetts: Harvard University Press.
Hacker, H. M. (1951) 'Women as a Minority Group', *Social Forces* 30: 60–9.
Hacker, H. M. (1975) 'Women as a Minority Group Twenty Years Later', in R. Ungo and F. Denmark (eds) *Women Dependent or Independent Variables,* pp. 103–12. New York: Psychological Dimensions.
Helms, J. E. (1990) '"Womenist" Identity Attitudes: An Alternative to Feminism in Counseling Theory and Research', paper in progress, University of Maryland, College Park, MD.
Heriot, J. (1983) 'The Double Blind: Healing the Split', in R. Hamerman Robbins and R. Josefowitz Siegel (eds) *Woman Changing Therapy,* pp. 11–28. New York: Haworth Press.
Josselson, Ruthellen (1990) *Finding Herself: Pathways to Identity Development in Women.* San Francisco: Jossey-Bass.
Marcia, J. E. and Friedman, M. (1970) 'Ego Identity Status in College Woman', *Journal of Personality* 38: 249–63.
Mowbray, Carol, Lanir, Susan and Hulce, Marilyn (1984) *Women and Mental Health.* New York: Haworth Press.
New England Association for Women in Psychotherapy (1982) *Current Feminist Issues in Psychotherapy.* New York: Haworth Press.
Ossana, S., Helms, J. and Leonard, M. (1992) 'Do "Womenist" Identity Attitudes Influence College Women's Self Esteem and Perceptions of Environmental Bias?', *Journal of Counseling and Development* 70: 402–8.
Stone, M. (1990) 'The Gifts from Reclaiming Goddess History', in C. Zweig (eds) *To Be A Woman.* New York: St Martin's Press.

Dr Shari TARVER-BEHRING is a licensed psychologist and assistant professor at the Educational Psychology and Counseling Department, California State University, Northridge, 18111 Nordhoff St, Northridge, California, USA.

INDEX

Abu-Lughod, Lila, 141
academic boycott of South Africa, 7,
   46–51
academic community and neighborhood
   organization, 22
acceptance by others, 88
acculturation, 120, 124, 127–30, 185
acting white, 140–1, 143, 163
action and agency, 12–13
action research, 43
affirmative action in USA, 103
Africa
   decolonization, 23
   white women in, 22–3
   see also South Africa
African-American women writers, 71
African Americans
   in *Oprah Winfrey Show*, 69–73
   patriarchy, 71
African National Congress, 46, 50–1,
   54–5
Africanist in white imagination, 139–40
agency
   and action, 12–13
   in group relations, 45–6
   and structure, 6
agreement and conflict, 8
Aitkenhead, M., 56
alliances, coalition politics, 188–93
Angelou, Maya, 71, 74–5
angst of women, 90
animalization, 29–30
anthropology, 33, 35–6, 141–2
Anti-Apartheid Movement (AAM), 47
anti-feminism and conservatism, 107
anti-professionalism in USA, 74
anti-racism, 42, 56, 86, 184–6
   and class, 158
   and feminism, 51–4
   and identity, 157
   and silence, 70

anti-semitism, 163–4, 166–7, 168
anti-slavery campaign, 157
anti-zionism, 168
Anzaldua, Gloria, 147
apartheid, academic boycott of, 7, 46–51
apes, 22–3
Applegate, C., 84
Aronson, E., 145
arranged marriages, 126
Asian Americans, 141–2
Asian women
   as category, 12, 130
   ethnic identity, 119–31
assimilation, 166–7, 185
attitudes and race-consciousness, 111
Ausländer, 13–14, 81–98
'authenticity', 160–1, 185
authoritarian personality, 43
autobiography, 160
   see also story-telling
autonomous grass roots activity, 180, 181
autonomous subject, 94
autonomy, 87, 89, 185

Baltimore, MD, 21–2
Barkley Brown, Elsa, 193
beauty, 68, 199–203
Bell, E., 100
belonging, 5, 88–9, 120
Bhavnani, Kum-Kum, 5–18, 19–39, 70,
   138
Billig, M., 45, 137
biological determination of individuals, 82
bisexuality in *Oprah Winfrey Show*, 71–2
'black', 5, 13, 69
black culture, in *Oprah Winfrey Show*, 70
black feminism
   and Jewish feminism, 163–4, 165, 167
   in *Oprah Winfrey Show*, 71
black masculinity, 71

HETEROSEXUALITY
A Feminism & Psychology Reader

Edited by **Sue Wilkinson** *University of Hull* and **Celia Kitzinger** *Loughborough University*

'Both psychology and, for the most part, feminist theory, have tended to assume heterosexuality as 'a given'. Heterosexuality needs to become a 'serious target for analysis and political action', because, quoting Adrienne Rich, heterosexuality is 'a political institution which disempowers women'. These arguments provide the powerful rationale for focusing on the attempt to theorise heterosexuality... this volume graphically recognises and registers the need to address heterosexuality as a political institution which oppresses women. In doing so, it represents an opportunity to address the continuing difficulties of understanding and criticising heterosexuality over and beyond our sexual and domestic arrangements' - *Trouble and Strife*

'a unique and exciting reader... Wilkinson and Kitzinger, as lesbian feminist psychologists, are in an interesting position from which to view heterosexuality. From the vantage point of 'the other' they are able to disentangle the experiences of heterosexual feminists from what is the, until now, unexamined normative existence of the 'Generic Women'... an important addition to feminist scholarship about women's sexuality. Within an historical context where early books on oppressed groups were written by members of dominant groups, we find it refreshing to see two lesbian feminists taking the lead with heterosexuality and feminism and recruiting heterosexuals to bring 'unexamined heterocentricity' into the light' - *Contemporary Psychology*

1993 • 288 pages
Cloth (0-8039-8822-2) / Paper (0-8039-8823-0)

SAGE Publications Ltd
6 Bonhill Street
London EC2A 4PU
England

SAGE Publications Inc
2455 Teller Road
Thousand Oaks
CA 91320 USA